How to Buy a Computer

Or Upgrade What You Have

D0731462

Myles White

M&S

This book is for my folks, Phyllis and John Andrews, in answer to their request for help in buying a computer of their own. It's also dedicated to the memory of the late *Vancouver Sun* columnist, Jack Wasserman, who saw something worthwhile that a kid couldn't see in himself.

Canadian Cataloguing in Publication Data

White, Myles, 1948-
    How to buy a computer, or upgrade what you have

Includes index.
ISBN 0-7710-8829-9

1. Microcomputers – Purchasing.   2. Computers – Purchasing.
I. Title.

QA76.5.W55   1995   004.16'029'7   C95-932230-2

The publishers acknowledge the support of the Canada Council and the Ontario Arts Council for their publishing program.

Typesetting by M&S, Toronto

Printed and bound in Canada. The paper used in this book is acid-free.

McClelland & Stewart Inc.
The Canadian Publishers
481 University Avenue
Toronto, Ontario
M5G 2E9

1 2 3 4 5   99 98 97 96 95

CONTENTS

ACKNOWLEDGEMENTS

Virtually every company mentioned herein has, at one time or another, provided products to review, technological background papers, answers to sometimes impertinent questions or gentle (and sometimes not so gentle) correction when I've done something wrong. Thank you.

Some provided extra assistance, allowed me to quote material at length here or in an earlier article, and/or allowed me to hold on to evaluation hardware longer than I normally would. In alphabetical order, these companies are ATI, ADI, AMD, Compaq, Corel, Creative Labs, Cyrix, Dell, Delrina, Diamond, Genicom, IBM, Hewlett-Packard, Hitachi, Intel Iomega, Lava Computers, Logitech, Microsoft, Motorola, NEC, Plextor, Symantec, Texas Instruments, Turtle Beach, and Xerox.

I also owe much gratitude to longtime colleague and friend, Walter Gollick, of Axiom Systems in Toronto, for his time and patience over the years helping me learn how to take things apart and put them back together again, to past and current editorial assistants, Jeff Mousseau and Tony Damourakis, and especially to assorted family members and pets who have had to put up with my late nights, deranged deadline-driven fits of panic, blank stares, or loud rejections in answer to reasonable requests for attention and other odd behaviors.

Thanks also to the publishers (David Carter, then Doug Alder) and the editors (the late Larry Bruner, then Mark Langton) of *Toronto Computes!*, editors Paul Barker of *Computing Canada*, Gordon Brockhouse of *Home Computing and Entertainment Magazine*, and Rob Wright of the *Toronto Star* Fast Forward section, as well as George Bachir and David Carter, owners of the Computer Fest shows, and (last, but not least) McClelland & Stewart senior editor Dinah Forbes, for the opportunity to work with them and for putting up with the occasional late filing and other bits of craziness.

INTRODUCTION

In the past several years, during my visits to various Canadian cities to conduct seminars for Computer Fest shows, I've often heard the plaintive cry, "I'm new at this and feel so confused. How do I sort out the choices when buying a computer? Where do I start?"

Buying a computer can be a daunting task, particularly if you're new to the high-tech marketplace. Given that you will be spending anywhere from several hundred to several thousand dollars on the computer equipment alone, you'll do your homework first. According to an IBM ad, the average person spends fifteen weeks, five days, twenty-three hours, and fifty-eight minutes searching for a new computer. If you're like most consumers, that time will be spent checking with a variety of sources for the information you need to make decisions: trade and consumer shows, glossy specialty magazines, and monthly newspapers. There are also user groups – gatherings of people who use a particular type or brand of computer and who get together to pool their knowledge, trade information, and share skills. As well, you'll talk to your friends and business associates. If you're buying something with your children in mind, you'll talk to their friends, too.

In other words, there's a wealth of information available to you when you're ready to dive into it. In fact there's too much to absorb in a short period. To make it even more interesting, just when you think you have a clear idea of what you want, the market changes. One of the headiest aspects of technology is the rate at which new products and methods are introduced. Something else you will have to cope with are the hundreds of retailers each shouting that they have the best, fastest, cheapest deals going. My job is to help you separate the good stuff from the junk, to cut through the hype and bafflegab, to alert you to new trends, and to put all of this into some kind of useful context.

You're probably thinking that anyone who would write a book titled *How to Buy a Computer* has to be some type of computer nerd (thick glasses, furtive expression, doesn't get out much). Not me. I am fascinated by computers and related products, but I only use them so I can have more time to play with my girlfriend, walk my dog, wrestle with my son (or one or the other with one or the other). In other words, I want my time with technology to be brief, efficient, satisfying, and fun. And I want it to serve me, not the other way around.

In this book I'm assuming that you and I are pretty much alike. Whether it's to make your work more efficient, to help your children with their homework, or just to have a new toy to play with, you want a computer to make part of your life better – and you'll shop till you drop to find something that works properly, fits your budget, and meets your expectations.

There are a lot of books about computers and their software programs boasting that they're written for idiots and dummies. I'm assuming you're neither an idiot nor a dummy, but an intelligent person who wants sensible advice and that you're just a little curious about what computers are and how they do what they do. In this book, I'll tell you. If, in fact, you don't really want to know how, say, the central processing chip (the vital organ of your computer) does what it does, skip ahead in that chapter. I won't mind. But if you're just a bit curious, you'll learn not just how the chip (or adapter or printer or what-have-you) works but also the real differences among the myriad options that face you in the computer marketplace.

There's one thing I need to share with you first – and that's the bias I bring with me (quick, Marge! Get the gun! He's got a *bias*!). If a particular bit of technology will make your life more efficient and enjoyable – especially if the vendor recognizes that your time and enjoyment are valuable – I'll tend to say nice things about it. However, if a product doesn't work as promised, doesn't install easily, or fights with other components, if it acts cranky and makes you crazy, if related software is poorly written or the manufacturers have somehow forgotten that real people use their merchandise, then I'll let you know.

The computer market is also full of traps – sink holes full of alphabet soup, flashy numbers, and chameleon chips – and you almost have to learn a new language, computerbabble, to understand what everyone is talking about. This book will, I hope, guide you through the major pitfalls. My recommendations, based partly on experience and partly on what my contacts in the industry tell me, are likely to annoy the odd advertiser and salesperson. *C'est la vie!*

You'll find that every item you want to purchase has its own terminology. Use a term incorrectly, or fail to understand what it means, and everyone from the computer zealot at your next dinner party to the nice salesperson in the computer store will pounce on you. There's no avoiding these terms, and so I've tried to explain them where they crop up in this book.

In short, I hope this book will be the "friend in the business" you need to give you some extra help in buying that first computer.

One last thing: the prices I cite in the book are only approximate, don't include taxes, and are in Canadian dollars. If you are in the United States, you'll find prices somewhere between the same and 20 per cent less, depending on the item and the vendor.

1

Shopping Basics

We need to talk about basic shopping strategies, because trying to buy your first computer without a little help can make you crazy.

Before you go shopping you'll have to learn the jargon – the names and acronyms of the thousands of gizmos and ways of doing things that make up a computer system – not to impress your boss or kids but to hold informed conversations with other computer users and salespeople. Then there's the task of learning what all the gizmos do, so you're not paralysed by the normal and healthy fear of paying too much and receiving too little. You won't find more untrustworthy people in the computer industry than in any other retail trade, but you won't find fewer, either. So I'll also warn you about practices that both I and reputable retailers abhor.

You'll want to choose a platform (see below), decide whether to buy a national name brand or locally assembled clone, and settle the issue of timing your purchase to get the best deal. We'll cover all of this and more in this chapter.

Choosing the platform

The first choice you have to make is what type of computer to buy (what platform). A lot of other choices become simpler once you've decided on an IBM-compatible PC (personal computer), Apple Macintosh (Mac), or the new PowerMac or PowerPC. There's a detailed discussion of the advantages and disadvantages of each plat-form in Chapter 3. For now, we'll talk about some less technical factors that will help you make up your mind.

Get what your friends have

The problem in picking a computer isn't a lack of choice. Far from it; there are several types of system available and choices of brand galore.

If you already own an older system and you're shopping for the next evolution in hardware, only extraordinary circumstances would prompt you to switch from a PC to a Mac or vice versa. We tend to stick with what we know, warts and all. For a new purchaser, however, the choices are still confusing.

The best source of information on what computer to get and where to go to get it is someone who already has one (according to a survey conducted in late 1994 by the COMPAS research firm, about 73 per cent of people shopping for their first computer turn to friends and family as their primary source of information). So, the first rule of choosing a platform, if you can't decide between a PC and a Mac, is to get what your friends have.

Your friends will tell you where they bought their computer and will tell you whether you should shop there, too. They'll likely teach you how to use your system or at least tell you about the software they use and what it can do for them, as well as give you tips on what to do when you're stumped. (Software is the umbrella term for the programs or applications that your computer runs.)

Your friends are the ones who are most likely to be available to help you out or share your misery one evening when you've just done something unfortunate on your PC – such as wiping out all your pro-grams by typing "format" and "C:" in the same sentence at the DOS prompt. The local store where you bought the machine won't be open then (unless you bought from a manufacturer with a twenty-four-hour hotline and paid big bucks for the service). In fact, if all of your friends have a Mac and you buy a PC (or the other way around), get set to look for a new group of friends.

Getting what your friends have is even more crucial if you're buying a system for your children. Failure to find out what their friends have, particularly if they're teenagers, will only land you in deep soup. Unless you're already skilled enough to teach your children how to use the system, their friends are going to be doing that job.

The concept extends into your work life, too. For instance, if your office has nothing but PCs and you plan to bring work home, using a Mac will only exasperate you while you try to figure out how to move your data painlessly between the two platforms – there are ways, but few of them are simple. (By "data" I mean the words, numbers, graphics, and so on that you create on your computer and store in files on the hard disk.)

If you plan to get a computer in order to retrain yourself, either to get back into the workforce or to improve your skills in it, a few calls to training schools or temporary help agencies will show you very quickly that most businesses use PCs and their software. Macs are a small (less than 10 per cent) share of the overall global market.

If you're buying a system for use in business, many of the same rules apply, but there are a few other considerations as well. Many companies, banks, and government-reporting agencies now make it possible (and in some cases mandatory) to exchange data via computer. I know of one pharmaceutical company, for example, that receives reporting forms from the federal government in PC format and has to return the data the same way. The only problem is that someone in the company once chose to equip the department that does the reporting with Macs. Major hassle.

What your clients and outside support companies use will play a role in your decision, too. For example, if you'll be using the computer to prepare advertising or other graphic and design material, you'll find most of the service bureaus (printers and film houses) you'll be working with have Macs. This is the case even though virtually all of the artistic design and desktop publishing software, which used to be the exclusive preserve of the Mac, are available for the PC, running under Windows. There are also excellent design programs, such as CorelDRAW, that won't run on the Mac at all. But the service bureaus turned to the Mac years ago when it was the only serious graphical game in town. They now have a major investment in Mac hardware, so they are predominantly Mac shops – something to think about if that's the type of work you intend.

The music industry, too, although most MIDI software (which lets you compose and play music on your computer) is now available in PC versions, is also predominantly Mac-based. That's important to know if you have aspirations to be a professional musician, but less important if all you plan to do is fiddle around on a MIDI keyboard at home for your own amusement.

User groups

If you have no friends or colleagues who own a computer, check out your local computer newspaper or visit a couple of stores for clues on finding local computer user groups, then pay several a visit.

Virtually every computer platform invented has groups of users who get together to share their experiences. The groups exist to help newcomers cope with the learning curve. There are skills exchanges where you can see demonstrations of new hardware and software, get hints on where to buy (and where there are traps to avoid), and where you can find deals, and hear news of secondhand equipment at reasonable prices. The groups have incredibly knowledgeable gurus, reasonably experienced users, and people who know even less about computers than you. The good news is that you don't have to own a computer to attend a few meetings. You can find Mac groups, PC groups, and everything-in-between groups. The people there will be more than glad to tell you why they got the computer they have and what's good about it (although there are fanatics everywhere and you may want to take some of the praise and the scorn you'll hear with a grain of salt).

Finally, ask your friends and acquaintances about their mistakes as well as their triumphs. Ask them where they bought their system. If they weren't treated well, don't go there! Remember: If you're still afraid of being ripped off *you haven't done enough homework!*

Bring in the Clones

Clone or name brand?

One of the questions asked most often by new computer shoppers is "Should I get a brand-name computer or a clone?" The answer depends entirely on your level of computing experience and on the type of person you are.

The first thing to remember is that computers aren't solid devices; they are modular assemblies of components that must work together for the whole system to work at all. The components include a main system board (also a collection of components), video adapter (also called a video card), drive controller, hard and floppy disk drives, keyboard, monitor, and so on. This is what can make buying a computer so complicated, but it has little to do with whether you choose a brand name or a clone.

Let's define a few terms first. By "brand-name" computer equipment, I mean products from nationally advertised manufacturers. These are both the mainstream names you'll recognize – such as IBM, Apple, Compaq, AST, and Packard Bell – as well as some mail-order names you may be less familiar with – such as Dell, ZEOS, or Gateway 2000.

"Clone" is a term used to describe compatible computers that are not made by the original developer. There have been IBM clones for years and, in 1995, PowerMac clones were just starting to appear (by spring of that year, Apple had licensed six, although none had made an actual appearance in the stores).

The major alternative suppliers hate the word "clone" because they feel it means cheap knockoff. They prefer the word "compatible," but you will still hear "IBM clone" and "IBM compatible," or "Apple clone" and "Apple compatible," used interchangeably. Today, however, "clone" is mostly used to refer to compatible systems assembled by local retailers and sold either without names or with the local retailer's own "brand name."

"Clone" has been replaced by "compatible" or "locally assembled system" because it has a long, bad, historical connotation, which you should know about as it explains the strange state of the market-place today.

In the very early days of microcomputing, long before IBM got into the act with the PC, there was another whole class of computers. They used variations of an operating system called CP/M and had names such as Epson, Kaypro, Osborne, and one you're more familiar with: Apple.

The Apple II was one of the most popular brands, but just as is the case with Macintoshes today, cost more than the others. Various unscrupulous folks copied them illegally and sold them out of small, dingy shops under a variety of fruit names. The machines tended to have bad reputations for quality, compatibility, and longevity.

Then IBM and two other U.S. companies, a little-known chip maker from California called Intel and an equally unknown small soft-ware firm from Redmond, Washington, called Microsoft, tried some-thing different. The result was the IBM PC, which used a new operating system called MS-DOS (Microsoft Disk Operating System). IBM was desperate to get software developers to start building appli-cations for its new platform. It divulged so much information to the developers to aid it in writing software and disseminated it so widely that the cloners were able to copy IBM's hardware designs. There was also nothing that prevented Microsoft or Intel from selling their prod-ucts to anyone who asked.

Because IBM failed to copyright the physical architecture of its PC, hundreds of companies were able to manufacture components to work in it. This "open architecture" allowed generic PC parts to become so widely available that local retailers could build their own PCs with little difficulty. However, because IBM was the first company to put its name on a computer using Intel chips and running MS-DOS, the clones made by everybody else were called "IBM compatibles." For the most part in this book, we'll call both IBMs and the compat-ibles "PCs" (as distinct from Macs and PowerPC/Macs).

Large companies grew up and made millions of dollars selling IBM compatibles. About the time Intel was on the verge of releasing the third generation of its central processing chips (the 80386, known simply as the 386), IBM was no longer the first company to ship a PC with new hardware (in fact, that year, Compaq was on the street with a 386-based system first).

Today there are myriad companies throughout the world manufacturing the components. They are engaged in a lively and cutthroat competition, which has brought the prices down to a point where anyone can buy them and put them together to create a working computer. In fact, if you knew where to find the parts (mostly at the same stores that sell locally assembled systems), you could build your own computer, too – although building one takes some skill and more money than buying it off the shelf.

A locally assembled system does not necessarily contain parts that are inferior or superior to those in a name brand. It does not necessarily mean that less or more attention was paid to quality control. It doesn't necessarily mean that the completed system will break sooner, last longer, perform worse or better than a name brand. But it could mean any of the above.

I have seen nationally advertised products come out of the box dead on arrival or expire before their time. I have tested both name brands and locally assembled models that exceeded my wildest expectations of performance and some that were dogs.

On average, however, a locally assembled system will cost less than a name brand (anywhere from 10 to 30 per cent less, depending on the brand and model). Some of the reasons are obvious. The local guys don't have the advertising overhead, the huge bureaucracy, or high-paid executives to support. Their storefronts tend to be in low-rent districts. Their sights are set on the bottom line, and they shop like demons for lower-priced (not necessarily lower-quality) components. Fierce competition among them keeps their prices down, too – forcing some of them to skimp on paying qualified technicians large salaries or on having dedicated technical support lines.

Support is largely what you pay the big guys the extra money to get. It costs them to provide twenty-four-hour-a-day, seven-day-per-week customer support services. Guaranteeing to come to your computer within two business days to fix or replace it for one to three years (depending on company and model) has a cost, too.

So where does that leave you? Only you know how good you are at dealing with life when things go wrong. Regardless of whether you buy a brand name or a no-name, things can go wrong (as an acquaintance at Intel once wailed, "Why don't these things always work?").

When something does go wrong while you're using your new computer, it will either be because you didn't understand an instruction or failed to carry it out, because of some flaw (bug) in the software, or because a piece of equipment got tired and headed south.

If this is your first computer and you don't have enough experience to do even a preliminary diagnosis of the problem, if you need the security of worry-free, on-site maintenance for the first year (or two or three, depending on brand and model), if you want a large amount of hand-holding (an around-the-clock technical support hotline), chances are you're looking for a brand name with a reputation for service (Dell, IBM, and Compaq come to mind, but there are others).

If this is your second or third computer or you've done your homework and know enough (or have an experienced friend to help you do at least a preliminary diagnosis), if you don't mind packing up the system and taking it to where you bought it, then politely but firmly standing on the counter while insisting that they make it work properly, you should consider purchasing a locally assembled system. Chances are it will cost you less.

Mail order

Mail-order systems advertised in U.S. publications may or may not be reliable (and several, such as Dell, Gateway 2000, and ZEOS have fine reputations), but the first thing I'd want to check is, if something does go wrong with the computer, where it has to go, how it has to get there, and for how long it has to be away. In Canada, you should check whether the company has Canadian offices (and so far Dell is the only company of the ones listed above that does).

Rip-offs

You can't get quality for $1.98

No one likes to spend more than they must, and with the fierce competition and brutally low markups in today's computer market, retailers don't have a lot of room to manoeuvre. But if a deal is remarkably better than the general competition while appearing to offer the same thing, start wondering why.

If the retailer is slashing prices to the bone and hoping to survive through volume sales, the company may not make enough to stay in business long enough to honour the warranty – or have enough staff to spend time on the telephone with you when you don't know what to do next or when your machine is acting funny. As well, without sufficient cash reserves to maintain a solid reputation with suppliers, the retailer may be forced to use low-quality parts in order to keep their prices down.

If you check the advertisements carefully, you'll notice that some of them are vaguer than others about the brand names of the components that form the system. You'll likely also discover that ads mentioning name-brand components tend to have slightly higher prices because they force the retailer to provide exactly what they've advertised. For instance, someone offering a "hard drive" rather than one of a half-dozen quality brand names isn't telling you anything about the quality of what you're really going to get

Some generic terms in advertisements such as IDE (a style of hard drive), SVGA (used to describe both video cards and monitors), 486 chip (without a manufacturer's name), tower or mini-tower (a style of case), MS-compatible mouse, and local bus (a form of the route data takes between components) are so broad that they are virtually meaningless. A brand name on a video card or a mouse doesn't necessarily guarantee better quality, but it does give you a more accurate basis for comparison and it also allows you to find out if your software is going to work with it.

Who's your best friend?

One of the advantages of the "open architecture" of the majority of the PC market is that there are hundreds of suppliers able to sell me computers and parts for those computers that are all interchangeable. But occasionally, I run across a brand of hardware or software that is deliberately designed to make me go back to that original developer if I ever want to repair or upgrade the system.

"Proprietary" schemes – methods of doing things unique to a single manufacturer – may offer some short-term advantages, but in the long term they are often dodgy investments. Avoid these products like the plague. They tend to have higher prices to begin with (although that's not always the case), and replacement parts, such as consumables (for instance, ink cartridges for printers) or additional enhancements (such as more memory), and so on, always entail a price premium.

It never hurts to ask whether you can buy industry standard parts for your system later.

Dealer tricks

The majority of computer retailers are honourable and reliable, but as in every walk of life there are a few notable exceptions. There are a few unscrupulous practices that you should note, just in case.

The price for SIMMs (single in-line memory modules, one of the components that determines how powerful a computer is) can go up and down like a yo-yo. Prices have held at around $50 a megabyte (MB) for a number of years, but there have been occasional bumps (such as around the time that Windows 95 began to ship).

When prices bump up, in order to avoid using the more expensive SIMMs, some unscrupulous local assemblers take older, slower memory out of recycled computers and install it into new systems. This can lead to unstable systems that report, among other ills, memory "parity errors" under some circumstances. You should check to see that all memory in the system comes from the same manufacturer and is rated at the same speed – either at 60 (fast) or 70 (slower) nanoseconds (ns).

"Shortages" of memory also prompt some suppliers to dump lower quality memory into the market. Looking at the SIMM chips themselves to see if there is a brand name on them (as opposed to either a serial number and no name, or nothing at all) may help you to discover the deception. Look for recognizable names (such as Toshiba or Hitachi and others) not only on the front of the SIMM (where the individual chips are located), but also on the back, to see if the same manufacturer assembled the whole component.

Forming a long-term relationship with a reliable dealer, particularly if you plan to upgrade your system often, can usually save you from this type of nonsense. It is also a good idea to talk to your friends about the quality of certain brand-name components and peripherals such as graphics cards, hard drives, monitors, CD-ROM drives, printers, motherboard chip sets, and BIOS (basic in/out system) chips. Comparison tests done by many of the glossy magazines are also valuable sources of information. Once you've decided on the mix of components you want, it's a good idea to specify them to the salesperson and have them written on the sales invoice.

Once that's done, still test what you've bought *as soon as you get it home* to see if you got what you paid for. Most of the time you will receive equipment as specified, but on occasion, a harried system builder may, either through error or design, install a less expensive component.

Ask what "burn in" really means. It is supposed to mean that your system is set up, turned on, then subjected to a battery of tests for a prolonged period – usually two to three days – before you take delivery. Any electronic component can fail within the first twenty-four to seventy-two hours (even from a brand-name supplier). In some cases, however, "burn in" is a euphemism for "We don't have the parts in stock and if we keep you waiting long enough maybe you'll agree to take something we'll tell you is just as good as what you wanted." This is a version of the old bait and switch tactic. The classic version is to be offered a pricier system because they just sold the last one of the system you wanted. It's just possible that the marvellous system advertised was so popular that they ran out the day the ad first appeared, but I'd hesitate to stick around after I heard the excuses.

"System comes complete with DOS and . . ." Does it come with just enough of the operating system to start, or do you get the full software complete with manual and disks? Does all of the software installed (from the operating system to the "application bundles" some retailers offer) come with registration cards, full documentation, and licences? Is this the first time that the software has been installed? Some retailers accept returned software, reseal the package, and offer it for sale again. There's a chance that it's been corrupted by a virus, so it's a good idea to subject all software going into your system to an anti-virus scan, just in case.

There will be more detail about non-Intel "486" processors in Chapter 3, but the following story may tell you something about how they and the "586-class" processors – the Pentiums – of today may be marketed. I was in a retail store in Vancouver a while ago helping a friend shop for parts. It was just after companies like Cyrix and Texas Instruments began shipping what they called "486" chips. On display at the front of the store was a beautiful unit in a mini-tower case with a huge monitor beside it. A decal on the case proclaimed, "Intel Inside." Next to the display was a placard saying in big red letters, "486 Computer System," and showing a ridiculously low price. At the bottom of the placard in much smaller print, it advised that the monitor was extra (fair enough), but in even smaller type were the words "includes additional math coprocessor." Oh?

Intel's 486 chips come in two flavours, a DX that includes a math coprocessor and an SX that doesn't, and that's usually stated right after the number, as 486DX or 486SX. So I asked the salestype who was hovering near the door whether the 486 was indeed by Intel or whether it might possibly be a Cyrix DLC. He shuffled his feet, then admitted that it was in fact a Cyrix chip in the system. When I pushed a little harder, he told me that "customers wouldn't know the difference," so there was no point mentioning the Cyrix name on the placard because, "it would only confuse them."

When I pointed to the "Intel Inside" decal on the case and suggested that the display was a tad misleading, he grumbled, but removed the placard, claiming it had been placed there by error. Sure it was. I have no doubt at all that he put it back as soon as I was out the door.

Last but not least, there's the CPU re-marking scam. When Intel produces a processor chip, it tries to make all of them as fast as possible. Those that don't pass the test for its highest speed are tested again at a lower speed. Those that pass at the lower speed are conscientiously labelled as such on the top of the chip. To take the 486DX4 chip as an example, they're all manufactured to run at 100 MHz and then they're tested at that speed. Those that fail are tested again at 75 MHz and, if they pass, are labelled and sold as 75 MHz chips. The nasty people who are out to cheat you have also been known to steal good chips and re-mark them, or worse yet, to steal discarded chips that fail the quality control tests entirely and re-mark them as well.

On a PC motherboard (the main circuit board) is a device which keeps the CPU (the processor chip) and various other components running at a constant speed. There are a variety of methods to do this using what are called "clock crystals" and other electronic timers. The important thing to know about these methods is that motherboard manufacturers and local assemblers can change the motherboard's speed. It is possible to take a 75 MHz 486DX4 chip, mount it on a 33 MHz motherboard, and have the CPU run at 100 MHz – for a while, until the additional heat or the chip's basic instability causes it to crash (generally just after your warranty runs out or sometimes sooner).

Modern design methods make this easier than ever to do. Many motherboards now will run a number of different processors. I saw one recently, for example, which simply by changing some jumper settings, would run Cyrix or Intel processors all the way from a 25 MHz 486SX up to a 100 MHz 486DX4. The same nefarious practice is also being carried out on Pentium chips, as well.

If you have reason to be suspicious, you may want to check your CPU. If it is covered by a label that says something like "warranty void if label removed," I'd really be curious about exactly what was under it, because Intel CPUs don't normally have such a label. Because this practice was so endemic in the days of the 486 chips, Intel has now started stamping the correct value on the bottom of the chip, but removing it to have a look isn't a job I'd recommend – and even if you did, you still might not be any further ahead. Some of the really unscrupulous folks in the re-marking game get rid of Intel's original markings and add their own. Unfortunately, there's almost no way to detect the fraud (and that's what it is).

Intel is very concerned about the problem, but as yet it hasn't developed a foolproof method of interrogating the chip to have it report back what it is – and unfortunately, software system checkers, such as Norton Utilities, PC Tools, Checkit, or Microsoft's diagnostic program, MSD, can't do it either.

The only way you can protect yourself is to ask around about the reliability of the vendor. It is highly unlikely you'll find this practice being carried on by brand name manufacturers – they have too much to lose if they're caught. And most local assemblers are honest, too. They don't want customers to lose their trust in local assembly because of a few crooks.

Homework

Know what your software wants

Your software needs will determine what type of computer you buy. More and more software is now available in versions designed for the different types of computers (i.e., there are word processors for both PC and Mac systems as well as spreadsheets, drawing programs, desktop publishing, and so on), so it may not affect your choice of platform. However, individual products will still determine how much memory your system has to have, whether it requires a math coprocessor or could benefit from a graphics card with its own coprocessor, determine how much hard disk space you need, and offer suggestions on compatible printers and other devices.

Some specialized software products – such as OS/2, Microsoft Windows and Windows NT, AutoCad, and Lotus 1-2-3 (just to name a few) – require special hardware, a lot of memory, excellent video graphics, and so on. The software itself will tell you what it wants and will suggest other brand-name products (both hardware and software) with which it is compatible. Check the small print on the software box.

One note of caution, however: the "minimum system requirements" listed on the box usually assume that you'll never run anything else at the same time. For example, Microsoft said Windows 3.1 would run with 2 MB of RAM (random access memory) and that was true. Windows 3.1 itself could, but you couldn't simultaneously run most of the programs written to work with it.

This is a rule: *You'll never be sorry if you get more memory and hard drive storage capacity than the software recommends.*

The only exception to this rule are some specialized television grabber boards used to manipulate TV video in computers (NTSC boards). If you plan to use a grabber board, there may be a restriction on how much memory you can have in your system, not to mention that there's a very short list of computer video cards and types of monitors with which it will co-operate. (For example, the Creative Labs Video Blaster version 1 won't work in a PC with more than 15 MB of RAM – version 2 of the board corrected the problem).

Drivers

Most of the concern about making software and hardware work together is about software drivers. Virtually every component in or attached to your computer has its own way of doing things – and special codes are required to tell it how to do what you want it to do.

The task is to get, for example, your word processor to provide the codes that peripheral devices such as your graphics card and printer understand. To do that, you need small software programs called drivers. They are used to translate what you're doing with the program into instructions the hardware can understand – so that what comes out bears at least a faint resemblance to what you intended.

Printers require drivers, so do pointing devices (such as a mouse), video cards, CD-ROM drives, and the list goes on. One of the best ways to buy yourself frustration is to purchase a device, only to discover once you get it home that the driver supplied with it is out of date or flawed and that the software you plan to use with it doesn't have a driver to support it. Failure to check the needs of the software you'll be using first causes more grief than any other factor when buying peripheral devices.

When to Buy

There's always something faster

You can't buy the fastest PC, Mac, or PowerPC/Mac there is because the next model is already in a truck between the factory and the store, while its successor is already in the factory. The next model beyond that is in a lab somewhere.

If you think I'm kidding, consider this: In early 1995, the 486DX was already pretty much off the market, and the faster DX2 series was more or less toast by late fall. Intel tracks its market and reports that, while it took nearly five years for the last XTs and 286-based systems to disappear from store shelves once the 386 started to ship, it took only three years for the 386 to sink without a ripple once the 486 appeared. When the Pentium (the 586 generation) first arrived, it took less than two years for it to become half of all systems sold. By early spring 1996, the 486 in all forms will be history as well. As I write this in the summer of 1995, there are already nine models of Pentium (up to 133 MHz) in three generations of design, and the P6 is due out before this book is back from the printer.

Trying to hedge against this rapid cycle makes you vulnerable to some folks who will try to pick your pocket. They know of your desire to have your cake and eat it, too, and will allow you to pay for the privilege – usually by making the "upgradeable" offer.

"Processor upgradeable" is a phrase that's always trotted out by retailers in that brief period between Intel's announcement of a new chip and its arrival in quantity – while retailers still have shelves full of the old product. For those planning to buy a system because its processor is "upgradeable," a word of caution: The performance increase you'll get is rarely commensurate with the cost of upgrading, and the upgrade processor is unlikely to be available until two years after you buy your system (that's been the pattern in the past). For example, although 486 systems were sold as being upgradeable to Pentium as early as 1993, there was no Pentium upgrade part for them until 1995 (and didn't show up until late that year for 33 MHz motherboards).

Prices always go down

If you wait, the system you want today will be less expensive in six months.

All other things being equal – without the addition of specialty items, but with enough memory, hard drive capacity, and a suitable graphics system to run most of the software you'll want – the locally assembled, leading-edge PC system is always around $5,000 (add 10 to 30 per cent for brand names). Complete systems that are one, two, and three steps back from the leading edge usually start at around $3,000, $2,000, and $1,500 respectively. Keep in mind that you can play games with these figures. Add better graphics, a bigger monitor, more than 16 MB of RAM, multimedia components, or a larger hard drive and you'll be pushing the price up. Cut back on some or all of them and you can push the price down.

The leading edge for the PC when I wrote this in summer 1995 was a system based on Intel's 133 MHz Pentium processor – with a 150 and 180 MHz Pentium on the books and the P6 (the 686 generation of processor chip) announced and due to ship. One step back was the 120 MHz Pentium, then the 100 and 90 MHz models, followed by the 75 MHz Pentium, then the 60 or 66 MHz Pentium, the 100 MHz 486DX4, and the 66 MHz 486DX2. Everything else, including the 33 MHz 486DX or SX, 386 (any X), 286, and earlier models, were obsolete. Obsolete doesn't mean it isn't a good computer and that it's not what you need (though you might have trouble finding a new one to buy). It means that you shouldn't buy one if your object is to have a system for three to five years before advancements in software and hardware, plus your own internal sense of how fast the computer should work, prompt you to start looking for a new one.

By the time this book is published (fall 1995), the 486DX2 will have more or less disappeared. By spring 1996, the DX4 will have followed, and my guess is that by summer or fall 1996 the new entry level system will have become the 90 to 120 MHz Pentium.

There's no such thing as "too powerful for you"

I constantly run into consultants and salespeople who try to convince the hopeful shopper that the system they can't afford is "too powerful" for their needs, and this cheaper, less powerful system will do just fine. I also understand retailers' motivation not to let a sale get away.

No one has a bottomless bank account, and some systems may be too expensive for you to purchase now, but regardless of whether this new computer is simply to do word processing or to run the odd game for the kids, the point of having a computer is to get it to do things for you as efficiently as possible. I repeat: There's no such thing as "too powerful."

You won't stop where you think you will. Once you discover how relatively easy it is to do the task you're buying the computer for in the first place, you'll find more things to do with it. Count on it. The more you ask it to do, the more you'll appreciate any of the power it can give you.

If your budget is limited (whose isn't?), here is roughly the order I'd recommend for spending your limited resources: processor (as fast as you can find), memory (as much as you can afford), hard drive capacity (as big as possible, then start saving for another), video acceleration and monitor size (see Chapter 4). If you have any money left after you find an affordable printer, then start pricing multimedia components (sound card and CD-ROM drive), backup systems (tape backup and power), case design, and software.

Everyone else knows better

It doesn't matter how much research you do. You can read my columns or the rest of this book, go to the library searching through back copies of every monthly magazine in the industry, and attend seminars until you're blue in the face. You may consult relatives and knowledgeable friends, find one of those rare salespeople who really does have your best interests at heart, and only shop during sales. Even if you do everything you're supposed to do, I'll make you a tiny wager. Within two to three weeks of unpacking your shiny new system, one or more of the following things will happen: You'll pick up a copy of one of the local computer newspapers and find ads for a fancier model at the price you just paid, or see ads for the one you bought for less money, or your smart-alec twelve-year-old niece will tell you where you could have purchased more power for less money.

Ignore 'em all. Simply enjoy the heck out of your choice until you're ready to upgrade (in about three years) when this will start all over again.

You're going to want another one

When I work with people new to computers, I tell them to type some words at the command line (the C:\> that appears on a PC once DOS has loaded itself) and press "Enter." Their reaction is invariably hesitant, fearful – almost as though they expect their computer to blow up and do them some damage. The fortieth time they type these same words, they don't bother looking at the screen to confirm what they've done. They know that the computer will do the same thing this time that it did the last thirty-nine times they tried it (unless they spelled the command incorrectly). Before the poor computer, which once worked faster than they could comprehend, has finished its first task, they're already issuing another command.

Eventually, this system, which used to appear to work blindingly fast, is being cursed as the by-now experienced users drum their fingers on the desk, muttering, "C'mon, c'mon, damn you . . ." Not long after this point is reached, particularly if they have the experience of working on someone else's faster system, they start doing shopping research again. Don't believe me? Talk to me again in a couple of years – or less.

What do you do?

None of the above means you should go back to bed and pull the covers up over your head. Rapid processor obsolescence does not mean you should wait for the next model you've heard is hovering over the horizon. If the object is to get a system that will run not only today's software, but also the applications coming next year and the year after that, you simply get the fastest system you can afford today and start using it. The time to buy a computer (or anything else) is when you need it.

Buy the best, fastest system you can afford today, use it to your heart's content, and start saving for your next one. By the time you're ready to upgrade, the system you wanted but couldn't afford will be available in quantity, will have any instabilities worked out, and will be less expensive.

Make them come to you

As you'll see in the next chapter, computer ads are seldom specific enough to use them as a decent basis for a price comparison. Local retail ads are often purposefully vague to allow the dealer to assemble a basic system from whatever parts were the least expensive on the open market that week.

The best way to get around this is to use the same tactics that both government and large corporations use: put your needs out to tender. It's my hope that by reading through this book, you'll get enough information to start tracking down the exact components you want in your system. At the end of the book you'll find a blank chart you can use, once you've identified the components, to fax out to various vendors – both of name brands and locally assembled systems. Feel free to photocopy as many blank forms as you wish, fill them out, then sit back and let the vendors come back to you with their quotes. Not only will it save a lot of shoe-leather, but it will allow you to ignore those who don't respond.

Don't leave the store without . . .

When you've made your choice of platform, vendor, and specific components you want in your system; when you've checked out the store's or the manufacturer's warranty policies; when you've had all of the promises and the components, complete with brand names and serial numbers, written plainly on your sales agreement; *before* you hand over payment, there are a few other items you must ask for. Don't leave the store without them.

Each of the main components inside and any attached outside your computer has a manual. I'm not talking about the no-brainer manual that shows how to switch the computer on or how to plug in the printer. I am talking about the technical manuals that come with the motherboard, the video adapter, the drive controller, the hard drive(s), the SCSI (small computer systems interface – pronounced "scuzzy") adapter, the sound card, the CD-ROM drive, the monitor, the printer, and the case (yes, the case!).

You have to have these manuals because, at some time in the future, you may want to upgrade or change parts of your system. For example, if you add more memory to your system, you should know how many SIMMs you require each time you do (some systems require you to upgrade in pairs or sets of four, instead of just one at a time). The motherboard manual will tell you. When you're shopping for additional SIMMs, it would also be useful to know what type and speed you need (adding faster SIMMs than you have now will cost extra and won't speed the system up, because it continues to run at the speed of the slowest memory you have). SIMMs are also user-installable parts; with the manual to show you where they go and how they're placed, you won't need to pay extra for installation or take your system to a shop for a couple of days to have it done.

The day your CMOS battery dies (see Chapter 2 under "clock/calendar"), and you have standard IDE hard drives in your system, you won't be doing any more computing until you can manually restore the hard drive descriptions. You could take your system back to the store to have them fix it, but what will you do if the store isn't there any more? It happens. You could call the company that made the hard drive; you could use a utility program's emergency disk, such as Norton Utilities or PC Tools, to find the drive's boot sector, read the physical description from it, then try entering the data – if you have the program and you're confident of your ability to make it work; or you could look up the information in the manual you should have received at the time you purchased the system.

By the way, when your CMOS data goes away, so does the fine-tuning information about your motherboard's chipset that's stored in the BIOS chip. Be warned: Don't try calling the company that made the BIOS to restore it. They won't know how. Get the manual.

How about the day you remove the case cover from your system and carefully vacuum away accumulated dust (it's a good idea because it keeps things running cooler), but accidentally knock loose one of the little wires connecting the motherboard to the case. Let's see now, was that the speaker wire, the drive light indicator, the turbo switch, or the keyboard lock? You'll need manuals for both the case and the motherboard to find out not only which wire goes where, but the correct position for it so you don't reverse polarity through it.

By the way, that little LED (light emitting diode) readout on the front of the case, the one with numbers indicating system speed, isn't really a speedometer. Those numbers are usually set by jumpers on the inside of the case to report any number you want. It's a neat trick you can use to impress friends and is seldom done by unscrupulous vendors anymore. Jumpers are little plastic connector caps placed over pairs of pins, designed to short them out and change how a hardware device operates, and they can be set in literally hundreds of combinations. Without a manual you'll *never* get them sorted out.

Speaking of jumpers, if you only have one standard IDE hard drive in your system and you can finally afford to add another, jumpers on both drives have to be set in order to tell each of them that there are two drives now and which one is the first drive in the chain. Set either one improperly and neither will work. Check the manual.

If your system has the normal complement of two external serial ports for connecting a mouse or external modem or what-have-you, there may come a day when you'll want to turn one or both of them off. See Chapter 8 and get ready to hunt for that manual.

If the video card you select doesn't have a specific setting for the monitor you choose, you may want to have the manual for each one so you can adjust them both so they work well together. The shop may make this adjustment for one resolution, but not for others. If you ever want to upgrade either component in the future, having the manual for both will be in your best interests.

Enough examples of hardware, what about the "free" software you got with the deal? If you don't get the original, properly labelled disks, then at the very least you'll want instructions on how to create backup disks of each program so you can re-install it if anything ever happens to the copy on the hard drive (and bad things can happen, either as a result of over-eagerly deleting things or because the hard drive dies – and they can die).

You'll also want the manuals for the software so you can learn how to work with it and to register your legal ownership of its licence. You wouldn't knowingly want to have illegal, pirated software on your system, would you? Once you've registered you can get technical support from the software developer if the manual baffles you.

You're entitled to these manuals, and smart vendors know this. If the vendor doesn't have extra copies of the original manuals (some buy parts in bulk and only get one manual for their own use), then you can ask for a photocopy of the one their technician will use to repair your system if it ever develops a problem. If they don't have the original manual, start worrying about how they will service the system if something breaks.

The last resort, and the one you can feel perfectly justified in applying if the hardware manuals (or copies of them) and the registration and manuals for the software aren't made available to you, is to explain politely but firmly why you're leaving the store – and shop somewhere else.

2

Reading Computer Ads

Unless you learn what the terms used in the newspaper ads and the brochures handed out at consumer shows mean, some salespeople will rub their hands together when they see you coming and think, *"Victim!"*

The single most important thing to understand about purchasing a computer is that it is not a solid, unified device. Portable notebook computers are a different story (see Chapter 8), but desktop systems are really assemblies of separate components that work together. Whether you buy a brand name or a locally assembled system (see Chapter 1), each component in the computer has a manufacturer's name (which is often different than the name on the case), a model name or number, and a set of characteristics and specifications that you can check. That's what makes a computer so difficult to buy and it's why you have to know not only what the bits and pieces inside it are called, but also why some are better than others.

A computer is comprised of a main circuit board (normally called the motherboard or – for those who wish to be more politically correct than accurate – the main system board). Attached to it are a number of devices, including a central processing unit (CPU), electronic

White's Computer Bargoon Emporium

486 system,
Math coprocessor socket
Upgradeable to Pentium!
8 MB, 256 k cache
540 MB HDD, 9 ms, enhanced
3.5 in HD FD
VESA or PCI local bus
1 MB SVGA 1024 x 768 VLB

MS compatible
mouse
101 enhanced
keyboard
"Green"
motherboard
Mid-Tower case
Local bus controller
2 S, 1 P, 1 G ports
Lots & lots of FREE
softwarol
Multimedia Upgrade
available

PRICES SO LOW, YOU SHOULDN'T BELIEVE THEM!

We've got DEALS!

random access memory (RAM), basic in/out system (BIOS), "expansion" slots, and various other widgets and gadgets that make it work.

The expansion slots hold other circuit boards with specialized functions, such as video graphics adapter (also called a graphics card) and disk controller. You need these two, but you may also have others (and to complicate things, the graphics card and disk controller may be integrated into the motherboard itself).

The motherboard, together with the circuit boards slotted into it, fit into the computer's case along with the hard disk drive(s), the floppy disk drive(s), and possibly some other toys such as a CD-ROM and/or tape backup drive. All of these boards and drives get electricity from a power supply that comes with the case.

Once you plug a monitor, a keyboard, and other devices such as a mouse and printer into the appropriate places at the back of the case (called ports), you're ready to go computing. All of which sounds really simple. Not!

If you're brand-new at shopping for computer hardware, the following composite set of specifications, with abbreviations culled from advertisements in various publications, may as well be written in Sanskrit:

486DX2 66 MHz (or 90 MHz Pentium)
Processor (or Pentium) upgradeable
PCI (or VESA) local bus
8 expansion slots, on-board video, and disk controller
8 MB RAM, expandable to 32 MB, 256k cache
Math coprocessor ready
American-made motherboard
Phoenix (or AMI or Award) BIOS
750 MB enhanced IDE HDD 12 ms
32-bit local bus controller
2 S/1 P/1 G ports
Clock/calendar
3.5-inch HD FD
14-inch SVGA monitor, .28dp, non-interlaced, 1024 × 768
1 MB local bus SVGA video card
101-key enhanced keyboard

MS-compatible mouse & pad
Mini-tower case, 5 drive bays, 250W power supply
MS-DOS, Windows (or OS/2), WordPerfect, Quattro Pro

Our composite ad appears to describe exactly what you're going to get, but in fact, it tells you nothing specific about any of the components. From the list above, you're supposed to be able to figure out whether the price they're asking is competitive. Good luck – because they're not giving you enough information upon which to base any type of price comparison.

As we take the ad apart line-by-line, you'll see what I mean.

486DX2 66 MHz (or 90 MHz Pentium)

The first line in the ad usually describes the central processing unit (CPU), which is the heart of the system – if you like, the computer inside the computer. It determines the computer's power and speed and may be described in several ways. Our ad, for instance, doesn't tell you whether this "486DX2" is made by Intel, Cyrix Corp., Advanced Micro Devices (AMD), or Joe and Harry. The "486" number suggests that it may be Intel's 80486DX2 processor, but unless you see the name Intel, or see it designated as "i486," you can't be certain.

As Intel's Pentium processor becomes more popular and the 486 fades from view, you're also likely to start seeing ads for "586" systems. There is no 586. When Intel discovered it couldn't copyright a number, it started using names for its processors instead. The 80586 would have been the logical progression from 80386 and 80486, but Intel started calling it the P5, then switched to the name "Pentium" (just as the P6 will be given a name of its own, possibly by the time this book is printed).

In the interim, other manufacturers started producing chips that they claim will work just like or better than the Pentium. AMD for example, has the K5, Cyrix Corp. has the M1 and M1sc, NexGen has produced the Nx586, and IBM is due to release its own version (which at press time still didn't have a name, either).

To keep it simple, use the following guideline: If everything you think you know about the performance and compatibility of a processor is based upon what you've heard and read about Intel's original design, then keep in mind when you pay less for a non-Intel version, less is what you're likely to get. The Cyrix 486DLC and M1sc are good examples. The DLC was closer to being a 386 capable of running a few commands in the 486SX instruction set than it was to being a 486, while the M1sc bears much the same relationship to a Pentium.

The "DX" part of the line suggests that the CPU has a built-in floating point unit (also known as a math coprocessor), special circuitry designed to speed up the calculation of numbers containing decimal points. If it had said "SX" (or SLC or DLC in the case of Cyrix or Texas Instruments chips, or "Blue Lightning" in the case of IBM "486" chips), this would indicate that it lacked a math coprocessor.

Folks trying to sell you either the less expensive Intel SX or a non-Intel chip, neither of which have a math coprocessor, will tell you the floating point unit isn't needed. They'll point out that Microsoft Windows doesn't use numbers with decimal points to operate; it uses whole numbers, also known as integers, to do most of its work. However, a partial list of the applications you'll run under Windows that use floating point math and benefit from DX circuitry includes Microsoft Excel, Novell Quattro Pro, and IBM/Lotus 1-2-3 spreadsheets, all computer-aided design (CAD) programs, drawing and painting applications such as Fractal Design Painter and CorelDRAW, databases such as Borland's dBase or Paradox and Microsoft's Access, and quite a few high-level games – the list goes on for some length. No one has ever complained to me about having a math coprocessor – but I've lost count of the number of folks who have moaned about not having one.

"DX2" – as opposed to "DX" – means this particular CPU works twice as fast internally as the motherboard to which it is attached. Our ad says this is a 66 megahertz (MHz) system, so that means the motherboard works at half the speed (33 MHz).

Megahertz is the metric equivalent of the old "cycles per second." In our terms, it's a way of measuring how fast a computer's central processor executes instructions. Because the way the chip functions most closely resembles the ticking of a clock, this is often referred to as the CPU's clock speed. The higher the number, the faster instructions are processed inside the chip. When we talk about local bus, below, we'll provide more details on how the speeds of the various components on the motherboard relate to each other.

If you're trying to figure out how relatively powerful a system is (using Intel-based systems as a guide), performance increases in the following order: 486DX/33, 486DX2/50, 486DX/50, 486DX2/66, 486DX4 (any speed), Pentium (any speed), P6 (any speed). (See the Intel iCOMP chart.)

Processor (or Pentium) upgradeable

The "Processor (or Pentium) upgradeable" portion of the ad is trying to reassure you that you can upgrade the system later if you can't afford a faster system now. Be prepared to pay through the nose for the privilege and to wait for a while, too. Intel took nearly three years to produce the special upgrade part containing Pentium technology for 33 MHz, 486-based motherboards. There already are ads for Pentium systems stating that they are processor upgradeable, too, but the chips don't exist yet. In any event, you'll want to check that the particular system advertised has been certified by Intel to work with any new part (not all are).

When the faster OverDrive upgrading parts do finally appear, Intel tries to make them provide a 50 per cent performance kick to whatever system they're supposed to fit. Whether upgrading makes economic sense is another story. If we take the Pentium upgrade part for 33 MHz 486 motherboards as an example, it cost around $800 when it was first released. That was at a time when the price difference between a 486DX2/66 system and a true 60 MHz Pentium, complete with architecture designed for the processor, was less than $500. Does this sound like a good deal to you?

PCI (or VESA) local bus

Local bus technology allows circuit cards for video display, information transfer, network connection, and other uses to communicate with the CPU at the same speed as the motherboard –instead of using the much slower information pathway from the motherboard's expansion

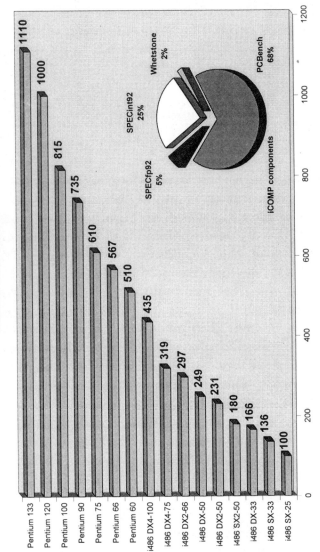

slots where the cards fit. Two methods have evolved to make this possible, but by the time you read this, particularly if it's close to the release of our second edition in 1997, one of them may have disappeared.

Computer designers borrowed the term "bus" from electrical engineering to refer to information pathways within the system. If you think of it as the equivalent to a pipeline, instead of the vehicle you may take to work, it will help. There are several information pipelines or buses on a PC motherboard, but for this discussion, we're only concerned about two of them. One of them connects the expansion slots to the CPU and is called the expansion bus. The other connects motherboard control logic, BIOS, system RAM, and external cache memory to the CPU and is called the local bus. (See below for descriptions of BIOS, RAM, and caches.)

The local bus is fast, but the expansion bus is dead slow. The expansion slots connected to it may have one of three designs: ISA (industry standard architecture – an 8- or 16-bit slot design); EISA (extended industry standard architecture – a 32-bit slot design), and MCA (microchannel architecture – another 32-bit slot design which has just about disappeared from sight).

One of the important things to understand about these slots is that components designed for a specific architecture may not fit a different slot type. For example, an ISA board will fit both ISA and EISA slots, but not an MCA slot. EISA boards will only fit EISA slots, and MCA boards are slot-specific, as well.

Data transmission speeds over the expansion bus of the three designs vary, too – ISA at 8 MHz; EISA, 8.7 MHz; and MCA, 10.3 MHz – and it doesn't matter how fast the system's motherboard or CPU are. In effect, the expansion bus is like the waist of an hourglass. When data hits it, the speed at which it moves is greatly reduced. A few years ago, when programs such as Windows made it desirable to move large amounts of information from the CPU to the graphics card or back and forth through a hard disk controller, SCSI (small computer systems interface) adapter, or network interface card, the slowdown became intolerable.

Fortunately, the computer industry is full of bright people who find challenges fun to surmount. Wouldn't it be better, they wondered, if a way could be found to move the same data over the much faster local bus instead? Sure it would – and it was. Local bus devices are always faster than expansion bus devices. The only problem is that two methods were developed to accomplish the task and have led to some consumer confusion.

VESA (Video Electronic Standards Association) and PCI (Peripheral Component Interconnect – developed by Intel) local bus schemes have exactly the same performance in 486 systems. Not even Intel has been able to measure a difference. VESA is less expensive for manufacturers to implement (and consumers to buy) and VESA local bus slots can be used by non-local bus ISA components. However, that's where its advantage ends.

Trying to run more than two VESA local bus devices will slow the whole system down, because of the way the VESA expansion slots are electrically connected to the local bus. Why use more than two? You'll want to if you ever choose to use a local bus video card, drive controller, SCSI adapter for a CD-ROM drive, and network interface card in the same system – and that's not uncommon.

PCI provides better performance in Pentium-based systems, but it's more expensive to implement, and PCI expansion slots will accept only PCI devices. These disadvantages are somewhat outweighed by two factors. First, there is a theoretical upper limit to how many PCI devices can be in the same system before performance is compromised, but you'll never have enough slots on a motherboard to get close to it. Second, even if your current system (or the one you are eyeing) is not a Pentium-class device, your next one will be (or better) and it *will* have PCI. Getting PCI devices now means you should be able to move them to your next computer and keep the cost of upgrading down. I'm less confident you'll be able to do that with VESA devices.

Here again, having your cake and eating it too exacts a price. Some motherboards currently on the market have a mixture of slot types available. It is not uncommon to see ISA or EISA, plus VESA and PCI slots all on the same board. While this may allow for a smoother transition from one type of system to another (i.e., a VESA-based system to PCI-based system), overall performance will likely suffer as a result. Tests performed by PC Labs in late 1994 found that motherboards with both VESA and PCI slots were up to 20 per cent slower than those with only PCI slots – even if the VESA slots weren't used for VESA devices.

8 expansion slots, on-board video, and disk controller

This one is fun. From this description, you have no idea how many useful expansion slots you're really going to get or what bus the on-board components are going to use. For one thing, there is no description of the slots themselves. Are they ISA, EISA, VESA, or PCI? If they're ISA, are they 8-bit or 16-bit slots? Once you have this information, you still may be in the dark.

The PCI specification allows for what is known as a "shared slot." This means that one of the PCI slots on the motherboard is so close to a non-PCI slot that you can use one or the other, but not both.

Having components that might ordinarily occupy an expansion slot connected directly to the motherboard instead will free up some slots. For example, I've seen at least one system with SCSI controller, dual IDE controllers, floppy drive controller, video controller, sound chip, and network interface all attached directly to the motherboard and run through the PCI-based local bus (the Compaq Deskpro XL 590).

I've also seen systems where, although some of these components were attached to the motherboard, they were wired into either the ISA expansion bus or through a VESA-compliant local bus. In several examples, the computer's expansion slots were PCI; it was advertised as a PCI-based system and it wouldn't be too big a stretch to assume it was a fully compliant PCI computer. Making assumptions is never safe. If you're not absolutely certain, ask questions.

8 MB RAM, expandable to 32 MB, 256k cache

This translates as 8 megabytes of random access memory, expandable to 32 megabytes, plus a 256 kilobyte external cache.

RAM (also called just "memory") is where a computer stores instructions until the CPU can get to them, and where the CPU places information while it is being processed. It's the place where you do all your work (or play) on the computer, and if you don't save the memory's contents to disk, it will disappear when you turn your computer off.

I'd want to know how fast the RAM I'm being offered is before I assess the price. Is it relatively slow (70 or 80 nanoseconds – ns) or fast (60 ns)? Does it include the newer 15ns "DynamiCache" memory, and if it does, will it comprise the full 8 MB RAM?

Is it extended data out (EDO) memory? If it is, is the price premium I'm likely to be charged for it worth the small performance improvement I may get? As I'm writing this in the summer of 1995, EDO memory was relatively new to the computer industry. Although several manufacturers were beginning to use it, implementation was still in the early stage of development and benchmark tests conducted by a variety of people were showing only a 1 to 2 per cent improvement over standard RAM. Whether this will change over time remains to be seen.

Knowing whether the memory chips used were 30- or 72-pin SIMMs (single in-line memory modules) would tell me how expensive buying more memory will be. Thirty-pin memory often has to be added two or more SIMMs at a time, while the newer, high-density 72-pin SIMMs come in larger sizes (8, 16, 32, or 64 MB) and can often be added one at a time.

A motherboard using DynamiCache SIMMs may require you to fill all of its special slots first, and because this type of memory can be in short supply, it may cost you quite a bit to upgrade.

While you're asking, check to see if the motherboard's design actually does take advantage of the 72-pin, single-SIMM upgrade. Some don't.

Thirty-two megabytes may sound like a lot of memory, but 8 MB is barely enough to run a robust Windows- or OS/2-based system. When you try to run numerous applications simultaneously, both the Windows and OS/2 start swapping program segments to your hard drive when they run out of electronic memory. This slows your system down. Always buy as much memory as you can afford, and don't think about starting out with less than 8 MB if you want to use Windows or 12 MB for OS/2. Sixteen MB or more is better.

Cache memory (sometimes called an external cache because it isn't inside the CPU) is used to make the CPU more efficient (see

Chapter 5 for a fuller discussion of how it works). The minimum is about 256 KB, while 512 KB to 1 MB will cost you a lot extra.

How much cache is enough? According to Intel, while there is a drop-off in performance increase for running DOS-based applications after 256 KB, performance of Windows keeps increasing as the amount of external cache memory goes up. In fact, Intel's iCOMP benchmark figures for Pentium systems use a 1 MB external cache to achieve the higher results.

A word of warning: two otherwise identical systems will appear to work quite differently depending on how large the external cache is.

Math coprocessor ready

Another mostly meaningless phrase. All Intel 486DX, DX2, DX4, Pentium, and P6 processors have a math coprocessor built into the chip. There is no math coprocessor in 386SX or DX chips, 486SX, SLC, or DLC chips.

"Math coprocessor ready" simply means the motherboard being offered has a compatible slot to allow you to add a separate math coprocessor later, when you've discovered that you should have purchased a CPU with one in the first place. Then you still have to pay for the extra chip.

Some math-intensive applications can also benefit from a second, additional math coprocessor (generally manufactured by Weitek). If software you want to use says it can utilize a Weitek coprocessor and you intend to add one later, don't assume that "math coprocessor ready" means you can do so. Ask the vendor about it specifically, then have the assurance added to the written sales agreement.

American-made motherboard

I don't care and I wonder whether anyone really does care where the motherboard was manufactured (or assembled – there's a difference). National origin has nothing to do with quality of work, components, or performance. However, we'll all care about some of the board's design points.

Take a look at the motherboard diagram. Aside from the problems discussed below about the location of various port connectors, there are some other physical items to check. Find the expansion slots. At this point we don't care what type of slot they are (see expansion slots above), but we're definitely concerned about what lies above and below them. If there is something between the end of the slots and the openings in the case, will it prevent you from properly installing a device in the slot? Some designers place keyboard chips or BIOS chips here and they can prevent adapter cards from getting all the way down into the slot. If the motherboard is too close to this end of the case, it will also make placing adapter cards difficult.

Similarly, the replacement battery terminal (see below under "clock/ calendar") may be located in such a way that when a battery is connected to it, the plug interferes with the slot. You want it away, to one side.

Now have a look at the other end of the slots – the one nearer the front of the case. While they are becoming rarer, it is still possible to find adapter cards that want to occupy the full width of the case. If there is a great, hulking CPU located at the end of the slots, complete with heat-sink and/or chip fan mounted on it, you may not be able to place a full-length card in as many as three or four slots.

Last, but not least, you'll want to see both motherboard and case together to see if they obstruct each other. If you aren't diligent, you may discover that in order to put more memory in the system you have to totally dismantle it because the memory slots are buried under the case's drive bays.

Phoenix (or AMI or Award) BIOS

When IBM lost control of the PC, about the only proprietary part it tried to protect was the BIOS (basic in/out system). It's a chip (or pair of chips or system of chips) holding software that directs a number of functions on the motherboard. The BIOS acts both like a traffic map and to a lesser extent like a traffic manager in the system. Its information is used by the CPU and consulted during a number of operations. The BIOS is one component that will determine how "compatible" the system is (i.e., whether it will run standard PC devices and software without too much trouble).

Flawed design

The PC motherboard to the left has three serious design flaws which may ultimately come back to haunt the purchaser:

1. The alternate battery connector is located at the end of the expansion slots. When in use, it may impede insertion of circuit boards such as hard drive controller, in as many as two slots.

2. The CPU slot is in an awkward place. If you have a 66 MHz 486 DX2 or Pentium processor and add a heat sink and/or chip fan, the height will prevent using 3/4-length or full-length expansion cards in as many as two or three slots.

3. The memory slots are in a very bad place. When fully populated with eight SIMMs, this location will also prevent 3/4-length or full-length cards from being used in two to four slots.

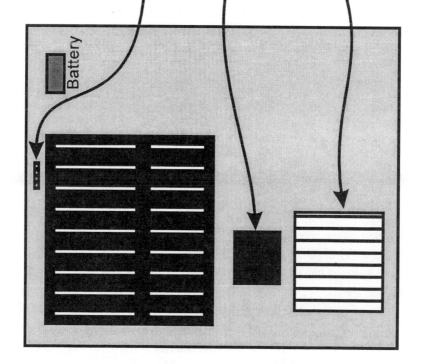

Battery

IBM and other name-brand manufacturers still produce their own BIOS software, but other suppliers have gotten into the act. Three of the best known are Phoenix Technologies Inc., American Megatrends International (AMI), and Award Software.

Most people, if they think about BIOSs at all, see the chip(s) and wonder why I refer to software when the BIOS appears to be hardware. The BIOS is really a programmable, read-only memory (PROM) chip. The chip is a standard part; what goes in it isn't.

The way it works? The motherboard manufacturer sits down with the BIOS programmers to figure out how to make the motherboard work efficiently. When done, the BIOS folks hand the manufacturers the software and a customization program that allows them to do any last-minute fine-tuning and tinkering – just in case they change the design slightly or start getting slightly different components from other suppliers, something that can occur with amazing rapidity.

That's why, when your CMOS battery goes dead (see "clock/calendar" below) and you call the BIOS manufacturer to find out how to restore the information required to fine-tune your system's chipset, all you get is silence. The BIOS house has no more idea of the exact settings than you do – and will refer you to the motherboard maker for the correct information.

By the way, one really desirable feature to seek in a system is what is known as a flash BIOS. These systems use erasable programmable read-only memory chips (EPROMs) that can be updated in case the manufacturer makes changes to the system after you've plunked your money down (it happens).

750 MB enhanced IDE HDD 12 ms

Without abbreviations, this line reads "750 megabyte, enhanced, integrated drive electronics hard disk drive, 12 millisecond access time." It refers to the hard disk (also called the hard drive), where you'll store all your data and programs.

The 750 MB number indicates how much information the hard drive will hold. IDE tells you what generic type of drive it is and also indicates the type of drive controller needed to operate it (see a fuller discussion of IDE and SCSI in Chapter 5).

When I was writing this in mid-1995, enhanced IDE drives were relatively new on the market, and a number of hard drive manufacturers had introduced models while the "enhanced" standard was still being developed. There was evidence that pre-standard enhanced IDE drives larger than 528 MB would not work properly with other drives in the future once the standard was completed, might not work properly with Windows 95 (there were also reports that they did not work with OS/2 Warp), and might be subject to unexplained data loss.

By now, of course, the inconsistencies may have been worked out. Well, at least we can hope. For safety's sake, however, my personal choice is as follows. I know that regular IDE drives (i.e., those 528 MB in capacity and lower) will work when the enhanced IDE standard is completed, because backward compatibility is built into the new standard. I can't be as certain about enhanced devices manufactured prior to the release of Windows 95 (and this includes IDE-based CD-ROM drives). I'm not telling you that the enhanced devices won't work properly, but I can't tell you they will, either. I plan to wait until mid-1996 before buying one for my own use. Until then, if I have to buy a large-capacity hard drive or a CD-ROM drive, I'll go with a SCSI device instead.

Yes, SCSI devices are slightly more expensive. Yes, they require a separate controller (to which I can attach seven devices). But I don't have either the time or the cash to squander on the bleeding edge. I'd rather get something I know works or wait until the cure for someone else's headache results in technology I can trust.

Average access time of 12 milliseconds (ms) tells you how quickly the hard drive finds information on its surface and lifts it into the read head. It does not tell you how quickly it gets this information to the computer (that is largely determined by the drive type and controller, see below).

Finally, our dummy advertisement is conspicuously lacking a brand name and model number for the drive. Hard drives are not identical. Some are slower; some are noisier; some have better reputations for compatibility, stability, quality, and service. You'll want to do your homework here and not simply accept whatever was the least expensive on the open market the week the system was put together for you.

By the way, hard drive prices have fallen rapidly in the past few years. You can get good quality 528 MB drives for under $300 without a lot of shopping and you can expect the prices to fall even further as time goes on. Get a large one now, then start saving for another because data always expands to fill the container and software programs are getting more and more greedy for space.

32-bit local bus controller

This line in an ad has nothing to do with controlling the local bus. It refers to a device used to control the functions of a hard disk drive (and more, as you'll see below).

Whose controller are we talking about here and which local bus scheme does it use? Drive controllers also have reputations and a range of features. Controllers costing under $40 don't add much ooomph to your system. Slightly more expensive models may contain a separate memory cache to improve drive throughput (how fast the data gets from the computer to the drive and back again) and may allow you to change the controller's characteristics to take full advantage of really fast hard drives.

A 32-bit drive controller will move data 32 bits at a time (as opposed to 16 bits), and explaining what this means will take a moment. If you consider that the information pathways (the expansion and local buses) in your computer are like roads, and that depending on the type of road, each has a maximum speed, you're halfway there. Now imagine that two vehicles are travelling the same road, at the same speed – except that one has sixteen passengers and the other has thirty-two. They'll both arrive at their destination at the same time, but one of them will deliver twice the number of people. A 32-bit controller moves twice as much data as a 16-bit device, which makes it appear to be working twice as fast. In order to take advantage of it, you have to have a CPU with a 32-bit external bus (which rules out some of the pseudo 486s not made by Intel), and you also have to have it mounted in a 32-bit slot (EISA, MCA, VESA, or PCI local bus).

"Enhanced" IDE controllers are also starting to appear on the market. They may allow you to attach more than two IDE devices, offer greater control over devices attached to them, and increase throughput, but like the enhanced IDE drives, the standard for these controllers was still under development at the time this book went to print.

Hard drive controllers have to be matched to the type of device they're controlling. For example, an IDE controller won't drive a SCSI device (or the other way around). They may also provide control and connections for floppy drives, serial and parallel ports, and a game port for a joystick. They also may not include any additional functions. In any event, make sure you get the manual for this device. (Why? Read on.)

2 S/1 P/1 G ports

"Ports" in computer terms are the places where you connect external devices to the system. Our ad says you get two serial ports (used to connect a mouse, an external modem, or other device), one parallel port (for a printer and/or CD-ROM drive), and one game port for a joystick or gamepad. These ports may be attached to the drive controller (see above), to a separate circuit board known as a multifunction I/O board (for input/output), or may be directly wired to the motherboard.

Brand name hasn't become a factor here, but characteristics definitely have. I'd want to know whether the serial ports have a special, high-speed "16550 UART" (universal asynchronous receiver/transmitter). The 16550 UART (as opposed to an older 8250 or 16450) chip is desirable if you're planning to use a modem operating faster than 9,600 bits per second (bps). Fax/modems are currently available at speeds of 14,400 and 28,800 bps, and without a 16550 UART, you won't like the results if you try to use one running at that speed. (See Chapter 8 for more on UARTs.)

I'd also want to know whether the parallel port is bi-directional and whether it is the newer, high-speed "enhanced parallel port" (EPP). Several new printers have arrived on the market that will report their status back to your computer while you work. They need the bi-directional port. Certain models of CD-ROM drives that attach to the parallel port also need the high-speed EPP version in order to achieve acceptable multimedia performance speeds.

One additional physical item to check is to see where the connectors for these ports are located inside the computer. If they are attached to the drive controller or separate I/O board, some ports will be available on the circuit board's backplate and will be accessible through the external opening leading to its expansion slot. Some models with ports connected elsewhere (i.e., directly to the motherboard) may use external slot openings to hold a plate with the ports on it, mounted in such a way as to make putting anything in that particular slot impossible. This is a sign of poor design, or worse, sloppy or lazy assembly, because most computer cases have port-shaped knockouts on the back designed to hold the connectors away from the slots.

Clock/calendar

So what? Every PC since the 286 has had an onboard clock/calendar, but some folks still mention it, because when XTs were still sold, a clock chip was often an optional extra. The clock/calendar may be housed in a separate chip or may be integrated into the same part that holds the computer's CMOS system. How the CMOS is powered when you turn the computer off is far more important and interesting, yet it is seldom mentioned in ads.

The CMOS (complementary metal oxide semi-conductor) is a form of memory that contains information vital to how your PC functions. For example, it will control the clock/calendar, contain a description of any IDE-type device(s) in your system and descriptions of the floppy drive(s), as well as providing information on any fine-tuning that's been done to the motherboard's control/support logic chipset (many modern motherboards have adjustable speeds and can accommodate a variety of CPU speeds, and this information on CPU speed has to go somewhere).

For the most part, the CMOS gets its information from the system's BIOS, and while it may acquire some of it automatically (such as how much memory you have on board), a lot of it was entered manually, either at the factory or at the place where you bought it.

CMOS memory is volatile. That means it needs power applied to it to hold its contents (i.e., when the power goes away, so does everything in it). When your computer is switched on, the CMOS gets a trickle of power from the computer's power supply, but when you switch the system off, it needs an alternate source. So, on every PC since the 286, there has been a battery on the motherboard designed to keep the CMOS happy when your computer is off. Eventually the battery dies, regardless of whether it's rechargeable. You can tell if yours is getting close to its natural end when your system clock starts behaving very erratically – other factors such as flaky software or a static-zapped clock chip can also cause this, but it's usually a good symptom to observe.

There are four methods of providing CMOS battery support, three of which are acceptable and one of which you'll detest.

When the Canadian government sets out tenders for computers, it insists that CMOS batteries be easily replaceable. Systems that fit the criteria may not have a rechargeable battery, but instead will come with a long-life battery similar to a watch battery. It fits into a clip and can be easily removed and replaced. Compaq, for one, uses this scheme but so do other manufacturers, because the government isn't the only one insisting on this method. You can, too.

A newer method of providing a replaceable battery is to have the clock/calendar, CMOS memory, and battery in a small black box that's soldered to the motherboard. The top comes off the soldered component and the battery can be replaced. Look for names such as Dallas Semiconductor and Benchmark. Why you'll want to be cautious here is because not all little black boxes are the same (as you'll see below).

More common is to find a small, cylindrical battery soldered to the motherboard. When these batteries die, you don't replace them. Desoldering and resoldering the battery can permanently damage the motherboard and even well-trained, qualified computer technicians are reluctant to try. Instead, look for a small, four-pin terminal (which may have one of the two inner pins clipped short) intended as an external battery connector. You can attach a plastic battery case with four AA batteries to it (good for about a year), or a more expensive long-life lithium battery pack (good for about five years). In either case, correcting the problem is inexpensive and relatively simple.

The method you'll detest started appearing in late 1994. In this instance, the CMOS, the clock/calendar, and the battery are part of one small, rectangular (and usually black) box soldered to the motherboard.

But this black box can't be opened and the battery can't be replaced. What you may not find on motherboards using this scheme is any kind of replacement battery terminal (I've seen examples without one). So, even though the battery is supposed to last from five to ten years (sure), when it does die, so does the whole motherboard, unless you really like restoring the CMOS data every time you turn the computer on. Bad idea. Don't buy a system using this method.

When I raised this issue at a computer show, one of the retailers selling motherboards using this scheme was furious with me. He argued that the lower cost justified the method. "Besides," he stormed, "the computer isn't expected to still be useful by the time the battery runs out."

Sorry, I don't buy the arguments – there are better ways to save money, and when I upgrade to a new system, I want to be the one who decides on the timing.

3.5-inch HD FD

Again, without abbreviation, this line refers to a single, 3.5-inch diameter, high-density floppy disk drive.

A floppy drive is the device you use to load new software into your system from the disks containing the programs (unless it comes on CD-ROM and you have a CD-ROM drive). A 3.5-inch diameter, high-density floppy drive will read disks of that size containing 720 KB or 1.44 MB of data. Brand name isn't crucial, but you'll be happier with something by Panasonic, Sony, or Fujitsu.

For all intents and purposes, the 5.25-inch floppy drive is dead. I haven't seen any software shipping on this type of disk for several years and even hardware device manufacturers have finally stopped shipping drivers on them. Still, if you need to exchange data with someone with an older system without a 3.5-inch drive, you have an alternative to putting two floppy drives in your system. Look for a "dual-diameter" drive by Canon, Panasonic, Teac, and others. It will occupy less space in your system (the same space as one half-height 5.25-inch device instead of two) and can read from and write to both high and low density versions of both types of disk. The drive also uses only one power lead (which makes it energy efficient).

Dual diameter drives have two slots, one wide and one narrow, and they treat the slots as drives A: and B:. You can copy data between them and, because the drives use only one connector on the floppy drive cable, you can nominate either one as the A: boot drive without having to open the case and swap cables. You merely change the description of which slot is A: in the onboard BIOS setup.

Dual diameter drives do cost slightly more than two separate drives (in mid-1995 they ranged in price from about $130 to $190 compared to about $55 for either type of single-slot drive), but their advantages far outweigh the price differential. If you need one, be prepared to place a special order, because few retailers have them as standard shelf items.

14-inch SVGA monitor, .28dp, non-interlaced, 1024 × 768

What brand of monitor? They aren't all the same. This line says this model is super VGA (video graphics array) and will work at a resolution as high as 1024 pixels horizontally by 768 lines vertically. While it does say non-interlaced, it doesn't say that it is non-interlaced at this resolution (interlaced monitors are inexpensive, but they flicker badly at any resolution higher than 640 by 480). It doesn't mention the monitor's vertical refresh rate (72 Hz is good, lower is prone to flicker even if non-interlaced, and higher costs more).

There is no mention of where the monitor's controls are located (front is good, back is awkward), no mention of whether it has any memory to store settings or adjustments, and no mention of any power-saving or low-level magnetic radiation shielding options.

The ".28 dp" is shorthand for .28 millimetre (mm) dot pitch – a measurement of the space between the phosphor dots on the inside of the monitor screen. Your picture is made up of the glowing dots and the space between them. A dot-pitch measurement higher than .31 mm is grainy. Beware of ads that don't mention the number at all – they're generally up around .39, .43, or even .47 mm, and they're awful. Sharp, clear pictures start at .28 mm, and .26 mm or lower is gorgeous (and expensive, but worth every penny).

1 MB local bus SVGA video card

Like monitors, video graphics adapters (the card that communicates between your CPU and monitor) are not all the same, and without a brand name and model number you won't know what you're getting.

Names for "standards" such as VGA or super VGA are meaningless, too. The card described above may be limited to a top resolution of 800 by 600, 256 colours, and have no special circuitry to accelerate its speed under Windows. It could also provide 16.7 million colours (at low resolution – higher would require more than 1 MB of memory), be capable of 1024 by 768 resolution or higher, and be accelerated to the teeth. Both video adapters could still be called SVGA.

You need to be specific here about resolution, the number of colours you expect to see at the resolution you want to use, and to see benchmark figures indicating how fast the adapter is. Then negotiate brand name and price. Keep in mind that mainstream brands such as ATI, Matrox, Diamond, Western Digital, and Video 7 are more likely to have operating system support not only under the next version of Windows, but also under the one after that – while odd brands at ridiculously low prices may not. See Chapter 4 for a more in-depth discussion of both monitors and video adapters.

101-key enhanced keyboard

Once upon a time, keyboards had only ten function keys located at one side and no separate cursor controls located between the alphabetic and numeric keypads. All keyboards sold with PC systems today have twelve function keys located at the top, separate cursor controls, and they're all "enhanced."

Like everything else, keyboards have brand names. More importantly, however, they have a different feel. Buying one without typing on it to see if you like how it feels – and sounds – isn't a great idea. Most keyboards are flat and can be inclined at the back, but there are some new, "ergonomic" ones on the market that are designed to relieve hand or wrist strain (see Chapter 8). You may want to check them out.

MS-compatible mouse & pad

The key word in this line is "compatible." It means this isn't quite the name brand you're looking for, but if everything works right, it should perform in almost the same way. Again, see Chapter 8 for more details on mice and other pointing devices.

It is never a safe time to buy any unknown or slightly funny brand-name device that needs a separate software driver to work properly. This includes pointing devices (such as a mouse, trackball, or graphics tablet), sound cards, CD-ROM drives, printers, and others. You'll want mainstream products from companies you can contact easily if you need updated drivers for Windows 95 or 96 or . . .

Mini-tower case, 5 drive bays, 250W power supply

PC cases come in a variety of shapes and sizes.

"Desktop" generally means the case lies flat on your desk, while "tower" generally means that it stands vertically (either on the desk, beside it, or under it). Your job is to figure out where to put it.

In terms of cases, "full-sized," "low profile," "mid-sized," and "mini" are meaningless terms unless you can see the beast. If it doesn't have a CD-ROM, tape backup, additional floppy or hard disk drives now, ask yourself if there's room to install these additional devices later. They fit into the drive bays accessed through the front of your computer's case.

The indication of how many drive bays are available in the case is semi-meaningful, but it would be more useful if it also said what size they were – 5.25-inch wide bays will hold anything, while 3.5-inch wide bays won't.

You'll also want to check to see how many of each type of bay has an opening to the outside of the case. It doesn't matter if you can't see the face of a hard disk drive, but you will want case-front access to bays holding a floppy, CD-ROM, and/or tape drives.

Also check to see if the manufacturer has used any type of proprietary bracket on the bays to encourage you to buy additional parts from them. Compaq, for example, in its Deskpro XL 590 (and possibly other models), uses a special front-mount bracket on its bays which won't hold other manufacturers' devices (and it told me it wouldn't supply the brackets separately, either – that it was up to the other manufacturers to do so). Compaq isn't alone in this type of shenanigan. At one time, Ambra computers (IBM's Canadian clone), because of their cute external case design, wouldn't accept non-Ambra devices either.

Mini-tower or low-profile desktop cases can be damned awkward to move around in. If you plan doing any upgrading yourself, you'd best have very long, very skinny fingers. Full-sized tower cases present other problems – particularly if the motherboard is mounted at the bottom of the case and the drive bays are at the top. Standard connector cables may not be long enough to reach the devices in them.

Not all power supplies are created equal. Some have quiet fans while others are noisy as hell. You'll want to hear the system when it's running.

The wattage of the power supply is important, too. The advertised rating may be sufficient for the components included at the time you buy the system, but may come up short if you intend to install additional internal components later (particularly hard drives, which spin all the time unless they're told to power down).

Does this system have any kind of power management options? In the United States, the Energy Star specifications call for monitors and other devices that turn their own power off if they are not used for a specified period of time, which can be modified by the user. There is no such requirement in Canada.

Last, but not least, modern PCs can get quite hot while they are running. While there will be a cooling fan in the power supply, the case design may not allow sufficient air flow to cool other devices. Intel, for example, says mounting separate chip fans on its higher-end CPUs isn't necessary in "a properly ventilated case," but by their definition, that means a case with an auxiliary fan designed to move air across the motherboard. It's a good feature and one worth seeking out.

DOS (and the other software)

Getting software pre-loaded takes a lot of the headache out of starting your system. Of course it works better if the version number of the

Typical configurations designed to run all the software

Light to Moderate	Moderate to Heavy	Very Advanced
Intel, AMD, Cyrix or TI 486DX2 at 66 or 80 MHz	Intel DX4/100 or 75 to 90 MHz Pentium	133 - 150 MHz Pentium or P6
8 to 16 MB RAM, PCI local bus, plug 'n' play BIOS	16 MB RAM, PCI local bus, plug 'n' play BIOS	As much RAM as you can afford, PCI local bus, plug 'n' play BIOS, Triton PCI chipset, 1 MB external cache (8.5 ns)
64 to 128 KB hardware cache	256 to 512 KB hardware cache	2 GB SCSI drive (16-bit caching controller)
350 to 528 MB standard IDE drive	528 MB standard IDE hard disk with cache controller & multi I/O or IDE-ATA-3 drive larger than 528 MB and controller	1 GB tape backup or larger
3.5" floppy or dual diameter drive	800 MB tape backup system (QIC 3020)	Keyboard, floppies, 150 MB Bernoulli drive & ports as at left
101-key keyboard, generic mouse	hi-density 3.5" floppy drive or dual diameter drive	250 to 350 watt power supply
1 parallel, 2 serial ports, 1 game port	101-key keyboard, Microsoft Mouse, or Wacom tablet	Uninterruptible power supply (brownout protection)
SVGA graphics controller with 1 MB memory	230 to 250 watt power supply	Accelerated hi-res, true colour graphics adapter, 4 MB VRAM
14" "SVGA" monitor at least .31 mm dot pitch and non-interlaced to at least 800 by 600	Accelerated hi-res graphics board with 1-2 MB RAM	Adobe-type 2 compatible, 600 dpi PostScript laser or high-end colour (phaser 340 or 540)
24-pin dot-matrix, ink-jet, or GDI laser	17" SVGA monitor, 72 MHz refresh .28 mm dot pitch, non-interlaced to 1024 by 768 MPR low radiation	20" high-resolution monitor with Trinitron tube (.25 mm dot pitch), MPR low radiation
14,400 bps fax/modem	Laser-jet 4 compatible or PostScript printer with max memory (600 dpi, 10 ppm)	28,800 bps modem, 14,400 bps fax
200-watt power supply	Backup (UPS) power supply	Wacom (or similar) graphics tablet and soft-stylus
250 MB tape backup drive (QIC-80)	14,400 bps modem and fax	6X CD ROM, 32-bit audio board with wave table synthesis
Note: x86 SX2 processors, because they lack a math coprocessor, are NOT recommended	CD-ROM (quad), 16-bit audio board, speakers	NTSC grabber board, colour scanner, deep pockets

software is included in the quote. In fact it's the only way you can figure out whether you're getting a good deal or not. Just make sure you're given the disks or complete instructions on creating a set of disks, the manual for each program, and, more importantly, the documents that allow you to register the software with its publisher.

Lies, damned lies, and benchmarks

Although not quoted in our composite advertisement, one other item you'll often see is the vendor's claims for how fast various devices are.

Each of the components in a system, as well as the overall system itself, will have characteristics you can check. For example, in various sections throughout this book, I suggest you find out how fast a component is before you buy it (for example, the CPU, memory, video controller, hard drive, drive controller, CD-ROM drive.)

There are a number of ways of testing a computer to assess the performance of its components individually and collectively. Intel uses its own "iCOMP" rating. There are industry engineering-level benchmark tests including SpecINT92 and Bapco. Publishers of various glossy computer magazines have created their own (such as the Ziff-Davis Winbench and Winstone tests and *Windows Magazine*'s WinTune).

At the consumer level, you get a choice between Norton Utilities and PC Tools tests (both now owned by Symantec) or a somewhat more specific testing utility such as TouchStone Software's Checkit or Aris Entertainment's MPC Wizard. Some vendors like to use Landmark (if for no other reason than it produces huge numbers).

I don't claim that this is the entire list of benchmark tests – they pop out of the woodwork with dizzying regularity. I've also not given you specific version numbers for each one, as they're constantly being upgraded and by this time next week there's liable to be a different version. What is important to understand is that the results you get from one version of a test can't be compared to results from a prior version, nor can they be compared to the results of an entirely different test. How long is one piece of string compared to another? One hundred sounds like a bigger number than sixty, but it isn't when you're comparing centimetres to inches. Unless you use the same ruler to do your measuring, it's easy to wind up comparing apples and blocks of wood.

Another problem you'll encounter is that vendors sometimes don't tell you how the performance of each part was measured. You can take two identical video cards and wind up with two entirely different sets of results from the same test, simply by putting one in a 486 and the other in a Pentium system, or by starting with the same processor and adding additional external cache memory and faster system RAM and/or by using a PCI local bus in one and VESA in the other.

In essence, the testing standard you settle on doesn't matter. You'll need to compile your results from the same test, with the same version number – and make sure the vendor reveals the environment in which the test was run. If you want to be really thorough, compile results from two different tests. Then ignore the specific numbers and assess the results for each component in relation to the others in order to get a sense of what's slow, what's fast, and what's faster.

Phew!

Already you've learned the essentials about a computer system. In the following chapters, I'll be describing in some detail what all the various components are and how they do what they do, so that you can make informed decisions about exactly what it is you want to buy.

3

Choosing the CPU

Regardless of the type of computer you have, there is a chip at its heart that turns what would otherwise be a useless set of electronic components into an amazing machine capable of performing complex tasks. The chip is called the central processing unit (CPU) or the microprocessor or simply the processor – and whether you buy a PC, a Mac, or a PowerMac/PC, you'll get one.

Mainframes and early minicomputers contained circuit boards full of integrated circuits that comprised the central processing unit. Single-chip central processing units are called microprocessors and they made personal computers and workstations possible.

Examples of single-chip CPUs are the Motorola 68000, 68020, 68030, 68040, MPC601, MPC603, MPC603e, and MPC604 chips. The "68000" series is what you'll find in Macs and the dearly departed NeXT, Amiga, and Atari systems. The MPC60x series shows up in PowerWhat-have-yous. Motorola is the sole supplier of CPUs for these types of computer.

The sole supplier of CPUs for the PC crowd used to be California-based Intel Corporation. Its 8080, 8088, 8086, 80286, 80386, 80486, Pentium, and P6 chips are still inside about 85 per cent of all microcomputers on the planet. More recently it has had some serious competition (see below under "Intel wanna-bes").

What do CPUs do?

Reading this and the next few sections will help you to understand some of what goes on inside your computer, but when you come right down to it, you don't have to understand this stuff in order to use it. If you want to skip ahead to the section on Intel's CPUs (which may help you to decide what generation of CPU to buy for a new PC), feel free.

At the simplest level, all a CPU does is add fast. It has abilities to fetch, decode, and execute instructions. The CPU can also transfer information to and from other resources over the computer's main data-transfer path, or bus. It is the chip that functions as the "brain" of a computer. In some instances, however, the term encompasses both the processor and the computer's memory or, even more broadly, the main computer console (as opposed to peripheral equipment).

Just because I said "brain" doesn't mean these things think. They don't. They're adding machines with pretensions. However, the folks who know how to give them instructions are brainy. As the abilities of CPUs in microcomputers have been increased (today's newest CPUs would blow a minicomputer from ten years ago out of the water), the instructions they get – the software – has increased in ability as well. Today's programmers can give us tools that do such remarkable things that you might believe your computer is thinking; but there's no need to keep a shotgun under the couch against the day it wakes up; trust me on this – all it's really doing is adding and moving digital codes several million times per second.

Everything that a CPU does is based on one operation: the ability to determine if a tiny transistor switch, or "gate," is open or closed. The CPU can recognize only two states in any of its microscopic circuits: on or off, high voltage or low voltage, represented by the binary numbers 1 or 0.

The speed at which the computer performs this simple act, however, is what makes it a marvel of modern technology. In essence, it sits there, ticking like a clock. On each "tick" something can happen.

The speed at which the CPU ticks is often called the "clock speed" because of the similarity. It is measured in megahertz (MHz), or millions of cycles per second.

MHz isn't everything

How fast the CPU "ticks" is not the only way of determining how powerful it really is or how a given computer system with a particular CPU will perform. CPU power is also determined by the amount of data it can handle during each cycle. If a computer checks only one switch at a time, that switch can represent only two commands – *on* (or 1) to execute one operation or number, and *off* (or 0). By checking groups of switches linked as a unit, however, the computer increases the number of operations it can execute at each cycle.

Computers in the 1970s, about the time the XT arrived, were generally able to check eight switches at a time. That is, they could check eight binary digits, or "bits," of data, each tick or cycle. A group of eight bits is called a byte, each byte containing 256 possible patterns of 1s and 0s. Each pattern is the equivalent of an instruction, a part of an instruction, or a particular type of instruction, such as a number or a character or a graphics symbol. The pattern 11010010, for example, might be binary data – in this case, the number 210 – or it might tell the computer to compare data stored in its switches to data stored elsewhere.

The subsequent development of processors that can handle 16, 32, and 64 bits of data at a time has increased the overall speed of computers. The complete collection of recognizable patterns, the total list of operations of which a computer is capable, is called its instruction set. All factors – number of bits at a time, size of instruction sets, and the speed of the clock cycle – affect how much power is available from any given CPU.

Maybe this example will help you to visualize why the factors are related. Imagine an hourglass full of grains of sand in the upper chamber. They have to pass through a narrow waist to get to the bottom. If the grains of sand are small and the waist is large, the sand will fall quickly. If the grains of sand are large and the waist is even larger, not only will the sand fall more quickly, but the top chamber will empty faster.

The speed of a computer's CPU is like the waist of our hourglass. The faster it is, the larger the waist. The amount of data it can handle in one operation is like the grains of sand. The larger the bit-rate, the larger the grains. So, a 16-bit CPU, such as the Intel AT-80286 or Motorola 68020, will have a slower processing rate than a 32-bit CPU, such as the 80386 and 80486 or the Motorola 68030 and 68040, running at the same speed.

Apparent overall system speed is another issue. Two 33 MHz, 32-bit computers running side-by-side can appear to perform quite differently. The video card, disk controller card, the disk drives themselves, RAM chip speed, and whether the CPU and/or system itself has a memory cache all make a difference. You can also make a difference by increasing the speed of the CPU compared to the system's mainboard (as is done with the 486DX2 and DX4) and/or by adding a local bus scheme (VESA or PCI) to speed up the rate at which data is transferred from its other systems.

Some examples? Add a 256 KB external cache to a system without any cache and performance will increase 26 to 31 per cent. Get rid of that video graphics card running on the old ISA bus and replace it with an accelerated SVGA card running on a PCI bus and watch performance jump about 43 per cent. Take a hard drive with 15 ms average access time and a built-in 64 KB cache buffer, then replace it with a hard drive with 12 ms average access and a 256 KB cache buffer, and your system performance will increase by about 11 per cent.

What the CPU is

The CPU is a collection of transistorized switches integrated into one small circuit. And I mean small. For example, the first P6 processors will have about 6 million transistors packed into a chip about the size of your thumbnail (compared to 3.1 million transistors in the Pentium).

Hardwired into the chip are a set of instructions accessible to programmers. Most CPUs are composed of four to six functional sections: an arithmetic/logic unit (ALU); registers; a control section; and an internal bus are common to all CPUs. The 486DX CPUs have two additional sections, a floating point unit, and a data cache, while advanced processors such as the Intel Pentium, the P6, and the PowerMac/PC have even more.

Let me explain what these gizmos do:

The ALU gives the chip its calculating ability and permits arithmetical and logical operations using primary integers (numbers without decimal points).

The registers are temporary storage areas that hold data, keep track of instructions, and hold the location and results of these operations.

The control section has three principal duties. It times and regulates the operations of the entire computer system; its instruction decoder reads the patterns of data in a register and translates the pattern into an activity, such as adding or comparing; and its interrupt unit indicates the order in which individual operations use the CPU and regulates the amount of CPU time that each operation may consume.

The internal bus is the pathway that connects the internal elements of the processor and also leads to external connectors that link the processor to the other parts of the computer system, such as the monitor and printer.

The three types of CPU buses are: (1) a control bus consisting of a line that senses input signals and another line that generates control signals from within the CPU, (2) the address bus, a one-way line from the processor that handles the location of data in memory, and (3) the data bus, a two-way transfer line that both reads data from memory and writes new data into memory. The P6 has a new bus – it connects the processor in the package to its companion cache chip.

One factor determining the power of your system is how many physical wires connect the CPU to memory via the address bus. If there are only 20 wires in the bus, 20 bits of data describing a memory address are all that can travel at one time, and the amount of memory the CPU can use is limited to 2^{20} bits or one megabyte (MB). If the address bus has 24 wires, the amount of addressable memory jumps to 2^{24} bits or 16 MB. Increase the bus width to 32 wires, and the amount of addressable memory leaps to 2^{32} bits or 4 gigabytes (GB).

Another factor is the width of the data bus. As noted above, a 32-bit bus will carry more information simultaneously than a 16-bit or 8-bit bus (and a 64-bit bus will leave them all in the dust). The same

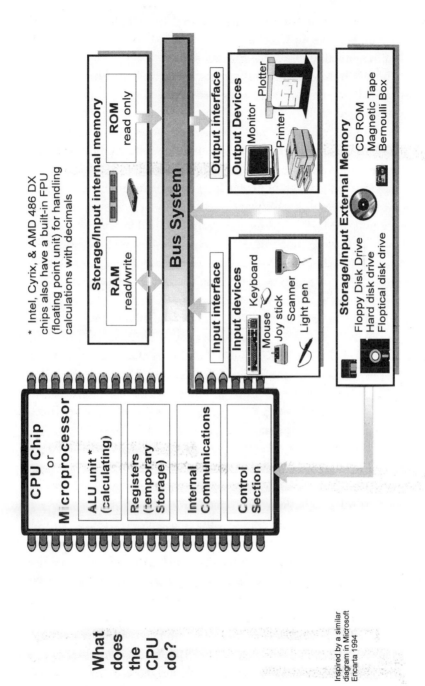

What does the CPU do?

CPU Chip or Microprocessor

ALU unit * (calculating)

Registers (temporary Storage)

Internal Communications

Control Section

* Intel, Cyrix, & AMD 486 DX chips also have a built-in FPU (floating point unit) for handling calculations with decimals

Storage/Input internal memory

RAM read/write

ROM read only

Bus System

Input interface

Input devices

Keyboard
Mouse
Joy stick
Scanner
Light pen

Output interface

Output Devices

Monitor
Plotter
Printer

Storage/Input External Memory

Floppy Disk Drive
Hard disk drive
Floptical disk drive

CD ROM
Magnetic Tape
Bernoulli Box

Inspired by a similar diagram in Microsoft Encarta 1994

holds true for the internal control bus that carries data among the other sections of the CPU.

Mathematical operations for numbers with variable decimal points benefit from special handling. In the case of both early Intel and Motorola CPUs, separate microprocessors, called math coprocessors, were developed to deal with these numbers more efficiently. In the 486DX, DX2, and DX4, and the Pentium and P6, as well as Motorola's 68040 and MPC60x chips, these circuits are built into the CPU, where they become known as FPUs (floating point units).

An additional section in newer Intel chips is the internal memory cache (or in Motorola's case what the company calls a memory management unit or MMU). It is used to store repeated instructions so the chip doesn't have to make as many trips outside to slower random access memory (RAM). This reduces the number of cycles during which the CPU is inactive while waiting for slower components of the computer system to catch up (called wait states).

Some Intel 80486 chips (SX, SX2, DX, and DX2s) have an 8 KB internal cache. Intel DX4 processors as well as IBM 486SLC and DLC processors have a 16 KB internal cache. Pentiums use two 8 KB caches, one for data and one for code, for the equivalent of 16 KB. The P6, however, is actually two chips in one package. On the processor chip itself are the same two 8 KB level 1 caches found in the Pentium, while the second chip consists of a 256 KB level 2 cache. The difference between level 1 and level 2 caches? Level 1 is faster and the first place where the CPU looks for data. If not found there, it then checks the larger but slower level 2 cache before finally going all the way to slower system RAM to get what it needs.

There are two basic flavours of CPU in use today, CISC (complex instruction set computing) and RISC (reduced instruction set computing). Microsoft's multimedia encyclopedia, *Encarta 95*, defines the difference as follows and it's as good an explanation as I've seen recently:

"Complex Instruction Set Computing (CISC) is a phrase describing a processor that uses complex instructions at the assembly language level. The instructions can be very powerful, allowing for complicated and flexible ways of calculating such

PC Memory Map

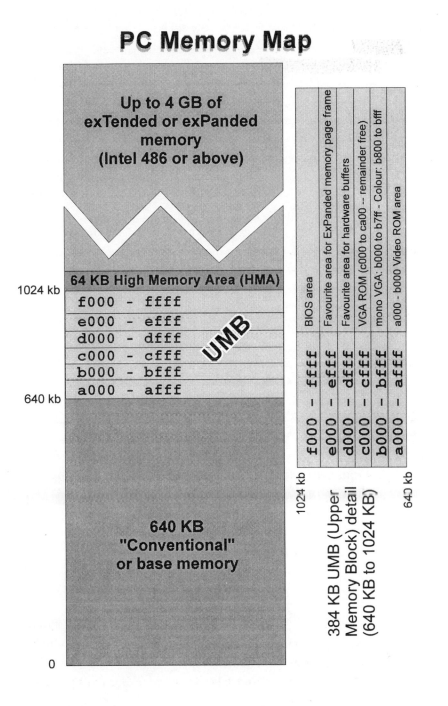

elements as memory addresses. All this complexity usually requires many clock cycles to execute each instruction. Examples of CISC computer families include all current IBM-compatible PCs, Apple Macintoshes, Amigas, and Ataris.

"Reduced Instruction Set Computing (RISC) is a type of microprocessor design that focuses on rapid and efficient processing of a relatively small set of instructions. RISC design is based on the premise that most of the instructions a computer decodes and executes are simple. As a result, RISC architecture limits the number of instructions that are built into the microprocessor but optimizes each so it can be carried out very rapidly – usually within a single clock cycle.

"RISC chips execute simple instructions faster than microprocessors designed to handle a much wider array of instructions. They are, however, slower than general-purpose CISC chips when executing complex instructions, which must be broken down into many machine instructions before they can be carried out by RISC microprocessors. Families of RISC chips that are gaining popularity include Sun Microsystems' SPARC, Motorola's PowerPC, Digital Equipment Corporation's Alpha, and Silicon Graphics/Mips' R4000 and R4400."

What this will mean to you in the short term when setting out to buy your next computer is that you will soon have more choices than ever before. Keep in mind, however, that most of the super-advanced systems are still under development and aren't quite ready to appear on your desktop to run your favourite word processor.

Intel

Intel's early CPUs

Until relatively recently, Intel was the sole supplier of CPUs for PCs, and its microprocessors are currently at the heart of roughly 128 million microcomputers in use throughout the world. Here's how Intel's CPUs have evolved in just over twenty years.

The first Intel CPU anyone paid any attention to was the 8080. Introduced in 1974, the 8080 has an 8-bit address bus and an 8-bit data bus. Despite the odd out-of-sequence numbering, the 8088 processor came before the 8086, which was released in 1978 and used in computers such as the IBM PC, PC/XT, Portable PC, PCjr, and compatible models. It was available in speeds of 4.77 MHz and 8 MHz. Both chips are now obsolete.

The 80286, also called the AT-286 (Advanced Technology) or simply the 286, was a 16-bit microprocessor introduced in 1982 and was included in the IBM PC/AT and compatible computers in 1984. With clock speeds of 8, 10, 12, 16, and 20 MHz depending on when it was manufactured, the 80286 has 16-bit registers, transfers information over the data bus 16 bits at a time, and uses 24 bits to address memory locations. It, too, is obsolete.

The 80386DX (also called the 80386, 386, and 386DX) was Intel's first 32-bit microprocessor. It was introduced in 1985 and used in IBM and compatible microcomputers such as the PS/2 Model 80, although Texas-based Compaq was the first computer company to ship systems using the chip.

The 386DX is a full 32-bit microprocessor, meaning that it has 32-bit registers, it can transfer information over its data bus 32 bits at a time, and it can use 32 bits in addressing memory. It came in 16, 20, 25, and 33 MHz models from Intel.

Like the earlier 286, the 386 operates in two modes, real and protected. Real mode in the 386 limits the amount of memory that the microprocessor can address to 1 megabyte, but in protected mode the 386 can address 4 gigabytes (roughly 4 billion bytes) of memory.

For a brief period during the reign of the XT, Intel had a competitor – the Japanese computer giant NEC – but its version of the 8086, which ran at 10 MHz, showed up in only a few North American machines. With the advent of the 386, however, Intel inspired another competitor that was due to give the company major headaches. Texas-based Advanced Micro Devices (AMD) produced a 40 MHz 386 processor and eventually took Intel's 386 market away.

The 386SX was introduced in 1988 as a low-cost alternative to the 386DX. The 386SX is basically a 386DX processor limited by a 16-bit external data bus. The 16-bit design allowed 386SX systems to be configured from less expensive AT-class parts, resulting in a much lower price. Like the DX model, the SX shipped in 16, 20, 25, and 33 MHz versions. Intel stopped manufacturing new 386 chips in early 1993, but may still be continuing to supply them from inventory for use in industrial applications (e.g., "smart" refrigerators and microwave ovens).

Intel introduced its 80486 chip, also called the 486, in 1989. Like its 386 predecessor, the 486 is a full 32-bit processor with 32-bit registers, 32-bit data bus, and 32-bit addressing. It includes several enhancements, however, including a built-in cache controller, a built-in floating point (math) coprocessor (in the DX, DX2, and DX4 models), and provisions for multiprocessing.

In addition, the 486 uses a "pipelined" execution scheme that breaks instructions into multiple stages, resulting in much higher performance for many common data and integer math operations. It also employs "burst mode," which allows the CPU to take four instructions in one gulp instead of the single instruction that a 386 takes. Despite these enhancements, when it was first introduced the 486DX was often called (primarily by companies wishing to sell their stocks of 386-based systems), "a 386 with a math coprocessor." Even though at 33 MHz it far outperforms a 40 MHz 386, this inaccurate criticism threatened the 486 market in its early days and led to the introduction of the 486SX (see below).

The Intel 486DX comes in 25, 33, and 50 MHz versions. A clock-doubled version, the DX2, comes in 50 and 66 MHz flavours, while the last variation of the chip is the clock-tripled DX4 running at 75 and 100 MHz. (Yes, the DX4 is clock *tripled*, not quadrupled as the number may lead you to think.)

The "clock-doubled" and "clock-tripled" versions of a processor can confuse you until you understand that the computer's system bus speed (the speed of the local bus on the motherboard) can be independent of the speed of the CPU. In DX systems, the CPU runs at the same speed as the motherboard's local bus – that is, 25, 33, or 50 MHz. A 50 MHz DX2, however, runs at that speed only inside the chip, while the local system bus continues to plod along at 25 MHz.

To give you some idea of how this affects overall performance, Intel says that a 66 MHz DX2 system runs approximately 70 per cent

PC Processors

Name	Chip	Made by	Long Name	Speeds	Good For...
PC	8086	Intel	Personal Computer	3.5 MHz	Obsolete
XT	8088	Intel	eXtended Technology	4.77 to 10 MHz	Obsolete
AT	80286	Intel	Advanced Technology	6 to 20 MHz	Obsolete
386 SX	80386 SX	Intel/AMD	16/32-bit 386	15 to 25 MHz	Obsolete
386 SL	80386 SL	Intel	Laptop power-saver	15 to 25 MHz	Laptops (obsolete)
386 DX	80386 DX	Intel/AMD	32-bit 386	25 to 40 MHz	Obsolete
486 DRX2	80486 DRX2	Cyrix	386 replacement chip	25 to 40 MHz	Supposedly to replace 386 chip in existing system and allow it to run 486 code.
486 DLC	80486 DLC	TI/Cyrix/IBM	Not a true 486	25 to 40 MHz	Souped up 386. Runs 486 code but doesn't match Intel chips in performance. See separate Chip Wars chart. Obsolete.
486 SLC	80486 SLC	TI/Cyrix/IBM	Laptop version	25 to 40 MHz	See above and below
486 xLC2	80486 xLC2	TI/Cyrix/IBM	Clock-doubled version	25 to 40 MHz	Competitors to Intel. Some compatibility problems reported with Cyrix chips. Not the same performance as Intel 486 DX chips! Obsolete.
486 SX	80486 SX	Intel/AMD	low-end 486	20 to 33 MHz	No math coprocessor but otherwise identical to Intel 486 DX. NOT recommended (obsolete).
486 DX	80486 DX	Intel/AMD/Cyrix	standard 486 DX	25 to 50 MHz	See ChipWars chart. Obsolete by 1996.
486 DX2	80486 DX2	Intel/AMD/Cyrix	clock-doubled 486	50 to 66 MHz	Not as fast as a Pentium. Obsolete by 1996.
IntelDX4	80486 DX4	Intel	clock-tripled 486	75 & 100 MHz	Clock-tripled, not clock-quadrupled. They contain a 16 KB cache and run at 3.3 volts, not the standard 5 volts. A 75 MHz Pentium may be a more economical buy. Obsolete by mid-1996 or sooner.
Blue Lightning	80486 DLC3	IBM	IBM clock-tripled 486	75 & 99 MHz	See above under 486 DX4 – clock-tripled chips with no math coprocessor, but 16 rather than 8 KB cache – see Chip Wars chart for other differences.
586 or P5	80586	Intel	Pentium	60 & 66 MHz to 75 MHz, 90 & 100 MHz, 120, 133 & 150 MHz	60/66 MHz models use 5 volts, .08 micron design, emit much heat and require a lot of real estate. Newer 90 & 100 MHz models use .06 micron design, run on 3.3 volts and are not pin-compatible with the first generation, but run cooler. The 120 to 150 MHz versions use .35 micron design of the P6. The 75 and 90 are a good buy in 1995.
"586"	K5, M1 & M1sc, Nx586	AMD, Cyrix, and NexGen	K5, M1 & M1sc, Nx586	?	Taking a chance on Intel's competitors. At press time only the Nx586 was showing up in some systems. The M1sc is described as a 486 with 586-like qualities
686 or P6	80686	Intel	?	?	The P6 is based on a .35 micron design and early reports indicate it will run at 2.9 volts. Optimized for multimedia and video-conferencing apps.

faster than a 33 MHz DX system, not twice as fast as the numbers may lead you to expect. The performance ratings of the various systems increase in the following order (from slowest to fastest): 486SX/25, 486DX/25, 486SX/33, 486DX/33, 486SX2/50, 486DX2/50, 486DX/50, 486SX2/66, 486DX2/66, 486DX4 (any speed), Pentium (any speed), P6 (any speed) – see the Intel iCOMP chart on page 34.

Intel has announced that it will not make a clock-doubled chip for 50 MHz DX systems, citing problems with excess heat and the fact that the VESA local bus standard tops out at 33 MHz. I predicted in late 1993 that these systems would wither up and ultimately vanish (and they have).

Introduced slightly later than the 486DX, the 486SX was put on the market by Intel to forestall the competition it faced from AMD with its 40 MHz version of the 386DX. The 486SX is identical in all but one respect to the 486DX – it has no built-in math coprocessor. The 486SX comes in 16, 20, 25, and 33 MHz versions, while the clock-doubled SX2 comes in 50 and 66 MHz flavours. There is no indication from Intel that they ever plan to release an SX4, but I wouldn't put it past them.

The 486 market is the arena in which Intel currently faces its greatest competition – from AMD, Cyrix Corp., Texas Instruments, and IBM. For more details on how its so-called 486 chips differ from the Intel models, see the section "Intel wanna-bes" below.

One last variant of Intel's 486 was originally developed for laptop and notebook computers, but the technology is now incorporated into all Intel CPUs. The 486SL, together with software to address the issue, can power down parts of the system (monitors, disk drives, and so on) when they are not in use.

Pentiums

The Pentium was first released for limited testing in 1992, then it was revamped and began shipping in quantity only in late 1993. Originally designated the 80586, and for a short time known as the P5, Intel gave it a name after it discovered that it couldn't copyright a number (and given the confusion over what actually constitutes a 486, perhaps it's just as well).

The Pentium employs a 32-bit internal bus, a 64-bit external bus, and a 32-bit address bus allowing access to 4 gigabytes of memory. Using over 3.1 million transistors, the Pentium 60 delivers approximately twice the performance of a 66 MHz 486DX2 system.

And that's not all. Instead of the single onboard 8 KB data cache, the Pentium has two 8 KB caches; one for data and one for code. It also uses dual "pipelining" and what Intel calls "superscalar" architecture to allow it to process two instructions per clock cycle instead of one. Intel has also re-engineered the built-in math coprocessor to deliver "five to ten times" the speed of the math coprocessor in the 486DX.

The Pentium currently comes in a multitude of speeds and three different sizes, but before we can discuss them, we have to talk about microns. A micron is a unit of measurement that is roughly equivalent to one thousandth of the width of a human hair and in computer terms is used to measure the average distance between connected components on the surface of the chip. The distance a signal has to travel between components will determine how much electrical power is required to move it. Electrical signals in the CPU move so quickly that the time it takes them to move between components becomes a factor in how well the chip performs. The original 486s were based on a 1.0 micron design.

The first batch of Pentiums shipped in two speeds (60 and 66 MHz), and were based on a 0.8 micron design. Like the 486, the P60/66 chips also used a 5-volt power supply and suffered from overheating as a result. People with 60 MHz systems shouldn't despair, however. Intel has promised an OverDrive component for release in 1996 based on its relatively recent 120 MHz Pentium processor, which should revive these older systems.

The second-generation Pentium chips were based on a 0.6 micron design and operated at lower power levels (3.3 volts). Not only were these 75, 90, and 100 MHz chips orders of magnitude faster than 486s, they ran cooler than the P60/66.

As of mid-1995, the fastest Pentiums on the market were the 120 and 133 MHz models. They're based on the same 0.35 micron design used in the P6 and also run at 3.3 volts, so that while they were the fastest Pentiums at the time, they were also smaller than their earlier cousins and ran at even lower temperatures.

Is that all? Nope. My sources at Intel tell me that there is room for faster Pentium processors and that the P6 will eventually reach close to 250 MHz. In the meantime, you can expect at least two more Pentiums before this chip reaches the end of its production cycle. The same Intel sources have confirmed that a 150 MHz model is slated for release by late fall 1995. Another is rumoured to be planned for roughly 180 MHz and, although its existence couldn't be confirmed before this book went to print, you can expect to see it some time in 1996.

P6

Just as the Pentium was originally called first the 80586, then the P5, the P6 was originally the 80686, then the P6. It was first demonstrated at an engineering conference in early 1995, but didn't start shipping in quantity until fall of that year.

Building on the superscalar, dual pipelining architecture of the Pentium, the P6 adds Dynamic Execution, a combination of three processing techniques, to speed up software. The techniques include some things that sound like magic to me – multiple-branch prediction (the processor looks ahead in the software and predicts which branches, or groups of instructions, are likely to be processed next), dataflow analysis (the P6 analyses which instructions are dependent on each other's results, or data, to create an optimized schedule of instructions), and speculative execution (instructions are carried out speculatively based on this optimized schedule, keeping all the chip's superscalar processing power busy, and boosting overall software performance).

In plain English, the P6 reads ahead, calculates some operations out of order, then guesses what comes next. If it works as planned, the software executes an instruction before it knows it has been asked (well, maybe not – let's just say it makes things *fast*).

What's next?

The team that developed the Pentium began work on the P7 in January 1993. It is tentatively due for release in 1997 or 1998. A second team, working in conjunction with Hewlett-Packard, is developing what we

may as well call the P8. In its literature, Intel predicts CPUs incorpo-
rating over 100 million transistors, operating in excess of 250 MHz
and capable of handling over two billion instructions per second, by
the year 2000.

Now, if we can just get Windows to run without crashing . . .

Intel wanna-bes

I'm not a flag-waver for Intel; however, I am concerned that when you
buy a computer you get what you thought you bought.

Although the 486 as a class will soon drop off the active computer market, there will still be a few of them around during the early
life of this book, so we need to have a close look at Intel's competition. Active competitors using the "486" label to describe their products include Advanced Micro Devices (AMD), Cyrix Corp., Texas
Instruments, and IBM.

All of the competing chips in the 486 wars cost less than Intel's
and are therefore tempting alternatives. To my knowledge there have
only been a few concerns raised about whether they will run software
compatibly. The other issue is whether the competing CPUs have the
same performance characteristics – and in most cases they don't. See
the charts "Chip Wars."

If you've read the sections above, you'll know that several factors
control how powerful a CPU is. The speed of its clock cycle and the
speed of the motherboard's local bus are one set of factors. Additional
performance characteristics include the width of the external data bus
(it determines how much data can arrive at the CPU in a single cycle)
and the width of the memory address bus (which determines how
much memory the chip can work with).

Whether the CPU employs what Intel calls "burst mode" will
affect the number of idle clock cycles, during which the CPU does
nothing. Also called "wait states," these idle cycles directly affect the
overall system performance. According to Intel, burst mode allows its
486 CPUs to do in five wait states what chips without burst mode take
eight to accomplish.

If a CPU derives its name from the type of slot into which it fits,
the bus upon which it operates, the bulk of the instruction set with

CHIP WARS 1	AMD 486 SX2-66, SX4-100	AMD 486 DX2-80	AMD DX4-100 / DX4-120	Cyrix 486 SLC/SLC2	Cyrix 486 DLC/DLC2	Cyrix 486S Cyrix microcode	Cyrix 486 DX Cyrix microcode	Cyrix 486 DX2-66 Cyrix microcode	Cyrix 486 DX2-80 Cyrix microcode	Cyrix 486 DX4-100 Cyrix microcode
Pin compatibility/chip set	486 SX2	486 DX	486 DX	386 SX	386 DX	486 SX	486 DX	486 DX	486 DX	486 DX
Internal cache size	8 KB	8 KB	8 or 16 KB	1 KB	1 KB	2 KB	8 KB	8 KB	8 KB	8 KB
L1 internal cache design	write-back	write-back	write-back	write-thru	write-thru	write-thru	write-thru	write-back	write-back	write-back
Burst mode	yes	yes	yes	no	no	yes	yes	yes	yes	yes
Built-in math coprocessor	no	yes	yes	no	no	no	yes	yes	yes	yes
Instruction set	486 SX	486 DX	486 DX	486 SX	486 SX	486 SX	486 DX	486 DX	486 DX	486 DX
Max processor clock speed (MHz)	66 / 100	80	100 / 120	33, 50	33, 50	33, 40	33, 40, 50	66	80	100
Local bus speed (MHz)	33 / 33	40	33 / 40	33, 25	33, 25	33, 40	33, 40, 50	33	40	33
Internal data bus	32-bit	32-bit	32-bit	32-bit	32-bit	32-bit	32-bit	32-bit	32-bit	32-bit
External data bus	32-bit	32-bit	32-bit	16-bit	32-bit	32-bit	32-bit	32-bit	32-bit	32-bit
Memory address bus width	32-bit	32-bit	32-bit	24-bit	32-bit	32-bit	32-bit	32-bit	32-bit	32-bit
Max memory addressable	4 GB	4 GB	4 GB	16 MB	4 GB	4 GB	4 GB	4 GB	4 GB	4 GB
Superscalar performance	no	no	no	no	no	no	no	no	no	no

Note: Cyrix SLC and SLC2 chips contain a "16-bit hardware multiplier" which they claim overcomes not having a built-in math coprocessor

CHIP WARS 2	IBM 486 SLC2**	IBM 486 "Blue Lightning" DLC2/DLC3	IBM 486 DX2-66	IBM 486 DX2-80	Intel i486 SX/SL	Intel i486 SX2	Intel i486 DX/DX2	Intel i486 DX4	Texas Inst. 486 SLC / 486 DLC	Texas Inst. 486 SXLC / 486 SXLC2	Texas Inst. 486 SXL / 486 SXL2
Pin compatibility/chip set	Proprietary/ 386 SX	Proprietary/ 386 DX	Proprietary/ 486 DX	Proprietary/ 486 DX	486 SX	486 SX	486 DX	486 DX	386 SX / 386 DX	386 SX	386 DX / 486 SX
Internal cache size	16 KB	16 KB	8 KB	8 KB	8 KB	8 KB	8 KB	16 KB	1 KB	8 KB	8 KB
L1 internal cache design	write-thru	write-thru	write-back	write-back	write-back	write-thru	write-thru	write-back	write-back	write-back	write-back
Burst mode	no	no	yes	yes	yes	yes	yes	yes	no	no	no
Built-in math coprocessor	no	no	yes	yes	no/yes	no	yes	yes	no	no	no
Instruction set	486 SX	486 SX	486 DX	486 DX	486 SX/DX	486 SX	486 DX	486 DX	486 SX	486 SX	486 SX
Max processor clock speed (MHz)	50, 66	50/75, 66/100*	66	80	25, 33	50, 66	25, 33, 50/ 50, 66	75, 100	25, 33, 40 / 40	25, 40 / 50	40. / 50, 66
Local bus speed (MHz)	25, 33	25, 33	33	40	25, 33	25, 33	25, 33, 50/ 25, 33	25, 33, 50	25, 33, 40 / 40	25, 40 / 25	40 / 25, 33
Internal data bus	32-bit	32-bit	32-bit	32-bit	32-bit	32-bit	32-bit	32-bit	32-bit	32-bit	32-bit
External data bus	16-bit	32-bit	32-bit	32-bit	32-bit	32-bit	32-bit	32-bit	16- /32-bit	16-bit	32-bit
Memory address bus width	24-bit	32-bit	32-bit	32-bit	32-bit	32-bit	32-bit	32-bit	24- /32-bit	24-bit	32-bit
Max memory addressable	16 MB	4 GB	4 GB	4 GB	4 GB	4 GB	4 GB	4 GB	16 MB/4 GB	16 MB	4 GB
Superscalar performance	no	no	no	no	no	no	no	no	no	no	no

Note: Texas Instruments will be releasing a 486 DX2-66 and DX2-80, identical to the Cyrix models in late 1995

CHIP WARS 3	Intel Pentium 60/66	Intel Pentium 75	Intel Pentium 90/100	Intel Pentium 120/133	Intel P6	Cyrix M1	Cyrix M1sc	NexGen Nx586 P75	NexGen Nx586 P80	NexGen Nx586 P90	NexGen Nx586 P100
Pin compatibility/chip set	Pentium	Pentium / Triton	Pentium / Triton	Pentium / Triton	P6 / ?	Proprietary	486 DX / ?	Proprietary	Proprietary	Proprietary	Proprietary
Internal cache size	8 KB code, 8 KB data	8 KB code, 8 KB data	8 KB code, 8 KB data	8 KB code, 8 KB data	16 KB code 16 KB data 256 KB L2	16 KB unified	16 KB unified	16 KB code 16 KB data	16 KB code 16 KB data	16 KB code 16 KB data	16 KB code 16 KB data
L1 internal cache design	write-back	write-back	write-back	write-back	write-back	write-back	write-back	write-back	write-back	write-back	write-back
Built-in math coprocessor	yes	yes	yes	yes	yes	yes	yes?	optional	optional	optional	optional
Instruction set	Pentium	Pentium	Pentium	Pentium	Pentium /?	x86 and ?	x86 ?	?	?	?	?
Max processor speed (MHz)	60 / 66	75	90 / 100	120 / 133	no data	100	100 (80?)	70	75	84	93
Memory/expansion bus speed (MHz)	60 / 30 66 / 33	50 / 25	60 / 30 66 / 33	60 / 30 66 / 33	no data/ no data	50 / 25	33 / 33?	70, 35 */ 35	75, 37.5 / 37.5	84, 42 / 42	93, 46.5 / 46.5
Internal data bus	64-bit	64-bit	64-bit	64-bit	64-bit	64-bit	64-bit?	64-bit	64-bit	64-bit	64-bit
External data bus	32-bit	32-bit	32-bit	32-bit	32-bit	32-bit	32-bit	32-bit	32-bit	32-bit	32-bit
Memory address bus width	32-bit	32-bit	32-bit	32-bit	32-bit	32-bit	32-bit	32-bit	32-bit	32-bit	32-bit
Max memory addressable	4 GB	4 GB	4 GB	4 GB	4 GB	4 GB	4 GB	4 GB	4 GB	4 GB	4 GB
Superscalar performance	yes	yes	yes	yes	yes	yes	no	yes	yes	yes	yes
Branch prediction	no	no	no	no	yes	yes	no data	no data	no data	no data	no data
Dual pipelining	yes	yes	yes	yes	yes	yes	no data	no data	no data	no data	no data
Out of order processing	no	no	no	no	yes	yes	no data	no data	no data	no data	no data
Data flow analysis	no	no	no	no	yes	yes	no data	no data	no data	no data	no data

*The Nx586 contains two memory buses. The line to the L2 cache runs at the same speed as the CPU, while the line to external memory runs at half that speed. Sorry, NexGen didn't reply to our queries and we don't know how large the L2 cache is.

which it works, and the surrounding chipset with which it is integrated, then the LC models from Cyrix, Texas Instruments, and IBM are 386 processors, not 486s. Aside from the DX models manufactured by AMD and Cyrix, which the companies claim are identical to the Intel 486DX, none of the rest of the other chips have built-in math coprocessors. You'll need one if you want to optimize the performance of such software as Excel, Lotus 1-2-3, MS Access, Fractal Design Painter, and CorelDRAW, to name but a few.

One last difference, then we're done. You'll note from the chart that the LC models from Cyrix and Texas Instruments have smaller internal memory caches than the Intel 486's 8 KB (and the DX4's 16 KB) cache. Aside from being less efficient because they hold less data, the caches have to be flushed of this data more frequently and therefore they are likely to be unavailable when required. The IBM-made "486" line also uses a 16 KB cache, which goes a long way towards improving its performance compared to the others, but in benchmark tests it still doesn't match the performance of an Intel 486SX running at the same speed.

As 1995 closes, you're also going to start hearing more about companies with "586-class" processors as AMD, Cyrix, NexGen, and IBM all trot out chips they'll say will work just like Pentiums. AMD is working on the K5; Cyrix is preparing the M1 and M1sc (more of a 486 modified to run some Pentium instructions); NexGen has produced the Nx586, and it appears as though it may be the first on the street with something a computer can actually use. Only people in blue suits know what IBM is up to. When these chips arrive and start appearing in systems you and I can buy, this whole topic of compatibility and performance will rear its ugly head again. Count on it.

What about the other end – the high-end RISC processors such as Sun Microsystems' SPARC, Digital Equipment Corp.'s Alpha, and Silicon Graphics' Mips R4000 – or for that matter Motorola's MPC60x series in the PowerThings? For now, forget 'em. When I've seen one run today's PC- or Macintosh-based software at speeds equal to or exceeding the systems I have now (or for less money than a high-end PC or Mac would cost), without forcing me to buy all new software to take full advantage of them, I'll let you know. Hell, I'll be one of the first to buy one.

Motorola

Unlike Intel in the PC market, Motorola doesn't have any competition for its products. Its chips were found in the now-defunct NeXT, Amiga, and Atari computers – and it has the market for Macintosh and PowerMac/PCs all to itself. As a result, there aren't nearly as many models of Motorola chip to describe (nothing breeds innovation like competition).

The ancestor of them all is the 68000. It was the original microprocessor in the 680x0 family from Motorola. The 68000 has 24-bit physical addressing and a 16-bit data bus. The 8 MHz variety was at the core of the original Apple Macintosh released in 1984. It is also found in the Macintosh Plus, the original Macintosh SE, the Apple LaserWriter IISC, and Hewlett Packard's LaserJet printer family. It had no built-in FPU (see above) and no way to add an external coprocessor.

The 68000 is able to address 16 megabytes of memory – 16 times more memory than the Intel 8088 in the original IBM PC could address. In addition, the 68000 has a linear addressing architecture as opposed to the 8088's segmented memory architecture, making programming large applications more straightforward. In a linear system, all memory is memory is memory. You don't get involved in figuring out how to manage base memory, upper memory, and extended/expanded memory as you do with the segmented architecture in a PC.

I've often wondered whatever happened to the 68010, but the next member in the series was the 68020. This chip has 32-bit addressing and a 32-bit data bus and is available in speeds of 16, 20, 25, and 33 MHz. The 68020 is found in the original Macintosh II and the LaserWriter IINT from Apple. It included a 256-byte (not kilobyte) instruction cache, but still didn't have a built-in FPU – although it did have connections to add a 68021 math coprocessor.

Next came the 68030, also with 32-bit addressing and a 32-bit data bus, plus built-in paged memory management, which precludes the need for supplemental chips to provide that function. A 16 MHz version is used in the Macintosh IIx, IIcx, and SE/30, and a 25 MHz model is used in the Mac IIci and the dearly departed NeXT computer. The 68030 is also produced in 20, 33, 40, and 50 MHz versions. It

included two 256-byte caches for instructions and code, used a form
of burst mode, and once again allowed external addition of a 68031
math coprocessor to make up for lack of a built-in FPU.

Nearly last is the 68040, again with 32-bit addressing and a
32-bit data bus. The 68040 started at 25 MHz, but by mid-1995 was
up to 120 MHz. It includes a built-in math coprocessor and two
memory management units (similar in function to the memory cache
built into the Intel 486), including independent 4 KB instruction and
data caches (for a total of 8 KB). In addition, the 68040 is capable of
parallel instruction execution by means of multiple independent
instruction pipelines, multiple internal buses, and separate caches for
both data and instructions. It includes support for systems with multiple processors and also uses a form of burst mode.

PowerMac/PC

The PowerMac and PowerPC, which use Motorola's newest series of
chips, developed in conjunction with IBM and Apple: the MPC601,
602, 603, 603e, and 604. They're RISC chips, with one main advantage over other RISC chips on the market or under development:
lower cost for the chip itself.

Typical of RISC architecture, the MPC601 has a lot of registers.
There are thirty-two 32-bit general purpose registers (GPRs) and
thirty-two 64-bit floating point registers (compared to the Pentium's
eight GPRs and a floating point stack). There is also a single 32 KB
unified data and instruction cache (compared to the Pentium's two
separate 8 KB caches). The chip is a superscalar design capable of
executing three instructions per clock cycle, including out-of-order
processing (i.e., calculations are completed when they can be, regardless of which order they take in the instruction stack).

The core of the PowerPC consists of three independent pipelined
execution units – one each for integer math, floating point math, and
branch execution. Like the Pentium, the PowerPC also uses a form of
branch prediction, trying to anticipate when program logic dictates a
change in the normal sequential flow of instructions to the processor.
The MPC601 has a 64-bit data bus and 32-bit address bus, runs at

3.6 volts, and is based on a 0.6 micron design. Available in 60, 66, 80, and 110 MHz versions, the MPC601 is found in PowerMac 6100/60, 7100/66, 8100/80, and 8100/100 models.

The MPC 602, 603, and more recent 603e are low-power variants of the 601. The MPC602 has four execution units instead of three (it adds a load/store unit) and three progressive power-down modes (nap, doze, and sleep), making it ideal for portable systems. The MPC 603 is also a low-power model, based on a 0.5 micron design and running at 3.3 volts. It adds a fifth execution unit, the system register unit.

The 603 has four power-down modes, including static nap, doze, and sleep modes, but adds a fourth dynamic power management mode that, according to Motorola, causes the functional units in the chip to "automatically enter a lower-power mode when the functional units are idle without affecting operational performance, software execution, or any external hardware." Wow.

Where the 603 and 603e differ is in the onboard caches. The 603 has two 8 KB caches for data and instructions, while the 603e uses two 16 KB caches. Both chips have selectable 32- or 64-bit data buses and a 32-bit address bus. At press time, I couldn't find any consumer-level products shipping with either 602, 603, or 603e processors. However, Motorola itself has a brand-name line called Power Stacks, featuring both the 603e and 604 (see below). Like IBM's PowerPC, showcased in the summer of 1995, these units are aimed at the high-end workstation market and are only capable of running AIX and Windows NT (instead of Mac System 7.5, OS/2, or either Windows 3.1x or Windows 95). The MPC602 is primarily used in industrial design and it's unlikely you'll ever see it in a computer − in a "smart" piece of manufacturing equipment maybe, but not on your desktop.

Last but not least is the MPC 604. First introduced in the PowerMac 9500 in the summer of 1995 in 120 and 133 MHz versions, the MPC 604 utilizes superscalar architecture, allowing it to process four instructions per clock cycle. It contains six execution units: floating point, branch processing, load/store, two single-cycle integer units, and one multiple-cycle integer unit. It has separate memory management units and two separate 16 KB caches for instructions and data, and runs at 3.3 volts. At the time of introduction, a PowerMac 9500 ran nearly twice as fast as the 8100/100, came with a CD-ROM drive, 16 MB of RAM, and a 1 GB hard drive, starting at $8,749 U.S. (monitor extra).

So what?

In terms of handling data, the PowerPC and Pentium have similar characteristics. Where they part company entirely is in performance with current software.

Pentiums don't run Mac software at all, while the PowerPC will run some (but not all). By itself, the PowerMac won't run PC software either – unless you add (and pay for) enough memory to get to at least 16 MB, then pay again for either a software emulator or a special circuit board with a separate 486 processor; then you can run PC software at about the level of a 286 or that of a 25 MHz 486SX.

The alternative for former PC users is to toss out all existing software and hope someone sells enough PowerMac/PCs to convince the software industry to write some RISC-based programs for them. To be fair, there were some applications written exclusively for the environment by mid-1995, but the choices were limited.

It might help to understand why there is a PowerMac/PC at all if we look at history. The idea for it was born at time when Apple, IBM, and Motorola had no reason to love either Intel or Microsoft. At the time, the Mac offered the only real graphical environment in town (despite their adherents' protests to the contrary, the Amiga and Atari were considered gaming machines not to be taken seriously). The Mac had a lead in desktop publishing, graphics design, and music composition, and its interface – complete with menus, icons, mouse, and the visual point-and-click motif – was considered easier to learn than the often obtuse DOS.

PCs, on the other hand, were dominant in the corporate, government, and big institutional communities (where the really big bucks were). Although it had a hard-to-learn, character-based, command-line-driven interface, weak graphics, and tacky sound, the PC also had a commanding lead in heavy word processing, accounting, financial analysis and modelling (spreadsheets), and data manipulation (databases).

Wouldn't it be wonderful, a few bright folks at IBM and Apple asked, if they could build a computer that could run both the Mac graphics and the PC DOS-based stuff? They'd clean up and put an end to those annoying folk at Intel and Microsoft once and for all.

Nobody anticipated the success of Microsoft Windows or that Intel would develop its processors to the extent that it since has, or that the small-office, home-office phenomenon would take on the computer market share that it has.

Between the time of the grand idea and delivery of the PowerMac/PC, most of the software applications that once ran only on a Mac became available in versions that run in Windows and so did most of the software products that kept DOS on corporate desks. In fact, DOS is virtually dead – the only segment of the software market still updating or releasing new DOS applications are the high-end gaming folk. There is no longer any reason for a PC user to have Mac envy, and no reason left for MacFolk to want to run DOS. A faster Mac, yes – but not DOS.

This prediction is going to annoy the PowerWhatever fans, but I doubt it will survive any more than the Mac will survive. In fact if Apple is still a hardware company by the end of the 1990s, I'll be surprised (and probably embarrassed).

There are a couple of factors that could prove me wrong. For the first time in its history, Apple has begun to license its operating system to other hardware manufacturers. I think it significant that as of mid-1995 no one has volunteered to clone any pure Macintosh systems (the LCS, Performa, and Quadra lines), but as of this writing, six companies have announced intentions to produce PowerMac workalikes. If this competition brings the prices down, PowerThings may be more attractive than comparably performing Macs or PCs.

The second factor involves the software industry. Members of this particular club have access to all the world's brightest minds. These software programming wizards need only be aimed in a particular direction and told to kill. They'll write for the PC, for the Mac, or for the PowerGizmo. Still, Macs comprise somewhere between 8 and 9 per cent of computers in the world and the current crop of PowerThings (to be generous, perhaps a couple of million) doesn't even register as a percentage. But there are approximately 100 million PCs that run Windows. (Evans Research concluded in mid-1995 that of the 2.1 million PCs in Canadian homes at the beginning of the year, over 1.5 million of them were running Windows and all of the half-million more that would be sold this year would run it, too). Where do you think this year's budget for software product development will go?

Just to give one last kick at the PowerStuff, it is interesting to note that IBM, the third partner in the PowerWhats-it trio, announced in June 1995 that its PowerPC "was never intended to replace Intel's x86-based PCs," and that it was destined only for "high-end enterprise computing solutions." This was shortly after demonstrating its latest version of the system during a PC Expo computer show in New York and being forced to admit that it could only run two operating systems, AIX and Windows NT, and that it wasn't quite sure when it would run Windows 95, OS/2, or Mac System 7.5 except that it wouldn't be much before mid-1996.

4

Video Cards and Monitors

After the CPU, the subsystem in your computer that most affects how well it appears to perform is the video graphics subsystem. It is composed of a video graphics controller and a monitor. The video controller is either located on a circuit board slotted into the motherboard or directly wired to it, so you'll hear it called a video or graphics board, a video or graphics card, video or graphics adapter, or video or graphics controller.

Together, they are the window into your computer (and the big glass eye that allows anyone looking over your shoulder to share in your triumphs and mistakes). As with any of the other component subsystems, tinkering with this one can allow you to take two virtually identical computers and make one appear gorgeous and the other quite ordinary. For example, replacing a standard ISA, unaccelerated video card with an accelerated PCI-based local bus version could jack up apparent performance by as much as 43 per cent.

Basic terminology

We need to straighten out a couple of terms before we proceed. To begin to understand the issues involved in choosing a graphics card you need to be familiar with pixels, resolution, colours, and palettes.

A *pixel* (short for picture element) is the smallest unit on the screen that can be addressed by computer memory. In other words, it's the smallest portion of the picture that the computer can change. Think of the screen being divided into points similar to the dots that make up a newspaper photograph. In a character-based (DOS) system, a pixel will be about the size of a period at the end of a sentence.

Resolution is the term used to describe how many pixels can be displayed on the screen at one time. A resolution of 640 by 480, for example, means 640 pixels horizontally and 480 pixels vertically (for a total of 307,200). Doing the math here isn't simply an exercise – it will help to understand why a graphics card requires more memory to provide additional colours at higher resolutions and why your system will slow to a crawl if you don't have it.

For instance, a low resolution of 320 by 200 means that 64,000 pixels get coloured. At 1024 by 768, there are 786,432 pixels. If each pixel at that resolution is called upon to be any one of 16 colours, we're dealing with 12,582,912 choices. If the number of colours jumps to 256, the card has to deal with 201,326,592 factors. At 16.7 million colours, my calculator gives up and goes home.

Colours refers to the number of colours that can be displayed on screen at any one time, while the *palette* is the total number of colours the system can generate. Old, low-resolution, low-colour standards such as CGA could only display four colours on screen from a total palette of 16 (which was actually a palette of 8 colours with high and low intensities). "True-colour" 24-bit video cards can generate over 16.7 million colours from a palette of over 16.7 million colours. Medical and optical research has shown that in the "best" of human eyes, each of the three colour receptors is capable of distinguishing up to 256 shades of colour (256 shades of red, 256 shades of green, 256 shades of blue). That's a total of about 16.7 million colours (16,777,216 to be exact).

Video Cards

Because they are obsolete standards, I'm going to ignore CGA and EGA and use VGA as a jumping-off point. Standard VGA uses 8-bit technology. It has nothing to do with the nature of the slot into which VGA cards fit in the motherboard. Instead, it has to do with how information is processed in the card. They use an 8-bit video "word" or byte to specify the colour of each pixel on the screen – by assigning a specific, predefined colour out of a palette of 256,000 colours to each of the 256 numbers that can be described with 8 binary bits.

The VGA card then uses a DAC (digital to analog converter) to translate these numbers into three analog signals – red, green, and blue – that drive the monitor. In effect, VGA paints by numbers: "Make this pixel colour 25, this one 12," and so on. The scheme is referred to as indexing.

Because VGA is capable of displaying only a limited number of colours, it also uses an additional technique called dithering (using patterns of available colours) to simulate unavailable colours and gradual shifts of tone. This technique produces, at best, a rough approximation of the desired colour.

As VGA technology improved, some video card manufacturers introduced cards that increased the number of colours that could be displayed on screen. These so-called "high" colour cards are 15- or 16-bit. A 15-bit card (such as those using the Sierra HiColor RAMDAC, or IBM's now mostly defunct XGA card) could generate 32,768 colours. A 16-bit card could generate 65,536 colours.

While high colour was a big improvement over VGA, the technology still fell short of producing the number of colours required for truly realistic rendering or colour-critical work – which brings us to 24-bit colour cards. The first models on the market came packed with memory, required their own graphics processors, and caused bank managers to see all 256 shades of red.

In this scheme, each of the image's three colour channels (red, green, and blue) is assigned its own 8 bits, allowing each pixel to be one of the possible 256 shades of the primary colours. The result is the same spectrum of colours the human eye can distinguish.

Video graphics history

When personal computers became stable enough to enter the home and business markets, choosing a graphics card and monitor was dead simple – you got what came with the computer, and each computer manufacturer supplied its own combination. You could have any on-screen colour you liked – as long as it was green on black – and in any resolution – as long as it was approximately 720 by 350.

The introduction of the IBM PC ended that. Suddenly, anyone could manufacture a video card or monitor and have it work in millions of systems. This huge base, the steady improvement of equipment, and the inexorable advancements in software have all prompted further developments in the graphics side of the hardware industry.

Graphics standards

We really thought we'd arrived when the VGA (video graphics array) cards came on the scene. Early VGA cards were only 640 by 480 with 16 colours on screen – but the palette jumped to 256,000 from the 64 colours the earlier and now defunct EGA (enhanced graphics array) cards provided. However, moving to this card usually meant you had to replace your monitor. VGA cards produced an analog signal – and EGA's output was digital. This was more than simply different connector configurations. Only folks with monitors able to run in either digital or analog modes were able to keep their monitors. Today, it's not an issue – you'd be hard pressed to find an EGA monitor for sale and even if you're not paying attention, you will get a monitor that is more or less suitable for use with the graphics card you buy (otherwise it simply won't work), but there are traps, so read on.

VGA was quickly enhanced to Super VGA (SVGA). Initially, the SVGA "standard" called for 800 by 600 resolution and, depending on the card and the amount of memory on the card, a possible 256 colours on screen from a palette of 256,000. Once again, however, if you were stuck with a "VGA" monitor that ran at a fixed 640 by 480 resolution, you were out of luck. The SVGA standard was later extended to include resolutions of 1024 by 768 (and if the graphics card had sufficient memory, you could still get 256 colours out of 256,000 at

Video graphics standards

	Long Name	Year	Resolution range	Colour bit-depth	Maximum on-screen colours	Palette
MDA	Monochrome Display Adaptor	1981	720 by 350 / 600 by 400	8-bit	2 (green, amber or white on black)	Different intensities (bright, dim, reverse)
CGA	Colour Graphics Adaptor	1981	320 by 200 / 320 by 240 / 640 by 200	8-bit	8	4 (with bright and dim intensities)
HGC	Hercules Graphics Card	1982	720 by 348 / 600 by 400	8-bit	See MDA	See MDA
EGA	Enhanced Graphics Adaptor	1984	320 by 200 / 640 by 200 / 640 by 350	8-bit	16	64
PGA EGA+	Professional Graphics Adaptor / EGA Plus	1984	EGA resolutions plus 640 by 480	8-bit	16	64
VGA	Video Graphics Array	1987	640 by 480	8-bit	64	256,000
8514/A	IBM's interlaced adaptor	1987	1024 by 768 (interlaced)	8-bit	64 to 256	256,000
SVGA	Super VGA	1988	800 by 600	8-bit	64 to 256	256,000
SVGA+	eXtended SVGA or SVGA Plus	1988	1024 by 768 (non-interlaced)	8-bit	64 to 256	256,000
XGA	eXtended Graphics Adaptor	1990	800 by 600 (15-bit)	15-bit	32,000 plus	32,000 plus
UVGA	Ultra VGA (a name we made up)	1991	1280 by 1024 or higher may be 16 or 24-bit	8, 16 or 24-bit	64 to 16.7 million	256,000 to 16.7 million
TIGA	Texas Instruments Graphics Architecture	1991	2048 by 1280 (2048 by 2048 virtual)	24-bit	32,000 +, 65,000 +, 16.7 million	16.7 million

PC Video Graphics Standards keep changing. If you order a video board using the name of the "standard" you may not get what you want. Describe it by the number of colours you want to see on screen, at what resolution(s), and with what degree of acceleration. Then start negotiating brand name, model, and price.

that resolution). The only problem here was that running 256 colours on an early 486 computer at 1024 by 768 by made you want to take up a hobby while you waited for the screen to repaint each time you changed what you were doing.

The 8514 standard was introduced by IBM in 1987 (8514/a refers to the graphics card while 8514 referred to the monitor that went with it). The 8514 offered two resolutions, 640 by 480 and 1024 by 768 with either 16 or 256 colours out of a palette of 256,000. It was dropped by IBM and replaced by the XGA standard in 1991.

The XGA was able to move blocks of bits (such as a window, which you'll use if you run Windows) rather than just drawing horizontal lines. XGA was also a 15-bit "high" colour card capable of generating 32,000-plus colours on screen from a palette of over 16 million. XGA did not offer 800 by 600, was available only with interlaced output, and was married to computers with 32-bit micro channel graphics architecture (MCGA) – which convinced lots of people not to run right out and buy one.

Accelerator schemes, TIGA, and other coprocessor boards

Handling and manipulating 16.7 million colours at resolutions of 1280 by 1024 or higher, or even at 1024 by 768 or lower, slows a CPU to a crawl – particularly if you're running either Windows or OS/2. This fact led to the introduction of graphics accelerator cards based on a variety of schemes.

A standard VGA card is a "dumb" video controller. This type of controller relies on the host computer's CPU to perform all of the actual image processing. With VGA, the computer's CPU is responsible for placing every pixel on the screen in its proper location and colour. That wasn't a huge task in the days of monochrome, character-based DOS. Most early video cards contained an onboard character generator with the letters, numbers, and symbols making up the ASCII character set already hardwired into them. When the CPU, in effect, said, "put the letter 'A' so many lines from the top of the screen, and so many columns to the right," the graphics card had very little calculating to do. Not only was the character always the same shape, width, and height, but the screen area to be "painted" was limited as well – if there wasn't a character at a certain screen reference point, the graphics card could ignore it.

In today's graphical interface environments, all that has changed. There are no pre-generated characters – each has to be constructed pixel by pixel – and the whole background has to be painted as well, even if it isn't "used." Now add the complexities generated by using up to 16.7 million colour variations on the same screen, then pick up a whole window of information and move it around. The amount of calculation required to perform these operations would bring even a powerful CPU to its knees.

Sophisticated graphics cards employ a number of schemes (one of the following three, all of them, or a combination) to speed things up. They can use a special kind of memory known as video random access memory (VRAM). It's also called dual-port memory, because unlike the standard DRAM (dynamic RAM) used in the rest of the computer, it can do two things at once, such as receiving instructions and writing to the monitor simultaneously. (Simply put, signals in and out of DRAM are either going in or coming out – not both at the same time. VRAM uses two data paths – one for data from the controller and another for data to the digital to analog converter and monitor.) As a result, the controller has access to the display RAM at all times and does not have to wait for monitor retraces before updating the video memory. A card with VRAM generally repaints and updates the screen faster, and it's what you're liable to find on an "accelerator" card that does not have a graphics coprocessor.

Video graphics controllers (whether they're on separate circuit boards or wired directly to the motherboard) can also utilize the computer's local bus instead of its slower expansion bus so that data between them and the CPU can flow faster (see the discussion of VESA versus PCI in Chapter 2).

The more expensive, but ultimately most efficient approach, is to provide a graphics coprocessor chip to handle the bulk of the calculations that a standard VGA card leaves to the host computer (a graphics coprocessor is similar to a math coprocessor, except that instead of being tuned to handle floating point calculations, it is rigged to deal with video calculations).

"Intelligent" graphics cards can be divided into two basic groups, according to the programmability of the graphics coprocessor. In the case of 8514/a, XGA, and S3-type controllers, the video chip is not a true coprocessor because it is not fully programmable like a CPU. These chips do, however, have built-in ability to handle basic and even sophisticated drawing functions such as line rendering, area fills, shading, cursor and font management, and so on. These processors are function-specific and are tailored to the environment they were meant to serve (such as Windows or AutoCAD). In other words, a graphics card that is blazingly fast in a Windows environment may be a dog working in DOS or in other specialized applications such as computer aided design (so it helps to know what you plan to do with it most often before you take it home).

That brings us to TIGA (Texas Instruments Graphics Architecture) cards and their ilk. They were truly programmable graphics coprocessors tailored to manipulate graphical data. The most popular of these chips was the Texas Instruments 34020 – a fully programmable, 32-bit microprocessor. Although more flexible than 8514/a and XGA, cards that used the TI34020 chip relied heavily on the skills of a programmer to write the firmware that made them work well in all possible environments and software interfaces. Not all companies were good at the programming, and failure to provide updated or even bug-free drivers (the software that handles the exchange of information between the card and the monitor) was often more than some of them could handle. (I have what was a $2,400 card from Number Nine Corp. sitting on a shelf gathering dust for exactly this reason.) The cards were also serious memory hogs and likely to interfere with other equipment's desire for base memory locations and IRQs (see Chapter 8 under "UARTs"). The components increased the complexity and overall cost, working with them was a constant irritant, and although some of the boards were able to produce 16.7 million colours at 1280 by 1024, they were still slow by today's standards. You won't find many left.

Yes, but what about MCGA? What about it? I don't want to know, and by now I suspect you don't really want to know either.

Confused yet?

One of the difficulties of writing about graphics standards is that everyone has their own idea of what they are (you wouldn't believe

640 by 480
800 by 600
1024 by 768
1280 by 1024

Resolution is defined as the number of horizontal by the number of vertical pixels (picture elements) you can see on screen. However, the typical illustrations used by graphics card and monitor manufacturers to show how higher resolutions will look are often slightly misleading.

The diagram above is similar to examples used in some advertisements to show resolution differences. While it demonstrates that you can see more data on screen when resolution increases, it also appears to indicate that objects remain the same size, but that's not what really happens.

As you increase resolution, the amount of information you see on screen does increase, but your monitor size stays the same, so the objects on screen get smaller, as the samples on the following page show more clearly.

640 by 480

At low resolution, you see fewer objects, but on screen, they appear large . . .

800 by 600

At higher resolution, you see more objects, but each one is smaller on screen . . .

1024 by 768

how many sources I read to prepare for this and how often they disagreed about basics).

To make things even more fun, none of the standards' names mean anything any more. Many graphics cards can produce resolutions and colour ranges that cross standard lines. Today, even a low-end, generic SVGA card can emulate resolutions and colour ranges for EGA, VGA, Super VGA, and 8514. With 1 MB of onboard memory, some of them can produce 16.7 million colours at 640 by 480 and 65,000-plus colours at 800 by 600 and up. What kind of card is it?

At today's low end are generic SVGA cards with 1 MB of memory and no special acceleration, but capable of at least 256 colours at a resolution of 1024 by 768. That resolution is almost overkill for a typical 14- to 15-inch monitor (800 by 600 is about as high as you'd be comfortable using at that size). It's more than you'll need for most multimedia CD-ROM games and interactive encyclopedias, too. They're aimed at the low end of the technical spectrum and anticipate that most home users will still be using the standard VGA resolution of 640 by 480.

Some multimedia applications will benefit from a larger colour palette (i.e., 65,000 or 16.7 million colours), but you can do yourself two bigger favours when operating under either Windows or OS/2. Add acceleration and look either for a brand name the two operating environments support directly or one you can contact easily for updated support when new versions of Windows and OS/2 appear.

Most of the mainstream graphics card manufacturers supply benchmark figures to tell you how fast their products can move images around on your screen. What has almost become an industry standard for measuring acceleration is the Ziff-Davis Winbench test, but there were three versions of it floating around in mid-1995 and unless the numbers you're quoted all come from the same version, it's like comparing apples to oranges and bananas. When you're quoted a "Winmark" figure (an aggregate graphics speed), check to see whether the test quoted was under Winbench 3.11, Winbench 4.0, Winbench 95, or whatever is the most current version when you read this (see "Lies, damned lies, and benchmarks" in Chapter 2).

Across the board, a local bus graphics card, using either VESA or PCI local bus schemes, will work faster than one that uses the ISA, EISA, or MCA expansion bus.

Based on graphics cards I've tested in my own and other systems, I'd recommend cards (or chipsets if they're part of the motherboard) by ATI, Diamond, Western Digital, or Matrox at the high end or middle of the spectrum. At the mid to low end, look for ATI or Cirrus Logic. Trident and Oak (at the low end) and Number Nine Corp. (at the middle and high end) have produced less than sterling results or have been difficult about software driver upgrades in the past.

The simplest and most practical advice I can offer about selecting the graphics card for your system is to see it in operation, using the software you want to run, on a monitor you can afford. And make no mistake, affordability is a major issue here. It is not only possible, but quite likely that you will spend more on the graphics card/monitor combination for your computer than you paid for the computer itself. An accelerated, high-resolution board, with enough memory to produce all the colours you want could set you back close to $900. Low-end boards in the $150 to $300 range aren't as fast and don't have the resolution range, but we haven't even talked about monitors yet. They're next.

Monitors

Once there were two basic flavours of monitor with variations, but one of them has virtually disappeared from the market.

Monochrome (one colour) monitors are the type you can, for all practical purposes, forget. They used to come in three colours: green, amber, or white on black. In choosing one of the three, folks just got the variant that made them the least crazy. There were also "VGA-mono" monitors capable of 256 shades of grey. These have pretty much joined monochrome monitors and dinosaurs in the pages of history.

Colour monitors offer a larger range of choices. The low-end, 14-inch, interlaced units with a large dot pitch and limited resolution live at the bottom of the heap at under $400. At the high end are the 20-inch or larger, multifrequency, multisynchronous, small dot-pitch monitors that will do everything except water your lawn for well over $2,000.

The primary factors affecting monitor pricing are size, location and number of controls, and special attributes.

The diagonal screen size of a monitor is the first factor that will determine its price range. The typical 14- and 15-inch models range from under $400 to about $900. The intermediate 17-inch models start at around $800 at the low end and rise to $1,500. Models at 20 inches and above start at $2,000 and keep going.

Just as this book was going to press, Toshiba announced the MM20E45, a 20-inch combined television-computer monitor, with a suggested list price of $1,399. However, although the Toshiba Integrated Multimedia Monitor (TIMM) sounds like a good deal with its 181-channel TV tuner, speakers, and VGA input port, its .58 mm dot pitch and maximum computer resolution of 640 by 480 should mute the excitement somewhat (see below). But where one company has gone, others are sure to follow. TIMM may start a trend that will be worth watching.

Once size is accounted for, the location of the controls is the next cost factor. Front-mounted controls are good. That's the part of the monitor closest to you and the easiest to reach. If the controls are only at the back and you have to hug the monitor to change anything, it won't cost as much or be as easy to work with.

The number of items the controls allow you to change is important, too. Simple brightness and contrast controls are barely adequate. You want to be able to change picture width and height as well as picture position in both directions. You may also want to fiddle with whether it bows or wows in the middle or top and bottom, and whether it leans right or left at top or bottom. A "degaussing" control is nice, too (for demagnetizing the beast occasionally). If your work involves changing the resolution a lot, you'll find having memory in the monitor to hold settings for picture width, height, and position from resolution to resolution useful.

The special features that will increase the cost of a monitor include shielding for low-level magnetic radiation. I've spoken to equally qualified, terribly intelligent, and scarily intense people on both sides of the debate about whether this stuff will harm you. I don't know the answer, but if it concerns you, there are units adhering to both Swedish and European minimum standards. They cost extra.

There's also still a guilt tax associated with the U.S. Energy Star requirements to allow monitors to power themselves down after a period of inactivity. There is no such requirement in Canada, but so much equipment comes from the States that this is rapidly becoming a non-optional item.

More terminology, and hints on pricing

Like other computer components, monitors have jargon associated with them, too – but in their case, the terms have a direct bearing on price. Once all factors above have been dealt with, the following items will also affect a monitor's cost.

Frequency, when used to describe monitors, refers to the number of horizontal and vertical pixels displayed on screen. It is the counterpart to the term "resolution" used to describe graphics cards. A multiscanning, or multifrequency, monitor will be able to handle a range of resolutions. The higher the numbers, the more expensive the monitor will be.

So-called "VGA" monitors (without any further description) are generally fixed at 640 by 480. If you have or later get a graphics card with a wider range of resolutions, you're out of luck; you won't be able to see them. If the card you have is a cheapie that stays on frequency on alternate Tuesdays and drifts slightly the rest of the week, you won't be happy, because the monitor won't have enough flexibility to follow the drift.

Generic "SVGA" monitors tend to have maximum frequency of 1024 by 768 and also tend to have dot pitches in the high 30s or low 40s – very grainy. They look more or less okay in the shop, but make you unhappy if your face is eighteen inches away for four hours at a stretch. I *don't* recommend that you save money by getting a fixed or limited frequency, high dot-pitch monitor coupled with a cheap SVGA card.

MultiSync is a trademark of the NEC brand of monitors. A *multisynchronous* monitor is a whole other kettle of fish. Without going into great detail, I'll simply explain that PCs, Macs, and other computer families (such as SunSPARC work stations) all synchronize their video signals in different ways. If a salestype nods and tells you that the monitor you're checking out is indeed a multisynchronous unit, clap your hands in glee and say something like, "Oh, goody. That means I can run it on my PC today, my Mac tomorrow, and my SunSPARC next week!" If the vendor's eyes glaze over, the chances are that she or he doesn't know what multisynchronous means either.

A true multisynchronous monitor can run on a number of different platforms and there are a couple of reasons you might want one. If you're buying for a large company where the administrators use PCs, the design and advertising folk use Macs, and the engineers in the wonder cave use SunSPARCs, it might make sense to have monitors that are interchangeable. It makes little sense if you are buying for home or small business use where there is only one computer, or all are of the same type, but there is one exception. There is a price premium on monitors designed to work with Macs of all shapes and sizes that makes them far more expensive than comparable technology for the PC. You can save a bit by shopping for a multisynchronous monitor for your Mac, but by doing it at a PC vendor – it's one way to get around the Apple *gotcha*.

Interlaced versus *non-interlaced*. This and the next section (vertical refresh rate) has a lot to do with *flicker*. The picture on your monitor is made up of lines of video images (one pixel deep by whatever your horizontal frequency is wide). When producing the image on screen, the focus of the electron gun(s) at the back of your monitor starts at (from your point of view) the upper left corner, scans to the right, then does the same for the next line until it reaches the bottom of the screen – then the focus goes back to the top and starts all over again. What gets hit by the electron stream are fluorescent dots on the inside of the monitor face. When they're hit, the dots glow – but not for very long. If not hit again and quickly, they begin to fade.

Interlaced monitors accomplish this scan slowly and must make two passes at the screen in order to get around this slowness. Just like your television set, they paint the odd numbered lines first (1, 3, 5, 7 . . .) then go back and do the even numbered lines (2, 4, 6, 8 . . .). At resolutions of 800 by 600 and above, this produces a noticeable flicker in the image because the scan doesn't complete before the dots begin to fade. The severity of the flicker is dependent on the vertical refresh rate and individual perceptions. Some people – myself included – can see the flicker at 640 by 480, too. Interlaced monitors are old technology, and they are cheap. However, don't bother trying to save money by buying one. You'll hate them. Interlaced: bad.

Non-interlaced monitors refresh themselves quickly enough so that they can paint all of the lines in one pass. Non-interlaced monitors are more expensive than interlaced monitors and the higher the speed at which they work, the more expensive they'll be. However, I find the rock-steady picture at high resolutions more comfortable to work with (and I think you will too). Non-interlaced: good.

As noted briefly in the chapter on reading advertisements, however, some manufacturers are willing to allow you to pay for the privilege of having your non-interlaced monitor and saving money (you think), too. Even though a monitor may be advertised as non-interlaced and may actually work that way at 640 by 480 and at 800 by 600, corner-cutting prevents it from working quickly enough to be non-interlaced at 1024 by 768, so it is interlaced at this resolution instead. Cute trick.

Vertical refresh rate (VFR) refers to the speed with which the image on screen is redrawn. Usually expressed in Hertz (Hz – or cycles per second), it is not uncommon these days to find monitors with a VFR of 70 Hz and above (i.e., the screen is redrawn 70 times per second). The two most important things about VFR to understand are that to have a non-interlaced picture, you're going to need higher than 50 Hz. A VFR of 60 Hz is better (but can still flicker slightly at resolutions over 800 by 600, even though non-interlaced). The median for today's monitors is about 72 Hz, while higher refresh rates are at the top end of the price scale (but you can run these monitors at frequencies up to 1280 by 1024 or higher with nary a flicker to be found).

The same shopping principle applies to monitors as applies to graphics boards. See it running your software, with a graphics card you can afford, and sit down in front of it for a while before signing the second mortgage to afford it.

Dot pitch is the least understood and most important specification for you to note when buying a monitor because it will determine whether the picture is sharp and clear or grainy and mushy. As mentioned above, the inside of the monitor screen is covered with fluorescent phosphor dots. Remember, however, that the picture is made up not only of the dots that glow, but also of the spaces between them. It's the distance between phosphor dots of the same colour (the dot pitch, measured in millimetres) that is quoted in monitor advertisements (or not, if the number is high). For example, a .45 mm dp monitor has a large space between phosphors and a .26 mm dp monitor has a smaller space (and more phosphors on the screen). The lower the dot-pitch number, the sharper the picture, and the more expensive the monitor.

You won't often find dot pitches higher than .31 (about the upper limit of acceptability) quoted in ads. Monitors with a dot pitch of .28 are quite nice, while those with .26 or lower are sharp, clear, a pleasure to work with, and worth every penny. Sony's Trinitron monitors use a different technology, and the measurement of dot pitch is a contrived figure. Nevertheless, they're about the equivalent of somewhere between .25 and .26, and based on my experience with them, I'm not shy in suggesting you look closely at any of the several brands using them.

Size isn't everything

It's easy to get caught up in the blaze of options and dazzled by the discussion of resolutions and frequencies when discussing graphics cards and monitors. I mentioned earlier that I found 800 by 600 to be about as high as I wanted to push the resolution on a 14- or 15-inch monitor. Likewise, I find 1024 by 768 to be about as high as a 17-inch unit does well.

The reason is simple when you think about it, but not obvious. When you increase the resolution, you can see more objects on screen – but they're smaller because the size of the screen doesn't change. For example, on a 15-inch screen at 640 by 480, a group icon in Windows Program Manager is about a half-inch square. Increase the resolution to 800 by 600 and you can see more icons, but each is now about three-eighths of an inch on each side. Bump the picture up to 1024 by 768 or higher and the icons are best examined with a magnifying glass.

Hard Drives and
Removable Storage

It doesn't matter what you intend to do with your computer; you'll need as much hard drive space as you can get. A hard drive (also culled the hard disk, or if you work for IBM, the hard file) is so called because the magnetic recording medium inside is on hard, inflexible platters (as opposed to floppy disks, where the material is flexible). Regardless of what you call it, the hard drive is where you'll store not only the data or documents you'll create, but also the software for your operating system and for the programs you use. One truism in the computer world is that data will always expand to fill the container and the best overall advice is simply to get the highest capacity hard drive you can afford; then start saving up for another one.

How much?

When you buy your new computer, you'll be faced with several choices of hard drive type as well as a wide variety of choices in storage capacity. I want to address the issue of capacity first so we can get it out of the way.

Capacity is a measure in megabytes (MB) of how much information the drive will hold. This has nothing to do with the amount of memory (RAM) in the computer. To use a car in a very crude analogy, think of the computer's central processor as the engine, the amount of memory as the gas, and the hard drive as the interior and trunk. The processor and memory determine how fast and far you can go, while the hard drive determines how much you can take with you and how much you can bring back.

As you become more familiar with what your computer can do, you'll find yourself adding ever more programs. With those programs you'll create and then need to store data – all your business accounts, the kids' homework, your homemade Christmas cards, "saves" in the games you play, and that rotating 3-D diagram of the whats-it you invented. *You will never get a hard drive that has too much capacity.* I repeat: get the largest you can afford, then start saving for another one. If you plan to run Windows, try not to leave the store without a drive of at least 528 MB.

Fortunately, this won't cost as much today as it once would have. The most expensive elements of a hard drive are the platters inside the unit. More platters require larger cases, additional read/write heads, head actuator motors, and so on. However, changes in technology have allowed the manufacturers to cram more data onto fewer platters. This, and the fact that over the past few years so many people have purchased large capacity drives, has drastically reduced prices. My contacts in retail tell me that calls come nearly weekly from their suppliers advising them of more price adjustments. (In mid-1995, 528 MB hard drives were available for around $250.)

IDE and SCSI

The other factor that will determine the cost of your drive is the type. All hard drives are not the same. Older, obsolete drive types include ST-506 (MFM or RLL) and ESDI (see the chart for a fuller explanation of what these terms mean, how these drives work, and how efficient they are). Newer drive types include IDE (integrated drive electronics), "enhanced" IDE, and SCSI (small computer systems interface), and while they are included in the chart, I want to spend some time on them here as well, because these are the three choices you'll face if you buy a complete system or a new drive today.

Hard drive types

Standard	Long Name	Information
ST506 - MFM	Modified Frequency Modulation	The hard drive interface developed for the PC, ST506 drives are marked by slow data transfer rates (625 KB/sec for MFM encoding, 984 KB/sec for RLL encoding). MFM drives create a one-one correspondence between data bits and magnetic changes (flux transition) on a disk.
ST506 - RLL	Run Length Limited	RLL drives use GCR (group coded recording - where bits are packaged as groups, with each group assigned to and stored under a particular code). Storing blocks of coded data allows larger storage densities and faster transfer rates than MFM. Not many still in use.
ESDI	Enhanced Small Device Interface	Designed to be the successor to ST506. Produces higher transfer rates (1.25 MB/sec to 2.5 MB/sec). Not many ESDI drives in use due to cost.
IDE	Integrated Drive Electronics	IDE used to mean any drive that integrated controller electronics into the drive itself. Today, there is actually a standard, the "ANSI AT Attachment Standard." Variance in standards in older IDE drives can cause glitches when adding a second unit. Getting the second drive from same manufacturer can at least reduce the possibility of radical mismatches. IDE drives have transfer rates in the 2 to 3 MB/sec range and are marked by using very small controller cards. Drive size limit 528 MB.
ATA/ATAPI	AT Attachment, ATA Packet Interface	The "enhanced" IDE standard championed by Western Digital and rapidly taken up by the rest of the hard-drive and CD-ROM industries with the collaboration of Microsoft. With Windows 95, a PCI local bus, ATAPI controller card, and upgraded BIOS, this superset of IDE is less expensive than SCSI for both controllers and devices – and could provide plug and play installation, up to 13 MB/sec data throughput, up to four IDE devices on two cables (including CD-ROM and tape), and drives up to 8.4 gigabyte capacities. Look for a flood of products soon, but wait until they get it right.
SCSI	Small Computer Systems Interface	Pronounced "scuzzy." Data transfer rate of 5 MB/sec to 12 MB/sec. SCSI allows up to seven devices to be connected to a single host adapter. SCSI drives can have huge capacities and, because of the 'ganging' abilities, lend themselves to drive arrays. Most current CD-ROM drives are SCSI devices, but expect this to start changing in a hurry in 1995. Don't assume all SCSI devices will work flawlessly together, or that the software with the device will work with your brand and model of SCSI adapter. (Check out the adapter with the device manufacturer before you buy.)

IDE drives are the most common and, compared to SCSI drives of equal capacity, will cost less – both for the drive itself and for the circuit board to control them (the drive controller). For example, as I write this, IDE drives are selling for, give or take a bit, about 50 cents per megabyte, while SCSI drives, depending on brand, capacity, and vendor, are selling for between 60 and 75 cents/MB. Both IDE and "enhanced" IDE local bus controllers without cache cost less than $100, while SCSI controllers go for anywhere from $145 to $350 depending on whether they are local bus devices and the amount of cache memory on board.

IDE drives can often find information just as quickly (the seek time) as a SCSI drive and may lift the information from the drive surface as quickly (the latency) for a very similar average access time (these days between 9 and 12 ms). However, SCSI drives are faster at getting the information to the drive controller and through it into the rest of the system (the data transfer rate or throughput – see the chart).

SCSI currently has three other advantages. The first is expandability. You can run up to seven internal or external SCSI devices with one controller. These may be additional hard drives, CD-ROM drives (and multiple CD units known as jukeboxes), CD-R drives (recordable CDs), Bernoulli drives, Zip drives, SyQuest removable cartridge drives, magneto optical disc drives, WORM (write once, read many) drives, tape backup drives, and some high-end scanners and printers. When SCSI first made its appearance in the PC world, this advantage often broke down in practice because the manufacturers of the various SCSI devices and of the adapter cards often ignored the SCSI standards in favour of proprietary schemes, which required a specific device to work only with a specific SCSI adapter (often supplied by the same company). This could make using extra devices dangerous to your mental health, but the industry has to a large extent corrected this problem by introducing a software driver/manager called ASPI (advanced SCSI programming interface), which has smoothed out most of the problems.

Another advantage is valuable. SCSI drives, unlike IDE, MFM, RLL, and ESDI drives, will generally work in the same computer as one of the other drive types. You can only mix IDE, MFM, RLL, or ESDI drives in the same system with great difficulty.

The final advantage may not last long. SCSI drives can have more capacity than IDE drives. Nowadays, really large drive sizes (in excess of 84,000 MB or 8.4 GB – gigabytes) are SCSI drives.

Some other SCSI advantages also may not last long because of the new "enhanced" IDE standard. You'd be ill-advised to take advantage of it until several months after Windows 95 ships, in order to give the industry time to sort out its confusion over how the new drives and controllers are supposed to work, but eventually it will be safe to buy IDE controllers able to handle four or more internal (not external) devices, including CD-ROM, and, eventually, tape – with hard drive throughput equal to or exceeding the current SCSI-2 benchmarks (up to 13 MB/sec), and with drive capacities up to 8.4 GB.

You may be tempted by high capacities, relatively low prices, and the salesperson's glowing reports that everything is okey dokey, but I'd seriously recommend against an "enhanced" IDE device unless you also have an "enhanced" IDE controller and compatible BIOS (basic in/out system) already present in your system. Otherwise you will be forced to use a software driver to have your computer recognize the drive – and if something goes wrong it won't be because you weren't cautioned.

Caching and defragmentation

How quickly the drive can find the information it holds and how quickly it can deliver that information to the rest of the system are important for your overall system performance. These speeds play a large part in determining how quickly a program loads when you want to run it. It's even more critical when running programs that do a lot of reading from and writing to the drive (such as a database program). It is a crucial factor when running Windows or OS/2.

Both of these operating environments make use of empty hard drive space to provide virtual memory (I know I said earlier that memory and hard drive capacity aren't the same – and they're not, but I fudged a little). By storing bits of program code that are not currently in use on the hard drive, Windows and OS/2 are able to juggle several programs simultaneously and make it unnecessary to load and unload programs when you want to switch from one to another. This can speed up your use of the software, but the speed of your hard drive will have a direct effect on how quickly the switchover takes place.

Electronic memory is always faster than a mechanical hard drive. If the data you wish to get is in memory, you don't have to wait for the drive mechanism to find it or for the controller to deliver it.

A cache is a pool of memory set aside to hold information that might otherwise have to be found on the hard drive itself. The cache could be located on the hard drive, on its controller card, or both. Drives and controllers with caching, whether IDE or SCSI, always cost more – often quite a bit more – but the results are worth it. For example, according to figures generated by Intel, switching a hard drive with a 15 ms average seek time and a 64 KB cache buffer for one with a 12 ms average seek time and 256 KB cache buffer will provide an 11 per cent improvement in overall system performance. The cache could also be in the computer's own memory, created by a software program such as Microsoft's SmartDrive, Iomega's SCPLUS, or Symantec's Ncache or Speedrive.

Regardless of where the cache is located, the methods used are roughly the same. An assumption is made that the next piece of data the system will require is located right next to the last piece requested. When a program asks for information, the cache intercepts the request and "reads ahead" to get additional information. When the next request arrives, the cache is checked first and if the data is present, it's delivered without having to refer to the hard drive.

Using some variation of a last-read, last-out formula, the cache keeps information that is requested often and replaces unwanted information with new data. One of the measures of how efficiently the cache does this is known as the hit ratio.

Now let's turn to defragmentation. To understand the concepts of fragmentation and defragmentation, it helps to know how DOS deals with hard drives. To begin with, when a drive is formatted (readied for use), the surfaces of the drive platters are magnetically divided into tracks (the circular path around the platter) and sectors (divisions across the tracks). Each sector will contain several clusters (the smallest portion DOS can read). The result is something like, but a little more than, the address of an apartment – the drive is the city, the track is the street, the sector is the building's location on the street, and the cluster is an apartment in the building. Each division is numbered, and

DOS keeps two copies of these numbers in an area of the disk called the file allocation table (FAT).

When DOS is told to write a file to a disk, it checks the FAT to see where space is available, then it starts at the first empty cluster and begins writing the file. DOS starts with the first empty sector and keeps writing in adjacent (or contiguous) sectors until it's done. Each time, DOS updates the FAT to indicate that formerly empty spaces are now occupied.

When you erase a file, or edit it to make it shorter, DOS changes the FAT so it knows that space has become available. Instead of having a nice, clean disk full of contiguous files, there are blank spaces. The next time DOS goes to write a file, it has a dilemma. If it only writes to spaces large enough to hold the whole file, the disk would quickly become full and unusable, so it checks the FAT to see where empty spaces lie. It makes some intelligent decisions (for example, it will first try to put the new file in a space large enough to hold it all), but ultimately it has no other choice than to put only part of the file (a fragment) into one space, another fragment somewhere else, and so on. Through the FAT, it keeps track of where the file starts, where it goes from there, and how to find the rest of the file fragments.

Eventually, the disk becomes littered with file fragments. This slows everything down (the drive has to work harder to consult the FAT so often, as well as searching all over the place to get the files requested).

Now we go briefly back to caching. One of the best things that caching does is to keep a copy of the FAT in memory. Right away that cuts down on the number of moves the drive's heads have to make. However, the other thing the cache does is to read ahead of data requests. If the files are all contiguous, this speeds things up considerably. If they're badly fragmented (over 20 per cent), the advantage of the cache is mostly lost because the data next door to the last request is more than likely to be unrelated. This lowers the hit ratio and destroys the efficiency of the cache.

Even if you don't use a cache, getting information from the drive is faster if all of the pieces are contiguous, so whether you use a cache or not you should defragment your drive from time to time. Various companies provide defragmentation software (Symantec through

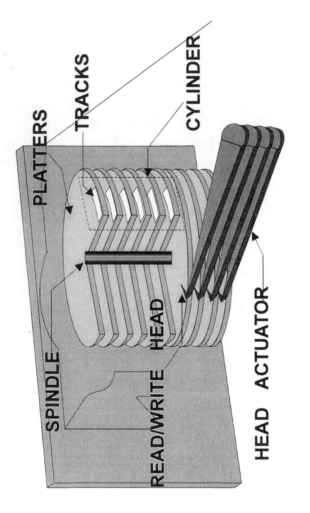

Cutaway view of a hard disk drive

Norton Utilities and PC Tools is the most common, and DOS 6 includes it). Data compression programs (about which we'll hear more later) also often come with a defragmenter.

Care, feeding, and maintenance

As the technology improves, it has become harder to hurt hard drives.

It used to be that the read-write head would crash onto the surface of the drive when power was turned off, causing physical damage and scrambling the data in the damaged sector(s).Today, IDE and SCSI drives come with what are called floating heads. Their position when the computer is turned off is away from the drive surface; power is required to bring them close enough to read or write to the disk (the heads don't and are not supposed to touch the platter surface, but they get real close).

What is more likely to damage a hard drive today is dirty power. In Chapter 8, there's a discussion of power conditioners and uninterruptible power supplies (UPSs). These devices prevent electrical spikes and surges from ripping into your computer and wreaking havoc. UPSs also prevent brownouts and blackouts from scrambling your data just as the cache is about to write it to disk.

Something else happens to hard drives that you don't hear too much about. They get tired. The surface of the platters is covered with a thin layer of a metallic oxide, the molecules of which are lined up magnetically. That's how data is stored, too, in molecular patterns in the oxide layer. The patterns are created by a weak electrical current and read later by the change in current detected by the heads. Over time, the magnetic force dissipates and the patterns begin to lose their coherency. How much time depends on many factors (not the least of which is how much power is flowing through the system), including temperature, humidity, static discharges, and the whims of the gods.

It's a good idea, particularly with older drives, periodically to make a backup of all of the data (onto floppy disks or tape) and to reformat the drive. I try to do it every eighteen to twenty-four months with my IDE drives. It's a pain to take the time, but not more painful than discovering that something I've spent days writing is in the "sector not found."

One last item, then we'll push on. Hard drives and their controller cards are connected by flat ribbon cables. Over time, particularly under harsh environmental conditions, these cables can become brittle. This isn't too crucial in a large, airy case with lots of room for the cables to run. In the new low-profile, small footprint cases, however, the cables are often severely crimped to get them to fit. Take particular care when removing the top of the case (and putting it back) that you don't pinch the cables to the point that one of their wires breaks. If you do get a message that your drive is out to lunch, examine the cable before panicking.

Speaking of backups

A basic maintenance step we all need to take and none of us likes to is making a backup copy of the contents of our hard drive(s) on a regular basis.

There are all kinds of nasty things that can happen to the data on your hard drive – from the obvious like fire and theft to less obvious catastrophes such as power surges, ill-behaved software doing despicable things, viruses, and the errors of our own fat fingers. Every time I mentally add up the amount of time it's taken to back up the contents of a drive compared to the frustration, angst, and time lost when I didn't, backups win.

The trick is to make backing up the drive a part of your routine and to make it as painless as possible. When you back up the contents of a hard drive, you're making a copy of everything on it, so that you can replace the contents if anything awful happens.

You can make the copy on floppy disks (the most painful and time-consuming method), to a tape backup system (one of the least time-consuming and more cost-effective ways, although not the fastest), to a removable storage device (like a Bernoulli cartridge or removable hard drive), or to another hard drive (the last two methods are very fast, but more expensive). See below, under "Removable Storage," for a more detailed examination of these devices.

In any event, you're going to need some kind of backup software. Good backup software will work quickly, will compress the data you're copying to require fewer disks (tapes, cartridges, or whatever), will offer a wide range of backup alternatives (not all will work with some tape drives or Bernoullis), and provide some type of scheduling routine to allow the backup to take place automatically when you're not present.

As with so many disk utility programs, the main player is Symantec (Norton Backup comes with Norton Desktop for DOS or Windows as well as being sold separately; Central Point Backup is sold the same way – and both are owned by Symantec). DOS and Windows 95 come with a backup program. It doesn't matter which you use, so long as you use it regularly.

Disk full

Sooner or later you're going to discover I was right when I claimed that what seems like a huge amount of storage capacity today will fill right up. When you've archived every bit of data you're sure you won't need this week onto disk or tape and still don't have enough room to add another program, when you use your backup software to provide temporary storage space for programs you don't think you'll need today, when you get a "disk full" message more than once a month, it's time to consider taking action.

You have three alternatives. Replace your existing hard drive with a larger one, add a second drive to the system, or if you haven't already done so, use a data compression program to increase the capacity of your existing drive.

Let's tackle data compression first. Incorrectly called disk compression (it's the data that is compressed, not the disk), it's the least costly alternative, but to some people it's the most controversial. There are two leading alternatives (or three, depending on which version of DOS you own): DoubleSpace (which comes with MS-DOS 6.2) or DriveSpace (with MS-DOS 6.22 or higher), and Stacker (which can be purchased by itself, or found with Novell DOS 7.0 or higher).

In its simplest form, data compression sucks all the "air" out of files on the disk by replacing repeating characters and spaces with symbols that take up less room. The technology behind the routine is anything but simple. Consider it high magic.

These programs create a huge file on a hard drive and stuff all of the drive's contents into the file, then make the file appear to be a hard drive with roughly double the capacity of the original. The remarkable part is not only that it works, but that it generally works so quickly you can't tell the difference in performance.

The controversy comes from several sources. Part of it, I suspect, comes from a Puritan sense that it's just not right to get something for nothing. More controversy comes from the fact that some software programmers play fast and loose games with the way DOS handles file access. The occasional program won't work properly in a compressed environment. And there are some files – sound or video files you've created for use in presentation software – that should always be stored on an uncompressed drive portion. Both types of files use their own forms of compression and the confusion among the different schemes can lead to unacceptable performance.

Lastly, Microsoft's first release of DoubleSpace (in MS-DOS 6.0) wasn't exactly spot on. They maintain that there were no bugs in it, but it gave enough people grief that the company released another version in MS-DOS 6.2 specifically to respond to the concerns about DoubleSpace. DriveSpace was born after a protracted lawsuit launched by Stac Electronics, which successfully claimed that Microsoft had violated some of Stac's patents in the creation of DoubleSpace. There are subtle differences between the two Microsoft offerings, but they're difficult to detect.

I use Stacker and have ever since its first release. Although I've had the occasional grief caused by other flaky software and version 4.0's unfriendly interface, Stacker itself has never let me down. Its primary advantage over DriveSpace is its ability to deal with drive volumes larger than 256 MB in size; DriveSpace won't use a larger volume. Versions of Stacker are also available for Mac and OS/2.

Data compression software has become a standard utility, and if used with care (make those backups first!), should be the first alternative to those below.

If you absolutely refuse to use data compression (or if you already have and you're still out of space), then you're looking at replacing the drive or adding a second. I would recommend replacement if you have an older style MFM, RLL, or even ESDI drive. For one thing, you'll have trouble finding a second drive to match the first one (remember, they can only work with a drive of the same type) and then you'll find it difficult to match the drives to your equally old controller card. For another, these drives are slower and less efficient than IDE or SCSI drives. While you may gain capacity, you won't gain performance.

You could try adding a SCSI drive to the system. If you already have a CD-ROM drive or other SCSI device, you may not have to add another controller card.

If your current drive is an IDE type, your chances of finding another one that will work with it are good, but not perfect. Occasionally you can run into trouble if the second drive is faster than the first, but this can often be resolved if it's by the same manufacturer and if you assign the new drive as the secondary, not the primary, drive in the system.

How do you tell what kind of drive you already have? You're going to have consult your manual or open the case and have a look. The drive type is rarely printed on the drive itself, and it's hard to tell the difference between an MFM and RLL drive by anything simple like looking at the cables. So write down the manufacturer's name and the drive's model number (which are on the drive), then ask a sales-person at the store where you plan to buy your new one.

When you add a second drive, however, you'll have to tell both the first drive and the new one that a second drive is in the system, and you'll have to tell them which is first in line (otherwise neither will respond). This is generally done by changing jumpers or switches on each drive, and without instructions, the manual for the drive, or a photo-copy of the one the store's technicians have, you don't have a chance of figuring out how.

Unless you're experienced or intrepid, you'll save yourself a lot of hassle by simply taking your whole computer to the store and saying, "Fix it, please."

Shopping tips

Here's your checklist for happy coexistence with your PC's hard drive(s):

- Get a big one and start saving for another.
- Get an IDE drive (that's a generic type, not a brand name).

Standard IDE drives under 528 MB are safe, while enhanced IDE drives over that capacity may not be until sometime after Windows 95 ships.

• If in doubt, if you can afford the price difference, and if you want a large capacity drive, try a SCSI.

• Average access time (in milliseconds) is more important than transfer rate (in MB/sec), but both are useful specifications to heed.

• For enhanced performance get caching, either on the drive, the controller, via software, or all three.

• Do get some sort of reliable power conditioner at the very least and seriously consider an uninterruptible power supply.

• Shop for a brand of drive that comes with a technical manual (Seagate, Quantum, Western Digital, Maxtor, and one or two others now provide one automatically), but in any case, don't leave the store without the drive's technical specifications including number of cylinders, heads, sectors per track, and the jumper or switch settings you'll need to accommodate another drive.

Removable Storage

If the idea of adding another hard drive is out for any number of reasons, you're left with looking for alternative ways to store data temporarily outside your system. The list of alternative removable storage devices includes solutions you'll find familiar such as floppy disk drives and tape drives as well as less familiar floptical drives, Bernoulli drives, Zip drives, magneto optical drives, the new recordable CD-ROM drives, and portable devices for use with notebook computers. With them, you can both back up your hard drive or archive portions of it (using compression software such as PKZIP to scrunch the data down into small packages for temporary storage and retrieval later).

Keep in mind, however, that as the price of hard drives keeps falling, few of these solutions are more cost effective than adding another hard drive. They do make sense as backup devices, but in most cases, less sense for use as hard drive overflow.

Floppy disks

Floppy drives for the PC or Mac won't go away until everyone has a CD-ROM drive or some other way is found to get new software into the system without making us copy-protection crazy.

However, the older 5.25-inch floppy disk *is* dead. It has been several years since either software developers or hardware manufacturers shipped programs or device drivers on anything other than 3.5-inch disks (or CD-ROM). The only excuse for having a 5.25-inch drive is a need to exchange data with someone who has only this type of device.

In most cases, you can be quite happy with a single 3.5-inch high-density (i.e., 1.44 MB) drive, but when there are exceptions, you should look for a dual-diameter drive. It will have slots for high-density versions of both types of diskette, require only one power and data connector, and take up only one half-height drive bay. You'll have to shop around and may have to place a special order because few retailers stock them on the shelf. Look for products by Canon, Fujitsu, Teac, Panasonic, and possibly others selling in Canada for between $129 and $200 depending on vendor and brand. That compares to around $55 (give or take a bit) for a new single-slot drive of either type.

With low-cost drives and cheap disks, the floppy is the least expensive method to use when backing up your hard drive. However, using floppies means you have to be present to change disks every few minutes and the cost of both disks and your time rises dramatically when your hard drive is larger than 100 MB. When you have truly large hard drives, there are less expensive and time consuming methods.

Tapes

Tape drives are highly desirable when you have a lot of data to protect (and you will). It's inevitable that sooner or later one or some combination of factors – your fat fingers, errant software, tired components, or the curses of passing wizards – will trash the contents of your drive(s) when you least expect it. When (*not* if) that unhappy day arrives, you will not panic; you'll simply reach up to a shelf and start restoring your system from your backups. You don't have backups? My, my, what a shame. Too bad.

Tape is the simplest and least costly backup system for large hard drives and there are several flavours of tape drive from which to choose in a variety of sizes. The rule of thumb, so you can back up your system while you sleep, is a tape drive at least twice the capacity of your present hard drive. This will cover you in case you get another drive, or in the very real possibility that sooner or later you'll use one of the real-time data compression schemes.

Unfortunately, one of the truly ugly things about the computer tape industry – regardless of the technology used – is that most companies quote tape capacities assuming your backup software will compress your data before storage. The real capacity of a drive is generally slightly less than half the value quoted in the advertisements. For example, the Colorado Memory "Jumbo 250" actually formats its tapes to 120 MB. I used to lambaste CM for this in public until some folks from Iomega pointed out to me that everyone else does it, too. "The first company to stop doing it will lose business because their products will appear to be overpriced," they moaned. Now, I simply mutter darkly about the whole industry.

Despite the amount of data tape drives hold, they are only suitable for archive storage – not for day-to-day use instead of a hard drive – because of the way they store and recover data. Tape drives lay information down sequentially. They start at the beginning of the tape and plod along in a straight line to the end. In order to recover any data, the drives have no way to get to the middle quickly – they need to plod along again from the beginning to the point where the information is stored – it's very, very slow compared to a hard drive's ability to find data stored on its surface randomly.

Starting at under $300 are the QIC (quarter-inch cartridge) 40 and QIC 80 drives (120 and 240 MB compressed) from Colorado Memory and others. In mid-1995, both Hewlett-Packard (in association with CM) and Iomega were releasing products using the QIC 3020 format storing between 700 MB and 1.7 gigabytes (GB). Again, cut the numbers in half. These units were still under $500 for internal models all the way to the top of the range. Both QIC 40/80 and QIC

3020 drives attach to a PC's floppy diskette cable, which keeps the cost and drain on system resources down.

Other more expensive alternatives include SCSI-based tape systems, DAT (digital audio tape) drives, and several others in the 2 to 10 GB range, but you don't even want to think about their prices.

On the other hand, if a 1.25 GB *portable* tape drive you can hold in the palm of your hand sounds interesting, you might want to have a look at the Datasonix Pereos. Using a tape cassette not much bigger than two postage stamps side-by-side, the Pereos runs off two AA batteries, weighs about ten ounces, runs through a PC parallel port, and will transfer data at a rate up to 10 MB/min. When introduced in early 1995, the Pereos had a list price of $749 U.S.

Floptical drives

This technology enjoyed a brief day in the sun in the early 1990s, but it is now dead. On the surface, the idea was a good one: use a laser-guided read-write head to get 21 MB of data on a magnetic 3.5-inch disk surface with very narrow tracks separated by the laser guide-track.

Unfortunately, the drives were expensive and so was the media used in them. Both main suppliers, Iomega and Insite Peripherals, tried valiantly to develop higher capacity systems, but both gave up.

Bernoulli drives

These drives won't die (and unless you seriously jump up and down on the cartridges, neither will the data they hold). It's often easiest to describe Bernoulli drives as being hard drives with removable platters, but the definition is a little inaccurate because the disk in each cartridge is flexible, not stiff. Aside from that, the description more or less fits. The principle, developed primarily by Iomega but sold by one or two others, is that a powerful stream of air is blown past an aerodynamically shaped head, keeping it very close to but not quite touching the surface of the recording medium.

Iomega's 150 and 230 MB drives have average access speeds – the speed at which the read-write heads can find data randomly scattered on the surface of the drive and then lift it – of about 18 milliseconds (ms). Hard drives are faster (down in the 9 to 12 ms range), but a Bernoulli is a whole lot faster than any magneto-optical drive, floppy drive, or tape system (with the added advantage of using random, not serial, access). Because they're SCSI devices, Bernoullis have burst throughput rates in excess of 10 MB/sec and continuous transfer rates (the speed at which data, once found, gets to the computer) closer to 5 MB/sec.

Bernoulli drives come in single- or double-drive units. The singles can be internal or external to the system. They have a range of prices starting well under $1,000 for internal models and, because you can use Stacker or DriveSpace on them, can hold twice as much data as the quoted capacity.

You're most likely to find these drives where a large amount of data needs to be close at hand, but not necessarily immediately available. For example, I use one to store clip art and archived faxes; an acquaintance uses his to store financial research data.

An alternative to the Bernoulli drive, heavily favoured by Mac users but also available for the PC, is the SyQuest removable cartridge. SyQuests range in size from 135 to 270 MB in 3.5-inch format and are readily available. The 270 MB model was selling on the street in mid-1995 for about $650 for the internal IDE version or $700 for the external SCSI version.

Another of Iomega's products, the Zip drive, started shipping in limited quantities just as this book was going to print. It can be connected to a SCSI adapter or a PC's parallel port and offers 25 or 100 MB of uncompressed storage (up to nearly 200 MB using Stacker or DriveSpace). One hundred MB Zip drives entered the market for around $329 with 100 MB replacement disks available for less than $30 (and if you do the math, it won't take long to figure out that a Zip drive and five 100 MB disks will cost nearly twice what a 528 MB hard drive would cost. They don't become competitive in price until you have ten disks or more).

Some U.S. publications predicted these drives might replace floppy drives as we know them in the future, but it's too soon to tell exactly what impact they will have on the market. Until there is widespread backup software support for them, they'll remain specialty devices, but because of their portability and price point, expect the parallel port version to be very popular among notebook users.

Magneto-optical (MO)

MO drives cost more than Bernoulli systems or other devices, such as SyQuests. MO drives have slower access times than either, but because they're SCSI devices, have about the same throughput. Despite cost and performance, MO drives are attractive in some niche markets because of the physical security of the data on one of the MO discs.

MO drives use laser technology but not to read or write data. Instead, a magnetic medium is coated with a layer of protective material that the laser heats before data on the magnetic surface below it can be altered. Once the protective surface cools, the magnetic media can't be changed until it is heated again, so magnetic fields produced by telephones or other sources won't scramble the contents. MO drives tend to pop up in lawyers' offices, government departments, and Mac-based graphics printing houses.

Compared to various other alternatives, the prices are hideous. For example, the Fujitsu 230 MB MO drive was selling for around $1,000 (internal) to $1,200 (external), while the external Pinnacle Micro Tahoe 230 MB MO drive for the PC sold for about $1,569. Both are 3.5-inch devices.

Recordable CD-ROM (CD-R)

These CD-Rs were just being introduced in mid-1995. The two models available then came from Pinnacle Micro and Sony. Both products were "double-speed" units (i.e., with maximum throughput of 300 KB/sec), which made them barely adequate for use as playback devices. Both had recording capacities up to 650 MB and, like the MO drives mentioned above, would be suitable for use where physical security of the data is important because stray magnetism can't alter the contents.

The CD-R format is relatively new and may end up being replaced by something still under development called CD-E (up to 5 GB capacity, high speed, double-sided, but don't expect to see any before late

1996 or early 1997). CD-R is still expensive, too. For example, the Pinnacle Micro RCD-1000 was selling in Canada for around $2,999, while the Sony had an "estimated retail price" of $2,595 for the CSP-920S (internal) and $2,795 for the CSP-9211 external model.

PCMCIA

This is the acronym for Personal Memory Card International Association. PCMCIA hard drives are about the size of a credit card and not much more than a quarter-inch thick and used to be the favourite solution for portable notebook computer users until the notebooks themselves started packing larger internal drives. They're still available from a variety of manufacturers, with models such as the Integral Peripherals Viper with a suggested Canadian retail price of anywhere from $489 for a 105 MB unit to $735 for a Viper 260.

However, several companies are offering alternatives. SyQuest, for example, says it will be offering an 80 MB removable PCMCIA cartridge drive "in the future." Available now, Kingston Technology Corp.'s 127 MB portable hard drive, the Data Traveller, connects through a parallel port, for a list price of $430 U.S.

6

Printers

A computer will help you to do your work more efficiently (and bring more enjoyment to your leisure), but without a printer, all you can do is invite folks over for dinner to show them what you've accomplished.

There are very few things you will want to do with a computer that you won't want to print. Of course, there are slide shows, demonstrations, and game playing – these activities rarely require printing – but word processing, spreadsheets, accounting programs, and databases are (in that order) the most common programs run on personal computers – and all of them will produce documents you'll want to print at one time or another.

There are three main printer technologies to consider for home use and a few more for use in certain types of businesses. We'll discuss each of them, some at length, below. To simplify your choices somewhat, however, it's safe to make some broad observations:

(a) The quality of dot-matrix print is not suitable for business correspondence. These printers are only recommended if you need multiple-impact copies or continuous-form banners, if you have children who want to print simple graphics in colour, or if you're on an excruciatingly tight budget.

(b) Ink- (or bubble-) jet printers have an attractive purchase price,

but also have the highest cost per page for consumables of any printing technology except dye sublimation (see below).

(c) Laser printers cost less than you think and the cost per page is
less than everything except dot-matrix.

(d) Offices in a box, also dubbed Swiss Army fax machines (combined fax/scanner/printer/copier), are *the* hot products of the mid-
1990s. Although many of them use ink-jet technology (with a
correspondingly inflated cost per page), others in the under-$2,500
price range use lasers and at least one, the LexMark Medley 4X prints
in colour for under $1,000.

(e) Good (although not professional) quality colour printers, using
either ink-jet, thermal wax transfer, or laser technology, are available
now. Other technologies (phase change, dye sublimation) that were
once far above the reasonable consumer price level should come down
in price as time progresses, but not in the very near future.

Before we turn to each of these technologies, there are a few notes
that apply to all types of printers. First, you should know that printer
drivers are the interpreters between your software and your printer. The
question of printer drivers was more crucial under DOS than it was
under Windows and other device-independent operating systems such
as OS/2 and Mac System 7.5, but an increase in the number of GDI
(graphic device interface) printers and of models providing two-way
communication between printer and computer has made it of increasing concern under graphical operating systems as well.

In the DOS days, each software application had to support a multitude of printers. If your word processor or accounting program didn't
have the driver for the printer you chose, you couldn't use it effectively
(and may not have been able to print at all).

Device independence means that the operating environment
(Windows, OS/2, and others) provides driver support for peripheral
devices, theoretically freeing the programs from the requirement.
Under Windows, for example, each program is supposed to use the
printer drivers Windows provides. This doesn't mean that Windows
supports every printer there is. And, just because a printer has been
on the market for a while it doesn't necessarily mean that the
Windows driver for it will still be present in future releases (support
for some dot-matrix printers is already dwindling). Nevertheless,

while printer makers adhered to the Windows 3.1 standard, the concern about driver compatibility nearly faded from view.

That was then and this is now. Two developments in printer and computer technology have revived the driver bugaboo. GDI printers derive their name from the way they handle codes instructing them how to print. Instead of having to spend processor power and memory in the printer to translate the data they get into understandable form, they take the information directly from Windows GDI. In effect, this puts the printing muscle back into your computer and allows the printer manufacturer to cut the cost of the printer itself. This is good in one way, but a disaster if the print driver to handle the GDI output isn't up to snuff. Just prior to writing this book, I had to send three printers from two manufacturers back without reviewing them, simply because the GDI print drivers were flaky.

The second development is use of the bi-directional nature of the PC's parallel port, using services provided by Windows 3.1 and higher, to do fancy reporting of how the printer is working. In the old days, when a printer was out of paper, had a loose cable, needed ink or whatever, it simply didn't print, and you either went to it and replaced the missing stuff, or spent hours trying to figure out why the letter to Aunt Peggy kept disappearing into the ether. Today, you'll get messages on screen, complete with animated graphics, sound and/or funny voices telling you what isn't right (and you might even get useful information such as the progress of the printing job, but don't count on it). To provide these services means adding virtual device drivers and dynamic link libraries to Windows initialization files (i.e., WIN.INI and SYSTEM.INI) and again, if the software is a little strange, not only does the printer not work, but the rest of your system may not either. Sometimes progress is a pain in the fundament.

By the way, while Windows is a long way from perfect, it still supports more printer models than either Apple's System 7, 7.5, or OS/2.

The most common problem encountered by technical support departments is complaints that the printer isn't printing from the software. If the print driver can't make the software and printer agree, you get gobbledygook on the page instead of the letter to your cousin. If you can't wait to buy your printer until after you buy your computer

Printers – always check the software first

Type	Advantages	Disadvantages
Dot-matrix	Impact printing, inexpensive, low cost consumables, fast	Low quality output, noisy, very cheap models wear out quickly.
Ink-jet (or bubble-jet)	Relatively inexpensive, better colour quality than dot-matrix, as well as letter-quality type. Very quiet.	Not very dense blacks, inks tend to run out quickly and are water-soluble. Colour models with black ink in same container not cost effective. Jets can clog. Cost-per-page for colour higher than any other printer other than dye sublimation.
HP II laser or compatible	Good quality print, wide software support, low prices in the 4 to 6 page per minute range, wide range of cartridges and soft-fonts available.	Can't print full-page graphics without memory upgrade to at least 1.5 MB). Limited font choices at set point sizes - not scalable. Consumables cost more than dot-matrix or ink-jet (but don't have to be replaced as often).
HP III laser	Better quality print, some onboard scalable fonts	See above except for scalable fonts. Not as wide software support as for HP II. No price advantage over PostScript.
HP LaserJet 4	600 dpi output, replaces HP III. 45 onboard scalable fonts, PostScript upgrade available for reasonable cost; uses industry standard SIMMs for memory upgrade. Prices in direct competition with 300 dpi models.	By the time you add postscript support, these tend to be a little pricey, and you may have trouble getting printer driver support for older DOS software.
PostScript Laser	Fully scalable font set, good software support from Adobe, excellent for graphics and desktop publishing – standard memory usually 2 MB (but 4 MB is better).	Postscript printers have been both coming down in price and going up in resolution (The new standard is 600 dpi). Frankly, the postscript crowd got scared to death of the HP 4.
"True Type" compatible	Can take full advantage of Windows 3.1 True Type fonts	So what? They generally cost more – not necessary.
"GDI" Printer	Uses Windows Graphics Device Interface commands directly, saving both memory and processor power in the printer itself. Lower costs. May be laser or ink-jet	If the software drivers are flaky, you've got a problem. The printer may not work properly and it just might freeze up Windows, too. Difficult to get enough memory to print graphics from DOS.
Microsoft at work compatible	New concept of two-way communications between printer and Windows to tell you when paper is out and other info	These printers will use a sound card and talk to you as you work – just what you need, a machine that talks ... and if the software drivers aren't right on, you may have problems.
Wax transfer	Excellent colour support – no banding	Shiny surface may crack when bent, some models at the low end of the price spectrum can produce blotchy output.

and software, at least have some idea of what software you want to use, and get the store to give you a written guarantee that the blasted thing will work with what you plan to do. *Otherwise, never buy a printer unless you've checked to see that the application, operating environment, or operating system you plan to use it with has a driver for that specific brand and model.*

Some manufacturers of newer printers on the market will supply drivers for a variety of programs and environments (including Windows and some DOS applications, but not necessarily including OS/2 or System 7). That's a good idea. It's not so good if you update a program, buy one not on the list of supplied drivers, or lose the driver disk that came with the unit – so make sure you can contact the company again should the need arise.

Other manufacturers will claim to "emulate" (work just like) another brand or model that has wider support. Emulations can be extensive or rudimentary – make certain your receipt carries the vendor's guarantee along with the manufacturer's that it will work in your chosen operating environment – then the two of you will share the headaches if it doesn't.

Many types and brands of printer within each type will seem like a really good deal when you first purchase them – right up until you have to buy more consumables – then the real headaches can start. Even at the low end of the price scale (under $200 for some dot-matrix printers), it's a good idea to do some additional research before you make your final decision. Check out your local vendors of business supplies. How easy is it to get brand-name ribbons, ink cartridges, toner, or whatever? Do you have to get them from the original manufacturer (expensive) or are they widely available elsewhere? Do third-party manufacturers have lower-priced alternatives (and do their products carry a warranty)? In the case of laser printers, can you save money by getting recycled toner cartridges?

After you've read the material below, you may still be undecided about which printer you should buy. If all else fails, here are a few more pointers:

• If the retailer won't let you try it in the store, with the software you plan to use, go to another retailer.

• Computer equipment generally has no trade-in value, and that includes printers. If you're really unsure about a printer, or any other piece of computer equipment, go to a rental agency and try it for a month. Then decide.

• A man who repairs broken computer equipment for a living offered this good advice about reliability: "Some models are more rugged than others. You can't expect to run a $200 printer all day long, every day, and expect it to handle a lot of five-part forms or heavy stock without it sooner or later wanting to visit the doctor."

If you're down to two or three models and just can't make up your mind, here are some other things to try: (1) ask people who own one; (2) check your software – pick the one supported by the majority of applications you'll use; (3) if there isn't a huge price advantage between them, take the brand that the others are emulating; and (4) ask people who fix them for a living which brand(s) they see more often and how they broke. Be nice; they don't have to talk to you, but you might get some useful advice.

Dot-Matrix

When the job of timing the events at the 1964 Tokyo Olympics was awarded to Seiko, its additional challenge was to find a way to print out the results. Seiko delegated the task to a small subsidiary – Epson – which designed the impact digital head used at the games. Then Epson redeveloped it for use in small calculators. Oops!

Despite the false start, Epson virtually created the market for the dot-matrix printer. Even IBM's first dot-matrix printers were Epsons in an IBM shell. For the smallest startup price and cost of consumables, the lowly dot-matrix printer is still the technology of choice for those who want a little colour on a small budget.

If you've decided upon a dot-matrix printer, however, one or more of the following is probably true: (a) you're on a tight budget; (b) you or your children want colour, but you're on a tight budget and low quality is not an issue; (c) the quality of your printed material is not crucial, and you're on a tight budget; (d) you're not going to be doing serious desktop publishing (because you're on a tight budget); (e) all or part of your printed material goes onto multipart forms like invoices, receipts, or order forms (but why is your data going into a filing cabinet instead of remaining on-line where they are useful?); (f) you don't mind a bit (or sometimes a lot) of noise, and you're on a tight budget.

If none of the above is true (and your budget isn't *that* tight), you may be in the market for either an ink-jet, thermal wax transfer, or a laser printer.

Dot-matrix printers come in three flavours: 9-pin, 18-pin, and 24-pin. They come in two sizes: narrow and wide carriage. Print can be in basic black or full colour. They can be connected to your computer through the parallel or serial port. Prices start under $200, with each step up the price ladder giving increased performance, paper-handling features, and print quality.

Dot-matrix printers form images by impact. The print head is composed of tiny wires, or pins, which are propelled into the ribbon (or not) as the printer receives a series of on/off signals from the computer. It's the pattern of dots on paper – and the spaces between them – that can give the output of a dot matrix printer a jagged, faded, grainy look.

The more pins there are in the print head, the darker and sharper the characters will be. The diameter of each pin in a 24-pin printer is smaller than that of a 9-pin, but there are more of them and they are able to plant more dots in a smaller area with fewer (and smaller) spaces. This also provides an increase in speed, particularly when forming "letter quality" print, because fewer passes of the print head are required to form the darker characters. There are also 18-pin printers on the market, but not many. Most people buy either 9- or 24-pin models.

The first choice you have to make, after deciding how much money you have to spend, is how good you want your print to look. If most of your printed output will be in draft mode (the fastest, grainiest quality), then there's not much advantage to a 24-pin printer – a 9-pin model will work just as well and just as quickly.

"Near letter quality" (NLQ) generally means that the printer has one or more built-in fonts like Roman or Courier to make the output look more like type. NLQ print takes longer for a 9-pin printer to do (two passes of the print head instead of one), but it's still an acceptable wait if your volume is low. Not all 9-pin printers have an NLQ mode; some of them simply make two passes over their draft font to make it darker, instead of forming characters shaped to look as if they came from a typewriter. If you have True Type fonts installed under Windows, the dot-matrix will print them, but it will take forever to do so.

Despite its name, using "near letter quality" print from a dot-matrix for business correspondence is today's equivalent of writing with a pencil back in the days of typewriters. If you're buying a printer for use in a small or home business, keep in mind that the larger companies you hope will take you seriously expect laser quality output or something that comes darned close – and dot-matrix quality doesn't cut it.

Where you might expect to see a dot-matrix used commercially is in a business that produces multipart forms. However, with the plethora of forms-based computer software and point-of-sales systems available today, there's no longer any excuse for not having sales, shipping, and inventory data on-line where it can be easily retrieved, audited, and analysed.

If you are printing a lot of graphics (line drawings, graphs) and have decided against a plotter, ink-jet, or laser, a 24-pin printer will give sharper resolution and finer lines than a 9-pin unit, but make sure your favourite graphics program has a software driver for the 24-pin printer you're thinking of buying.

Number of pins aside, dot-matrix printers also come in two sizes: narrow and wide carriage. You can get away with a narrow carriage if you never want to print on paper wider than 8.5 inches. Most brands of three-across labels will not fit a narrow carriage; neither will large envelopes. If you plan to use a lot of spreadsheets, or to print labels three or more across a page, you'll need a wide carriage. Wide carriage printers are more expensive and so are their ribbons.

The dot-matrix market has been dwindling for several years with the advent of and falling prices for alternative technologies. They'll probably never vanish entirely because: (a) they are the only impact printers left (an early victim of the laser and ink-jet was the daisy wheel printer – essentially a computer-driven typewriter); (b) they're the only device remaining that will handle continuous-form paper to produce "Welcome back Harry!" banners for the office; and (c) the cost of consumables is less than for any other computer printer.

Ink-Jets

"Pssst, c'mere . . . Ya wanna see somethin' neat? No, don't look around . . . come closer . . . closer."

I don't know what it is about ink-jet printers that reminds me of a street hustle. Maybe it's the emphasis the various manufacturers place on how close the quality is to what you might get from a laser and how expensive lasers are compared to how inexpensive the ink-jet is. Maybe it's how they fudge the cost-per-page figures by using unreasonably low coverage rates to make it appear less than it really is.

Ink-jet printers (they are called "ink-jet" by Hewlett-Packard and "bubble-jet" by Canon, and both terms are used by other manufacturers) have become an important segment of the computer printer market. They've surpassed the other low-end alternative, the dot-matrix, and have definitely cut into the laser market. There are good reasons: ink-jets are quiet, they produce high-quality print, and the price is right. Ink-jets start at around $300 and go up to over $4,250, with a number of models from various manufacturers grouped at the lower end of the scale.

Compare the price to the cost of monochrome dot-matrix printers, all sorts of which can be found for under $300. While you're at it, also compare it to monochrome lasers. At the low end, they can be found for under $600. Then there's colour.

While colour lasers are more expensive than the high end of the ink-jet market covered here, at least one other technology, thermal wax transfer, produces better and less expensive colour than ink-jets and is still relatively inexpensive (see the separate section on colour, below).

Let's get the cost-per-page problem out of the way before we start describing the various technologies involved in ink-jet printing. The advertising and marketing material on ink-jets is full of cost-per-page figures. In some cases, the cost of the unit itself is factored in, while in others, the cost of paper and the unit itself isn't. Some manufacturers are more diligent than others; they'll add the cost of regularly scheduled replacement of the print head.

The biggest game of all is played with the percentage of the page covered in ink. A typical letter-sized page of 12-point, single-spaced type gets about 30 per cent of its surface covered in ink. When you add graphics (charts, pictures, or drawings) or larger typefaces, the percentage of coverage goes up to as much as 80 or 100 per cent. However, typical cost-per-page figures quoted in ads are for between 5 and 7.5 per cent coverage.

Ink-jet printers have the highest cost per page of any widely used printing technology, including dot-matrix, laser, and thermal wax. For example, 100 per cent coverage of a letter-sized page on the Genicom 7025 thermal wax printer costs about 76 cents (including the cost of the special paper), while a comparable page on a typical ink-jet will cost over \$3.00. A typical text-only page (25 to 30 per cent coverage) on both a laser and a dot-matrix will cost less than 1 cent per page, while the lowest price for an ink-jet I was quoted when researching an article in early 1995 (for the Epson Stylus 800 series, which has a head design that prevents clogging) was 13.2 cents per page. Other models using a standard head design will run around 43 cents per page for that coverage.

While we're on the topic of cost, ink-jet printers are thirsty, and no one has yet made one big enough to hold enough ink. A typical toner cartridge for a Hewlett-Packard (HP) III laser printer costs around \$90 for a recycled replacement and is good for between 2,000 to 3,000 pages. Other models cost slightly more, but are good for as many as 8,000 pages. The highest ink-jet rating I've found (again, the Epson Stylus 800) is for 700 pages, while more typical models are lucky to produce 250. Plan to spend time replacing cartridges and print heads. (Canon makes this simple (and expensive); when you replace an ink pot, you replace the head at the same time.)

Ink-jets are also slower than dot-matrix and laser printers. Colour printing is always slower than monochrome printing and we talk in terms of minutes per page, not pages per minute. But most of the printing you'll be doing will be black and white, and here's where the real differences lie. It's not unusual for low-end lasers to print four pages per minute and there are 10 ppm models available on the street for under $1,500 (the NEC Silentwriter 900 series for example). If you can find an ink-jet that will do better than five pages per minute in letter-quality mode (about 150 characters per second), I'd like to see it.

As noted above, ink-jet printers produce better print quality than dot-matrix printers, but it's largely because they user smaller dots and the ink bleeds into the paper to reduce the jagged appearance some-what. However, they can produce jagged effects on artistic text or thin, curving lines.

Another contributing factor to the difficulties encountered by dot-matrix and ink-jet printers has to do with the matrix grid they employ. High resolution for 24-pin dot-matrix printers and early ink-jets was a grid of 360 horizontal by 180 vertical (for a maximum of 64,800 dots in a square inch). Today you can get, but pay extra for, ink-jets with much higher resolutions.

There are a number of ways that ink-jet printers do what they do. The four basic technologies are drop-on-demand, thermal bubble, continuous flow, and electrostatic. Technically, the Tektronix Phaser models, using phase-change technology and solid ink, are also ink-jets of a sort but are outside the scope of this section (see alternative colour technologies, below – but, with prices starting at close enough to $14,000 they'll remain alternatives for some time). You can also ignore electrostatic technology. It's old and I couldn't find any current models using it. I also couldn't find anyone using continuous flow technology, but that doesn't mean someone isn't.

The descriptions below are somewhat sketchy because the illus-trations do a much better job of explaining the differences than words ever could.

Thermal bubble

This technology is by far the most common used today. The ink is heated in the printhead, then cooled, forming a tiny bubble of ink that is forced onto the paper where it both splatters and spreads into the paper. The tendency for the ink to spread when it hits is one of the primary reasons why ink-jet print looks less jagged than dot-matrix print. The other is the number of dots produced by the head. It's not

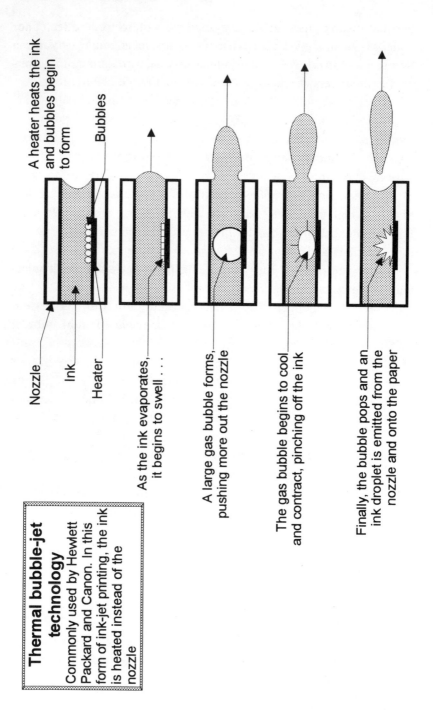

A heater heats the ink and bubbles begin to form

Bubbles

Nozzle

Ink

Heater

As the ink evaporates, it begins to swell . . . .

A large gas bubble forms, pushing more out the nozzle

The gas bubble begins to cool and contract, pinching off the ink

Finally, the bubble pops and an ink droplet is emitted from the nozzle and onto the paper

Thermal bubble-jet technology
Commonly used by Hewlett Packard and Canon. In this form of ink-jet printing, the ink is heated instead of the nozzle

unusual for ink-jets to have anywhere from 48 to 64 nozzles (finer dots, less room between them, smoother lines than you'll get from a 24-pin dot-matrix). This is the technology used by the majority of ink-jet manufacturers, including both Canon and Hewlett-Packard.

Drop-on-demand

This used be another name for piezoelectric technology, but there's a new variant introduced by Epson in its Stylus 800 series printers. In the piezoelectric, drop-on-demand system, small crystals in the print-head heat the nozzle and force ink out. In Epson's piezomechanical scheme (also called MACH, for multilayered actuator head), the nozzle is vibrated, rather than heated, and ink is shaken out of the head.

Epson says its method produces smaller droplets that don't splatter when they hit, producing a finer and sharper result (samples I've seen are impressive). It also says that because of the way the system is designed, you won't have to replace the head as often because it

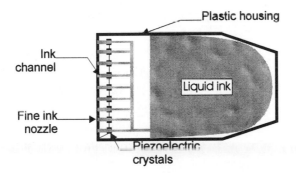

Ink-jet piezoelectric drop-on-demand printhead
Fine droplets of ink are squeezed out of the nozzles when the crystals heat the nozzles

doesn't gum up with dried ink. This keeps the cost of cartridges down and the overall cost per page as well. As of mid-1995, Epson was the only manufacturer using this technology.

Continuous flow

This technology could, in theory, work faster than the others. In this case, ink flows all the time. Each droplet passes through a chamber where it is either given an electrical charge or not. Charged droplets hit deflection plates and are literally sprayed on the paper, while those without a charge, and the residue, return to the ink reservoir for reuse. Why this system isn't in wider use is fairly simple to explain. In this case, the head doesn't move; the paper has to move, otherwise you'd get a big mess – and the extra cost of a relatively quiet and reliable paper movement mechanism would make them hard to market.

There are a number of factors affecting the cost of ink-jet printers and their effectiveness over the long term that you'll want to watch for when you're making your buying decision:

Number, cost, and availability of ink cartridges. In a monochrome printer, you get one black cartridge. In a colour model, you may get one cartridge (with all four or only three colours). This is the least desirable scheme, because most of your printing will be black and when the black is exhausted, you'll have to throw away the rest. An acceptable compromise is two cartridges, one with black, the other with the other three colours, but nothing works better than a model with four separate cartridges, one with each of the four colours.

Some cartridges cost more than others because the manufacturer, acknowledging that ink-jet nozzles gum up with dried ink, attach the head to the cartridge. When you change ink, you change heads at the same time.

Before you buy your printer, check with a few suppliers to see whether you'll be able to get replacement ink pots easily, or whether you'll be forced to keep buying them directly from the manufacturer at inflated costs.

Number of printhead nozzles. Heads with 64 nozzles are better than any smaller number. They'll give you the best quality of print.

Resolution. The higher the resolution in dots per inch (dpi) the printer will do – i.e., the number of horizontal by the number of vertical dots in a one-inch square – the sharper your image will be. A resolution of 360 by 360 dpi is fairly common. Hewlett-Packard offers models capable of 600 by 360, while Epson's Stylus 800 will do 720 by 720.

Software and font compatibility. If the printer requires a special driver for use in Microsoft Windows, it may not work properly in OS/2 or with your DOS applications. Ask if the company is working on a driver for Windows 95. Other questions to ask are: Does it have enough memory to allow you to download fonts or does it require cartridges for those not already in its own ROM (read only memory)? And, does it support Windows True Type fonts or do you have to get special fonts to make it work? (Hewlett-Packard has recently started providing True Type compatibility in some of its newer models.)

Emulation. If you're down to a choice between two or three models, pay the extra money to get the one the others are emulating. Their emulation may not be perfect.

Carriage width. Wide-carriage models cost extra, but may be worth it if you have to print on surfaces larger than 8.5 inches wide. While here, ask about envelopes. Hewlett-Packard has started to place sensors in some of its models to move the printhead away from the paper to accommodate thicker stock, such as envelopes.

Check the output. Print samples produced for promotional purposes always look great (you never get to see the rejects). If you can't see the printer make a page with graphics on it in the shop, make sure you can take it back if you're not satisfied once you get it to your home or office.

Regardless of promotional claims, ink-jet printers are not as good as lasers, and can't even come close to the quality you get from a Postscript printer or one emulating the page description language in the HP LaserJet 4.

Colour quality is better than any dot-matrix can produce, but because the head moves only horizontally, while the paper moves vertically, it *will* show banding. The colour will be darker and less precise than you hoped. In spite of this, have a look at the output of the Epson Stylus Colour 800 in 720 dpi mode, using their special paper.

You'll opt for an ink/bubble jet printer if: (a) you want better print quality than a dot-matrix or as close as you can get to laser quality monochrome output, but don't have enough money for a laser printer (see below); (b) you don't have a high volume of work to print (these things are slow compared to lasers); (c) you want higher quality colour than a dot-matrix can provide, can't afford a thermal wax transfer printer, and don't mind the hideous cost per page; (d) there are no clumsy people with coffee cups or nervous people with sweaty hands in your life (the inks used are water-soluble and will both run and smear. Humid weather isn't kind to ink-jet pages either; and even in dry weather they tend to curl up until the ink dries, particularly if you've covered a large area); or (e) you don't believe me about the cost per page and choose to believe the folks who want to sell you the unit, instead.

Lasers and LED Page Printers

The future is already here. Just when you thought you were ready to plunk down some cold cash for a 300 dot-per-inch (dpi) laser printer, the stakes in the game have changed. Today 300 dpi lasers are history, with models capable of 600, 800, and 1200 dpi now at a price that serious purchasers can justify getting one.

Blame Hewlett-Packard. After popularizing laser printing with its 300 dpi LaserJet, LaserJet Plus, LaserJet 500 Plus, LaserJet II, and LaserJet III models, HP's LaserJet 4 (non-PostScript) and 4M (PostScript) have done more than change the name from Roman to Arabic numerals.

Hewlett-Packard has been setting the standard to beat in laser printing since the introduction of the LaserJet in 1984. By 1991, it had sold over 6 million units. Today, laser printers produced both by HP and its competitors, using variations of HP's proprietary Printer Command Language (PCL), account for 80 per cent of the laser printer market (PostScript language accounts for the other 20 per cent).

All laser printers, regardless of the page description language, use a process known as electrophotography. The physical mechanics differ from model to model, depending upon who made the original "engine" that powers the beast. While there are dozens of brands of laser, only a handful of companies make the internal components. Among the most prolific are Canon, Ricoh, Sharp, and Minolta. With the exception of some models by Okidata, Epson, and Panasonic (i.e., LED page printers), they actually do use a laser somewhere in the process.

Early laser printers used helium/neon gas lasers (HeNe). While you may still find one or two gas laser models in larger industrial, high-speed units, it is far more common today to use a light emitting diode (LED) laser. Yet another method has liquid crystal shutter arrays arranged in line just before the drum and the shutters are opened or closed to form a latent image. Okidata's variation of this scheme "has no moving parts." It uses a series of LEDs (2600 of them) in line, which are turned on and off as appropriate.

Lasers printers all work the same way. Once the instructions from your software leave the computer and arrive at the printer, a laser is directed through a series of lenses and mirrors onto a photo-sensitive drum. The drum acquires an electrostatic charge on its surface, which attracts black dust from a toner container. The toner is transferred to the paper and heat-fused to its surface.

How all this takes place, the speed with which it happens, and how the printer figures out how to get onto paper an image that more or less resembles what you sent it is what costs you money. Together with the various paper-handling mechanics, it makes laser printers wonderfully complicated machines.

Even the earliest models of laser printers were capable of producing smaller dots than any mechanical printer, using a one-inch matrix grid of 300 by 300. Together with enhancements to the physical technology of both the printers and the toner they use, and particularly advancements in the software that drives the printers, edge jag has become less of a concern.

In the earliest lasers, descriptions of the characters they could produce were in the printer's firmware (ROM chips with software instructions permanently stored). The job of the software driver was simply to get them out of the firmware onto paper. Because memory storage space is always limited, there was a narrow range of characters, typefaces, and fonts available.

In order to produce characters in, for instance, a 10-point Times Roman typeface, all of the characters in the set would have to reside in the printer. To produce 12-point characters required another set. To make them bold required another, italic another, and bold italic yet another. The range of print styles from these early machines was, to say the least, limited.

One of the first advancements allowed the user to add character sets by purchasing separate cartridges that could be plugged into the printer. They were little more than ROM chips containing the typeface descriptions in a plastic box with connectors. It was common for really intensive users to have dozens of them (but given the prices, there was a limit to what most people could afford).

The next advancement allowed people to have typeface descriptions stored outside the printer on their computer's hard drive, together with software that allowed them to "download" the font descriptions to the printer's memory for use as required. The disadvantage was the time it took to send the font to the printer. Again, memory restrictions limited the number of fonts that could be used. Remember, at this point we're still dealing with the situation that required a separate character set to be used each time there was a change in size, weight, or orientation of a character. If you are thinking of buying a printer that is said to be HP II compatible, you'll still be dealing with these problems.

The first major breakthrough came from a U.S. company called Adobe. It developed a combined hardware and software solution dubbed PostScript, which for the first time allowed the printer to store an outline of the particular typeface. That outline could be scaled (that is, expanded or contracted), boldened, slanted, rotated, or filled with a wide variety of shades and shapes.

Doing something even more magical, Adobe also managed to play mathematical games with the dots that virtually eliminated jagged edges and produced wonderfully smooth curves. Adobe's patents on both the hardware and software were also airtight, and they extracted a hefty licence fee from any company that built a printer around Adobe technology. Even today, PostScript laser printers demand a price premium.

The next breakthrough came from Hewlett-Packard. Beginning with its HP LaserJet III series, it changed its traditional page description language to one that used an approach similar to PostScript, in that font descriptions could be scaled. HP also began using something it called "resolution enhancement technology." What it did, in effect, was to vary the size of the dots in order to fill in some of the edge spaces. It has continued with the same technology in its 600 dpi LaserJet 4 series (and has also introduced it in some of its ink-jet products).

Mind you, the image is still composed of dots. Even though a 300 by 300 matrix, providing 90,000 individual data points within a square inch, gives a sharper and clearer image than is possible with impact printers, the results are still not sharp enough for more than business correspondence or neighbourhood newsletters.

Over the years, various third-party manufacturers have developed add-on or add-in boards, together with special software drivers, to provide higher resolutions for HP printers – 600, 800, 1,000, or 1,200 dpi. Within the past couple of years, printer manufacturers other than HP have attempted to move the industry to these higher resolutions as well. Perhaps the most successful of these has been the LaserMaster Corp. line of 600 dpi WinPrinters (available only for the Windows environment and only with addition of a sometimes cranky print driver).

Before HP itself was willing to move, however, it had to change the toner its laser printers used. A 600 by 600 matrix produces four times the number of data points that a 300 dpi matrix can produce. There was no point attempting to place 360,000 data points within a square inch if the toner particles weren't fine enough.

They also had to beef up the printer's processing power. If dealing with four times the data took quadruple the time, few users would be willing to wait. They solved the problem by (in essence) giving the printer a computer of its own, an Intel 80960 KA-20 MHz RISC processor.

You're unlikely to see any difference between a 300 dpi image and a 600 dpi image when you're looking at the middle of a black object. While the LaserJet 4/4M produces very solid blacks, this has more to do with toner quality and internal mechanics than it does with dot density. Where the differences do appear are at the edges of curved or slanted objects, in fine curved lines, and in halftone screens.

When I ran some test documents through a 300 dpi NEC Silentwriter 2 model 290 and a 600 dpi LaserJet 4 equipped with PostScript (both operating in PostScript mode), I couldn't see much difference in large text characters with the naked eye, but there was a difference in the appearance of text at smaller points sizes (12 and under). The LaserJet 4 produces much finer lines. A halftone square, with 10 per cent saturation, was definitely grainy at 300 dpi and much smoother at 600 dpi (again, I couldn't see the individual dots without a magnifying glass). An EPS (encapsulated PostScript) graphic of an apple, with a gradient fill, showed the greatest difference. The gradient at 300 dpi was choppy. At 600 dpi, it was much smoother.

Once upon a time this stuff would have cost you an arm and a leg and a lease on your next three grandchildren, but like so much else in the computer industry, competition has forced prices down steadily over the past several years. Four to six pages-per-minute (ppm) 300 dpi lasers (and LED page printers) can be had commonly for under $600 to $1,000. Look for names such as Okidata, Panasonic, Epson, and Hewlett-Packard. You can easily find 300 and 600 dpi PostScript and HP III (or 4) compatible lasers in the five to ten ppm range for under $2,000 (NEC, Texas Instruments, Xerox , and others).

Shopping tips include:

(a) Check the availability and price of toner cartridges (and inquire about recycled products), keeping in mind that the rated number of pages per cartridge assumes normal business correspondence and will go down if you're printing a lot of graphics or a mixed document such as a newsletter.

(b) The number of pages per minute a laser printer can produce is important only if you're making multiple copies of the same document. A far more important figure is the time it takes to print an original page.

(c) If you're running on a small network, particularly a peer-to-peer setup, a printer with its own network interface will save you having to check that another computer is on when you need to print, but just because a printer contains a network hookup doesn't mean it will run under Windows by itself. Check to see that you don't need to be using Novell Netware or some other client-server network scheme.

(d) Prices for HP II compatible lasers often include only 512 KB of onboard RAM and they seldom include enough memory (at least 1.5 MB) to produce a full page of graphics. A PostScript laser with only 2 MB of RAM on board is going to struggle. On the other hand, GDI printers commonly ship with only 512 KB or less and seem to do all right.

(e) A number of new models of laser come with software to allow you both to get messages from them (such as, "I'm out of paper") and to have more control over them. This won't help you if you don't have a high-speed bi-directional parallel port in your system, it won't help if you're not running Windows, and if the software is buggy (as it was with some of the NEC SuperScript 660 and 660i models tested in mid-1995), you may not get the performance out of your printer that you wanted.

(f) Printers that rely on the processor in your computer to do their work for them (i.e., GDI models) cost less, but assume you have nothing else to do except watch the hourglass icon on screen instead of working (some don't release the system and let you get on with more work until they're done). It may make them dodgy investments if your time is valuable.

Colour

Dogs, it is said, can only see in black and white. People, on the other hand, see in colour. Rich, vibrant, and expressive, colour can take an average, ho-hum image and put it right in your face.

In the computer industry, there has been an explosion of sales of colour monitors and increasing sales of graphics cards capable of producing up to 16.7 million colours on screen.

As a yardstick in your hunt for a colour printer, you can assume that anything inexpensive (under $1,000) isn't going to look great. Once over $1,400 you begin to approach the low edge of acceptable (about the quality of newspaper colour in the 1970s) to reasonable quality. Highly acceptable will cost you $5,000 to $12,000. If you're looking for professional pre-press quality, don't leave the house without $10,000 to $20,000 in your purse. If you want glossy-magazine-quality colour, go see your local service bureau or commercial print shop instead.

Before we get to the technologies involved in colour printers, it's important to understand some basics:

Printing in colour will always cost more than printing in black and white. The printers themselves are more expensive, regardless of technology, and their supplies (including the special papers you'll need for some printers) cost more, too.

Quoting an exact cost per page for each technology is difficult because it changes with specific models of printer within each class and with the amount of page surface covered with coloured image. When I discuss the various technologies below, I'll give a cost-per-page estimate based on the assumption of about 30 per cent coverage, gleaned from several companies who make the printers.

Printing in colour always takes longer than black and white because colours are added one at a time, either in strips or by passing the whole page through the mechanism more than once. So, it's going to take at least three times as long from when the data reaches the printer, and because your software has to work harder to calculate and send a colour image, that takes longer as well.

Software compatibility is crucial in colour. It's important with any printer to have a matching print driver. It can either come from the printer manufacturer or from the software publisher, but without it you'll only come to understand the true meaning of frustration.

As a simple rule of thumb, check the software first to see if the printer you plan to purchase is supported. If it isn't specifically mentioned, view the salesperson's assurances that it emulates a better known brand with caution. Have it demonstrated that it will work with your software and operating environment (such as Windows or OS/2) before you buy it, or at the very least have the guarantee that it will work written on the sales invoice.

A funny thing is going to happen to your artwork when it arrives at the printer. Graphics cards and monitors don't produce colour the same way the printer does. You'll likely use software and hardware that can reproduce 64, 256, 32,000-plus, 65,000-plus, or 16.7 million pure colours on screen. Only very high-end printers produce more than 64 colours clearly and 57 of them are dithered – that is, small dots of different colour values are placed close to the pure colour to make an area look like a shade in-between from a distance. All three- and four-colour process printing technologies use dithering, with the exception of dye sublimation.

To make life even more fun, your graphics card and monitor combine the colours red, green, and blue – RGB – to paint your screen, while most printers use cyan, magenta, yellow, and sometimes black – CMY(K) – to build their images. Even some dot-matrix models that use blue and red, use yellow instead of green.

Add to this the curious effect your own perceptions have on the often idiosyncratic combinations of certain graphics cards with certain monitors and you can see how difficult precise matching can be.

What you're going to get on paper is at best going to be an approximation of what you saw on screen. Printers that allow you to calibrate them to match your screen or printers that have built-in references to a standardized colour chart (such as Pantone or TrueMatch) are desirable – and cost extra. Software that allows you to calibrate your monitor to match a specific brand of printer, and/or comes with a Pantone or similar colour palette, is also desirable. You may also begin to see how having the correct print driver to match your software takes on high importance for colour printers.

The relatively inexpensive printers won't produce quality good enough for publication. You may get away with acceptable overhead transparencies, kids' drawings, the occasional Christmas letter, and so on, but aside from that, anything under $5,000 is only marginally adequate to use to check a colour image you plan to have printed by a service house or commercial printer later.

There are six basic types of colour printers: dot-matrix, ink/bubble-jet, thermal wax transfer, dye sublimation, solid ink/phase-change, and finally, after a lot of years, laser.

Dot-matrix

Dot-matrix colour printers are suitable only for your children to print drawings for school, for party banners, or for proofing material destined for a higher-quality printer.

They produce images by hurling their pins against a multi-coloured ribbon. Generally, the printer moves the ribbon up and down to bring the various coloured portions in line with the print head, but regardless of how that's done, the technique used to build up an image is the same.

The print head moves across the page in each coloured strip: first yellow, then cyan or red, then magenta or blue. Black may be produced as a combination of the three colours or in a fourth pass. This continues until one strip of the full image is built. Then the paper advances and the whole thing starts again.

The advantage to dot-matrix colour is the same as it is for black and white: the relatively low cost of ribbons and the use of standard paper produce the lowest cost per page of any scheme. Dot-matrix machines are also the only product left that will use continuous form paper for making long banners. They're also relatively inexpensive to buy, with a host of 24-pin models available for between $500 and $1,500 that give an average cost per coloured page of 5 to 10 cents.

The disadvantages are legion. They are noisy, the images are grainy, and curved or slanted lines are jagged – and they always show banding. The dithering used to produce halftones is awful.

As the ribbon becomes drier and fainter, not only will the images become more grainy and banded, but they will often be lighter at the end of a job than they were at the beginning. The ribbon makes full contact with the paper and it will pick up colours from one strip and pass them on to another.

And finally, even though you're expecting to print coloured images, you'll be unpleasantly surprised by how much of your printing is actually done in black. One of the first things to wear out on a coloured ribbon will be the black strip, whereupon the whole ribbon, including the still-useful coloured strips, is toast. I know of no model of dot-matrix printer that uses two ribbons – one for black and the other for colours.

Ink- or bubble-jet

Everything I said above about how ink-jets work and how expensive they are to use, although they're relatively inexpensive to buy, goes for colour ink-jets, too. Keep in mind that liquid ink-jet images are composed of dots and the spaces between them, laid down one strip at a time. The colour image is also produced one strip at a time as all four colours are added separately. You can expect to see banding.

Depending on the model of printer and quality of the ink, ink-jet images can be vibrant, although there is a tendency for colours to be somewhat darker than you thought they'd be and for blacks to be lighter than you'd hoped they'd be. You can plan on having any page containing a high surface coverage to curl up as the ink dries and had best be prepared to handle it with care until it dries thoroughly – and after as well, as ink-jet images run and smudge just as easily in colour as in black and white.

The typical ink/bubble-jet cost-per-page range is roughly 20 to 30 cents for a 30 per cent saturated page (rising to over $3.00 for 100 per cent coverage).

One last caution. Low-end colour jet printers will often come with all three colours, plus black, in the same ink cartridge. Once again, the black will go south very quickly, leaving you with the necessity of replacing a cartridge full of colour, but lacking black. Slightly more expensive models will come with a black cartridge, plus a second cartridge with the colours. In the long run, these are more cost-effective. At the top of most product lines are units with four separate cartridges. These tend to cost within shouting distance of $2,000, take up just slightly more room on a tabletop than your old miniature hockey game, and can often dislodge nearby ornaments as their carriages whack back and forth across the page.

For the most sophisticated of the lot in terms of features, check out the Canon CJ-10. It's not only a colour printer but a photocopier and scanner as well. Have big pockets. Dig deep. The LexMark Medley 4X is also worth checking. It will fax, print, scan, and photocopy, but only printing from a PC or Mac is in colour (the faxing, scanning, and copying functions are in shades of grey only). For this unit, you can have shallower pockets.

In no circumstances buy any colour printer unless you've seen it print out the kind of material you plan to use it to do.

We're about to leave Kansas, Dorothy. From here on in I'm describing technologies that start at $1,300, easily cost over $3,500, and soar to over $20,000.

Thermal wax transfer

This is the least expensive technology of the group, with prices ranging from roughly $1,300 to over $10,000. At the low end are models by Genicom (it's the Canadian version of the Fargo Primera sold in the United States) and the NEC 3000. I actually bought the Genicom 7025, a 203 dpi printer that lists for under $1,300, and have been happy with the results. There is no banding because the whole paper is moved through the mechanism three times (or when using the four-colour ribbon, four times) in one continuous flow. Since its introduction, both Genicom and Fargo have introduced 300 dpi models.

Other manufacturers of thermal wax transfer include Brother, CalComp, General Parametrics, Mitsubishi, QMS, Seiko, and Tektronix. Prices within the range will be determined by the amount of onboard memory, whether the printer includes its own processor, the number of onboard fonts, the dots-per-inch print resolution, and whether it will produce PostScript.

The costs of consumables are considerable, with typical four-colour ribbons costing over $100 and producing about 150 pages. When you factor in the cost of the special paper required by most units, you are up to 75 cents to a dollar per page. One slight modifying factor is that this price holds regardless of the amount of paper covered in any one page. It's the same for 10 per cent or 100 per cent coverage.

Thermal transfer, thermal wax transfer, and wax transfer are all terms used to describe roughly the same process. It sounds simple in theory, but getting it right requires some tricky technology and sophisticated paper-handling mechanics. There is a film ribbon that is the same width as the printer carriage. It contains the colours in a waxy ink in sections that are the same length as a page. Think of a roll of Saran Wrap. As you pull it from the package, there is, for the sake of example, first an 8.5 inch by 11 inch yellow section, then a magenta section, then a blue section (and possibly a black section as well).

The film passes over a heated head and is applied to special, clay-coated paper or a transparency, one colour at a time. The whole sheet of paper is fed through the printer, then it's sucked back and fed again for the next colour, and so on.

The only exceptions to the need for special coated paper currently on the market are the Tektronix Phaser 220i and 220e introduced in 1994, which will print on standard laser printer paper. A press release from Genicom says it will also use "plain laser paper," but my tests were invariably disappointing – the results were faint and full of dropouts where the ink failed to adhere.

Once applied, the ink is fused to the surface, and the combined effect can produce brilliant, rich, highly saturated colours, glossy images, and gorgeous transparencies. However, both Genicom and NEC 3000 also showed signs of small areas on the page where the wax failed to adhere properly, giving the image a patchy appearance.

Wax transfer printers are generally slow (anywhere from two to three minutes per page, down to one and a bit pages per minute, with the Phasers leading the pack in terms of speed). However, they're faster than dye sublimation and most solid-ink/phase-change technologies.

Thermal wax transfer printouts resist smudging, but folding the page may result in cracking and flaking. This isn't a bad test for you to do in the store to see if the model you're contemplating is more or less prone to the problem.

Dye sublimation

This technology is called dye-sub for short and is sometimes also called D2T2 (for dye diffusion thermal transfer). Among the companies using this technique are GCC Technologies, Kodak, Mitsubishi, Seiko, and Tektronix.

Like wax transfer, this technology uses heat and special coated paper, but the similarity stops right there. "Sublimation" is a term used in physics to describe what happens when a solid goes to vapour (or vice versa) without passing through a liquid stage on the way. Dry ice does this and so does the coloured dye used in these printers.

The dye comes in sheets, which are passed over a heated head. This head can vary its temperature quickly, and the hotter the head, the more ink vapour is applied to and absorbed by the special porous, polystyrene-coated paper that these printers require.

The print head can apply up to eight different heating levels for each colour, producing the full 16.7 million colours available from high-end graphics hardware and software. There are no dots, no bands; colours are continuous tones – not dithered. They're intense and awfully hard to smudge – but face it, folks, if you spill coffee on anything, you're going to do it over. And you won't want to do it again. These printers are also achingly slow, often taking well over three minutes per page at a cost of $8.00 to $10.00 per page.

The price range is from $7,000 to $13,000, and some models cost over $20,000, depending on the amount of memory, the speed of the onboard processor, and the width of the paper path, plus a hefty premium for PostScript.

Curiously enough, even though this class of colour printer is very good at graphic images with solid fills and at continuous tone photographs, it is not preferred for text or images with fine lines (they have a tendency to blur on both paper and transparencies).

For a lower-end dye-sub emulation, once again we turn to Genicom and Fargo. While they do not use precisely the same technology as a true dye-sub printer, they use a special ribbon and paper to emulate it. The quality of the printing (again at 203 dpi for the lower of the two models) is quite good, but the $8.50-per-page cost makes it unsuitable for casual use and will want to make you lock it up when the grandchildren visit.

Solid ink or phase change

This printing technology is virtually the exclusive preserve of Tektronix (it has over 90 per cent of the market for this technology, and I don't have the faintest idea who the competition is).

The Phaser uses solid sticks of a wax-like ink that are heated and blown onto any paper that will go through the mechanism (I've seen them print on paper towels). The ink dries very quickly, and the medium is passed through pressure rollers that flatten and fuse the dots of colour. Multiple colour passes are done inside the unit with the paper passing through the handling mechanism only once.

Because the ink dries so quickly, it resists smudging and the colour doesn't bleed or flake off when the paper is folded. Although it will print well to plain paper, some people are less happy about how well it works with plastic transparency material (although examples I've seen from the Phaser 340 make me wonder why they weren't happy). Depending on the amount of surface coverage, the newer models (i.e., the 340 and 540) can push a page out every 15 seconds (about 4 ppm).

These printers are more expensive than wax transfer and some dye-sub models, but the cost per average page is down to around 30 cents for wide paper and 5 to 15 cents for standard letter-size pages. The fat crayon-like ink sticks are not only relatively inexpensive compared to dye-sub and wax-transfer rolls, but they can be added on the fly while the printer is still working. There are a number of Phaser models ranging in price from around $14,000 for models with wide paper-handling paths for industrial pre-press proofing (the 220i for example), down to $7,195 (Canadian list price) for the

Phaser 340. In tests I've conducted, the output has been better than colour lasers.

Colour lasers

When I first wrote about colour laser printers in 1992, there were no models available on the market for under $60,000 or that didn't weigh as much as a small car. By mid-1995, QMS, Hewlett-Packard, and Xerox were all in the market with models selling for as little as $8,500 (QMS), and ranging up to $12,000 (Xerox 4920). By the end of 1996, I would expect to see many more models available, but suspect we'll have to wait awhile before these units approach the price of today's monochrome lasers.

Several factors will likely lead to lower prices: higher consumer demand, downward pressure from competing technologies (if the phase-change, dye-sub, and thermal wax folks aren't careful, they'll be left wondering where their market went), and improved technology.

All three of the currently available models use four toner cartridges (cyan, magenta, yellow, and black), pass the paper three or four times (you can generally select whether to use three or four colours) through the system, but otherwise they behave just like a standard laser printer. Once all four colours are laid down, a voltage drop releases a dry toner, which is fused on in a single pass through another part of the mechanism.

The advantage of colour lasers is that they use plain paper and a familiar technology. You generally get a choice of page description language, which will include PostScript. Most of your printing will come out at 300 dpi, but if the length of time to get your first page out isn't critical, and if you can afford the whopping cost of getting enough memory to do the job, the Xerox 4900 will produce up to 1200 dpi, giving it a very sharp output.

Despite the use of three or four toner cartridges, this is still laser, not ink-jet technology, so it's not a consumable resource hog, with a cost per page of about 32 cents at 30 per cent colour coverage.

If this is the printer for you, then items to watch for while shopping are:

(a) The base price quoted often doesn't include enough memory to reach the highest resolution stated in the advertising.

(b) Check on toner availability – this is new stuff and it may not be widely available in your area without ordering from the manufacturer.

(c) Get a friend to help you move one – these units are smaller than a car, but still weigh as much as a small refrigerator.

Offices in a Box

They slice; they dice; they make beautiful radish rosettes! Oh, oh, wrong commercial, but it's easy to get carried away about machines that will send and receive faxes, make copies, print from your computer, and scan images back into it – the office in a box.

This is the technology I've been waiting for the computer industry to introduce for a number of years, but when I first ranted in print that fax machines, scanners, laser printers, and photocopiers all used similar technologies and should be in the same box, manufacturers scoffed and offered to make one if I had in excess of $100,000 in my jeans. Gee, how the popularity of the home office and its growth of market share has changed things.

Today, there are a variety of models on the market, and during 1995, the year of their first mass introduction, they were coming on the market at the rate of two a month, so don't be surprised if you don't see specific brands or models mentioned here. Instead of comparing features among boxes, then, I'll focus on some you'll most likely want, but that will be downplayed or missing from the marketing material you'll see at the store – then it will be up to you to find the model that has the largest number of them within your budget.

The price range, by spring 1995, had dropped below $1,000 on the street for home-office boxes, but still had a high end – over $20,000 for industrial-strength, high-output, network-ready models that would fill most of a small room. There were three price clusters, with home units from $950 to $2,400, small business units in the $4,500 to $7,400 range, plus the monster machines noted above.

The advantages of the home-sized models are numerous. Instead of four separate machines running up your monthly electric bill and cluttering up the place, there's only one – with a single power supply. Despite the cost of the systems in the $1,500 to $2,500 end of the home market, you'd be hard pressed to find a fax/modem or stand-alone fax machine, plus printer, plus scanner, plus copier for anywhere near the price of a single office in a box.

Feature sets

All of the cautions noted above under sections dealing with ink-jet printers and lasers apply here as well. Although the majority of home-based/small-business machines in 1995 were ink-jet based, there were some models well within the price range that offered laser technology (which ounce for ounce and pound for pound is simply better and less expensive over the long haul).

One of the first innovations you can look forward to seeing (as in the LexMark Medley) is colour, and all the cautions about the consumable costs of colour ink-jets, the need for compatible print drivers, and others listed above will apply, too.

How fast is the fax/modem contained in the box? If it is still running at 9,600 bits-per-second (bps), it will be less efficient than one running at the higher fax rate of 14,400 bps. If by the time you read this, fax speeds have increased to 28,800 bps, these will be the more desirable units, particularly if you do a lot of long-distance faxing.

Does the fax/modem for the system live in it or in your computer? If it is in the box itself, does it also transmit and receive data as well as fax? If the fax/modem is external to the box, you'll have to leave your computer on at all times to receive unscheduled overnight messages. However, if the modem is only in the box, will you be able to use it to retrieve your e-mail as well? It may be a better alternative to have a modem in both systems so you can have a choice about which to leave running and to provide better fax/data flexibility. However, this will increase the overall cost of the system.

Some of the really low-end systems, although they say they work with your computer, actually require you to print from the computer, then fax the resulting pages using the fax component (for example, the original HP OfficeJet, which also didn't scan – the upgraded LX model corrected these oversights). Better boxes allow you to work in conjunction with computer fax software to generate faxes directly. They'll also allow you to scan other documents into your fax software in order to send combined documents back out (see TWAIN in the discussion about scanners in Chapter 8, and don't get a model with a scanner that isn't TWAIN compatible). Check to see how the box interfaces with computer-based fax programs and which ones it supports (for example, even though I've mentioned the LexMark Medley several times, I'm less than happy that it will only work with the fax software shipped with the unit, not with standard Windows fax software such as Winfax, Bitfax, or even Microsoft At Work Fax).

How tight is the integration between fax software and the box? At least one model (the HP OfficeJet LX) allows you to enter group dial and delayed transmission information (i.e., send after midnight when I'm asleep and the rates are less expensive) into the fax software, yet have it stored in the box, so you can turn the computer off and still have your instructions carried out.

The availability of consumables is an issue I've harped on a couple of times in this chapter, and it is a crucial factor when considering relatively new technologies, while the original manufacturers are still trying to get the most profit they can from proprietary designs. I won't bore you here with the nightmare I encountered trying to get ink cartridges for the Xerox 3006. Although it had (despite being an ink-jet) the best set of features of its immediate competition, its product-ordering department needed to be swept out with a giant broom.

All of the offices in a box I checked in mid-1995 were designed to be used as both stand-alone units and either PC or PC/Mac companions. That means that you get feature sets of scanners, printers, fax machines, and copiers to consider when you buy one.

For example, some scanner components were TWAIN compatible and offered optical character recognition software as part of the bundle, but some weren't and didn't. Depending on what you want to scan (i.e., photos, line drawings, or text for documents), the same considerations I delve into in Chapter 8 are due here about resolution (high for art, low for text), feed mechanisms (sheet-fed for standard business letters and documents, flat-bed for odd sizes or textures such as newsprint), and connection to your computer (through the parallel port or serial port or through the addition of another circuit board).

See above for the features of printers in the offices in a box.

Stand-alone fax machines have a language and feature set all their own. I normally review fax software and have managed to stay away from stand-alone fax units over the years, so I'm not the most experienced person you could ask. However, if faxing without a computer is important to you, then you'll look at things like the amount of memory on board to hold either incoming or outgoing faxes (or both) while the unit is busy copying or printing or out of supplies. I've seen figures all the way from a half-megabyte (512 KB) all the way to 4 MB, and this will affect price. Group polling, fax broadcasting, speed-dial numbers, paper bins (for both output and input), whether there is a separate phone handset, whether the unit will recognize caller ID or distinctive rings, and whether it also includes an answering machine are all important considerations.

None of the systems under $2,500 promise to be able to handle corporate office-level copying. Think of these as more along the lines of a personal copier where you don't need to make more than ninety-nine copies and have all day to do it. Most of the models will copy at up to three pages per minute, and may take nearly a minute (or more) to feed an original page. Features to check here are the ability to reduce or enlarge (and the subtlety of the degree of zoom) and the number of shades of grey that the system can both see and reproduce.

The offices in a box are aimed at the home-office market, and are definitely worth checking out if you work out of your spare bedroom or basement or in a small office with a couple of colleagues. If your office is likely to expand in the near future, however, you'll be better off with a separate printer, copier, and a fax/modem in your computer or networked to it. Everything will work faster than in an office in a box.

7

Multimedia Add-Ons

It burbles; it chirps; it plays the tarantella, and does the hootchie kootchie. It's multimedia computing. You can thank Microsoft and, to a lesser degree, IBM for bringing sound and moving pictures to the PC. Before the advent of Microsoft Windows and OS/2, these treats were virtually the exclusive preserve of Apple (the Macintosh line), Commodore (the Amiga), and Atari. But once a graphical interface became viable for PCs all that changed. It's no longer enough to buy a PC with lots of memory, a large hard drive, and a powerful processor. Today's systems seem incomplete without a sound card, speakers, CD-ROM drive, accelerated video card, and quality colour monitor.

Because multimedia is all the rage, it has changed how PCs are sold. What used to be primarily retrofitted upgrade items – CD-ROM drives, sound boards, and speakers – are included equipment on a growing number of new systems. I know of few name-brand manufacturers or local systems assemblers without a multimedia special of some kind. They come complete with everything you need to fill your environment with sounds and flickering light. Because they're pre-assembled, tested (we hope) with a wide variety of software applications, and will most likely come with pre-installed software, you have a good chance that they'll work properly within your needs. More importantly, the whole system, including the multimedia bits, will be covered by a warranty. If it doesn't work the way it's supposed to, it's the vendor's problem, not yours.

The second way to add multimedia to your system is to shop for a basic system – without multimedia components – then negotiate with the vendor to add the sound card, speakers, and CD-ROM drive before you take it home. Like the pre-assembled system, all the hardware in this one should be covered by warranty, too – but you're less likely to have it pre-tested with the applications you want to run and you may get surprises.

The last way is to retrofit your existing system, and there are a couple of ways to do this. You can shop for multimedia kits. They come with sound card, speakers, CD-ROM drive, and a handful of CD-ROMs all in one box. At least you can be sure that the multimedia components worked together in computers at the manufacturer's factory. It could be another story entirely when you take the kit home and try to install it in your system. It's not a bad idea to ask how much extra it would be to have the kit installed at the shop where you buy it so they can fiddle with it (or replace it) if it doesn't work in your machine.

The truly adventuresome can study the computer papers and magazines, then select components separately, getting a sound card from here, a CD-ROM from there, speakers from wherever, and a SCSI adapter from somewhere else. This is lots of fun, but don't expect to see your loved ones for a few days while you try to install the hardware and software, swear at the manuals, and curse the computer. Here's a hint: don't tell your kids about the wonderful things you'll be able to do with the new stuff until after you've got it working (and had a good night's sleep).

All other things being equal, you can expect to end up paying a little less for the multimedia components in a pre-assembled system, a little more for them if the system is upgraded in the shop, and a fair amount more for components you retrofit. The economics make this so: vendors generally have a higher markup on individual components than they do on pre-assembled systems. When discussing the idea of assembling your own PC at computer shows, I generally advise people to expect to pay anywhere from 10 to 20 per cent *more* for doing it themselves than for buying off the shelf.

If you're still in the mood to spend more than you may wish, start with a Mac. Although it comes with a sound source (and does excellent MIDI sound after you pour a lot more into it), add-ons such as a CD-ROM drive will cost more than those for a PC – they're better implemented in the Mac environment, but there's always a price.

Regardless of the shopping strategy you choose, there are some component characteristics to keep in mind. We've covered PC video graphics cards in Chapter 4, so we'll deal with sound cards (also called sound boards) and CD-ROM drives here.

Sound Cards

When composer Claude Debussy said music was "the arithmetic of sounds as optics is the geometry of light," you have to wonder if he was clairvoyant. He couldn't have anticipated today's computer sound cards, could he?

As you'll see below, all sound cards (or CD-ROM drives or speakers) aren't equal. If they've been tacked onto an existing system, you may get so distracted dealing with what kind of processor the computer has, how much memory, how large a hard drive, which brand of graphics card it has, and how much the monitor will cost (yikes!) that the characteristics of the multimedia components get lost in the shuffle.

Pay attention. Having a sound card is fun; having an underpowered 8-bit card with slow sampling rate and lacklustre components may not be as much fun. Tacking $10 speakers onto a $4,000 PC may provide more disappointment than rapture.

Market madness

Little has changed in sound card technology over the past year or so, but the market has undergone some significant adjustments. At anything other than the extreme low end, 8-bit cards have virtually disappeared, which is not surprising considering that 16-bit boards are selling today for less than 8-bit boards cost when they were introduced.

Gamers drive the sound card market. More than 90 per cent of boards being sold today are being purchased for game use only, and Creative Labs' Sound Blaster product line dominates the mid-level of the market. Microsoft tried to create a business audio market with its Windows Sound System, but its lack of smooth Sound Blaster compatibility kept sales down.

My research tells me that over six million sound cards were sold throughout the world in 1994, nearly a 100 per cent increase over the previous year and only a portion of the anticipated sales in 1995. Main producers include Creative Labs, Turtle Beach Systems, MediaVision, Microsoft, Diamond Multimedia, Logitech, ATI, Orchid Technologies, Advanced Gravis Computer Technology, Aztech Labs, Cardinal Technologies, Computer Peripherals, Genoa Systems, Reveal Computer Products, Sigma Designs, and a host of smaller companies.

Bit stuff

The most important characteristic of a sound card is the number of digital bits it uses to describe the sound it's trying to reproduce. Eight-bit boards are old technology. They can only handle 256 "shades" of sound, and they don't produce high-quality results (think of the tinny quality of your telephone). You don't want one if it's part of the incredible deal you're being offered for a pre-assembled multimedia system.

The results are better with 16-bit boards, which can deal with 65,536 shades of sound. They're promoted as "CD-quality" sound cards, but that's pushing the description more than a little. The middle of the market is dominated by 16-bit cards.

Why are the shades of sound important? Sound is composed of a rich variety of nuances. It has resonance and harmonics. It has pitch. The higher the frequency of the vibration, the higher the pitch. In music, low-frequency vibrations produce low notes while high frequencies produce high notes. It has tremolo (oscillation of pitch), volume, and vibrato (oscillation of volume). Sound also has timbre – the quality of sound that distinguishes it from other sounds of the same pitch and volume, such as the distinctive sound of a particular musical instrument – and it has tone (a combination of pitch, intensity, and quality).

What this has to do with sound boards will become clearer after I explain two other terms first: "analog" and "digital." Analog means a one-to-one representation of real events as they happen in the world around us. When you use a microphone, a membrane in the device vibrates and is translated into a pulsed electrical signal, which in turn vibrates a speaker membrane somewhere else. One-to-one relationship: analog. This is the sound we get when we play those old vinyl albums.

When an analog event gets translated into numbers, it becomes digital. For instance, when I use the microphone attached to a sound card, it is an analog process right up until it gets to the chips on the board. However, then it hits an analog-to-digital converter (ADC) and the original sound ceases to be analog. The ADC and some other circuitry on the board convert the electrical impulses into numerical data, which are passed on to the computer's CPU, then stored on the hard disk.

Going in the other direction, the digital data comes off the hard drive, through the CPU, to the sound card where yet another chip – this time a digital-to-analog converter (DAC) – turns them back into electrical signals, out to a speaker plug, through speakers and air and into my ears. This is the kind of sound you get from a CD: precise, exact, crystal clear, and – some would say – cold. It is, as Debussy foretold, the arithmetic of sounds.

There is no "sound" stored on your hard disk or CD-ROM, there are only numbers describing it. The higher the bit-depth of the sound card, the more numbers it can use to describe the sound. Rather than leaving out high and low frequencies, you get a wider range. Sounds are fuller, less tinny. But that's not the whole story, either.

The next characteristic you'll hear used to describe a sound card is it's sampling rate. Converting analog sound into digital form takes time and it can also produce lots and lots of data. Those are two factors determining how often the sound card "samples" the instructions you're feeding it. When you and I hear noises, we hear them constantly in a continuous stream – no gaps or pauses (unless our hearing aids are on the blink or we're under twenty).

Quite simply, the human brain is a great multitasker. It can listen to sound, process all of it, and read a book at the same time. Computer hardware is much slower, and the PCs most of us have can't do two things at once, so the sound card has to read the instruction, then process, then send it to the CPU, then go back to read again.

Low sampling rates are 8 and 11 KHz (8,000 to 11,000 times per second). Mid-range and high sampling rates are 22 and 44.1 KHz, while some really high-end boards can sample at 48 KHz. At low sampling rates, the accuracy of the reproduction suffers and the sound gets fuzzy. At higher rates the accuracy improves, but 16-bit sound sampled at 44.1 KHz in stereo will eat up your hard drive at a rate of about 11 MB per minute.

Bit-depth and sampling rate together largely determine the quality of the sound processed by the card, but there are a few other issues as well – and here, I'm afraid, we're going to get a bit technical.

If you're getting a sound board simply to play back Windows sound files or to tinker with voice recognition or telephony (voice mail), the following won't matter much to you. If you want to take full advantage of both the voice *and* music tracks in high-end DOS games, or use your sound card to create MIDI music, then it may matter a lot.

A nice, simple Windows Sound System card or compatible model will give you what you need for voice recognition, telephony, and what is euphemistically called "business audio." It won't break the bank, but it may also not meet all your needs. Before you leave the store you'll want to check to see if the card has a full complement of connectors, including one for a microphone (some of the higher end cards with full MIDI connectors – see below – lack mike inputs).

Most mid-level to low-end sound cards use a process known as FM synthesis to support MIDI (musical instrument digital interface – a protocol for connecting electronic musical devices to computers. The protocol covers both hardware and software standards and is currently maintained by the IMA (International MIDI Association). Invented over twenty years ago, FM synthesis, usually produced by a Yamaha OPL2, OPL3, or compatible chipset, synthesizes musical instruments, drums, special effects, or the human voice by mathematically manipulating two to four *sine* waves. The result is only a loose approximation of the real thing, but the advantage to sound card developers is that the technology is inexpensive.

MIDI files tend to be very small, because all they are is a simple data file that tells the synthesizer when to play which notes and for how long, and that makes them popular with game developers, too.

The alternative is wave table synthesis. Instead of manipulating sine waves, boards with wave table synthesis use digitized recordings of the real thing, stored in ROM, as a basis for creating sounds. For example, it could have a piano's middle C plus a C one octave higher. Using technomagic, the card will compare the signal it receives to its built-in table, then extrapolate the rest of the notes in between. One item for you to check when you're shopping is to find out how many notes are compared. You'll get a better result if the card is checking two notes – before and after – not just one.

To give you a benchmark to aim for, check the following quote from Creative Labs' description of the advanced wave effects synthesis used in its Sound Blaster AWE32 board (the italics are mine):

"The Sound Blaster AWE32 supports 32 channels with 32-voice polyphony, utilizes a 6-part *amplitude envelope*, an additional 6-part *auxiliary envelope* for independently controlling pitch and timbre, distortion-free *pitch shifting* techniques, *resonant filters* which change the timbre of each instrument when played at different dynamic levels or with different types of articulation, two *low frequency oscillators (LFOs)* for independent control of *vibrato* and *tremolo*, and advanced effects like chorus and reverb which add richness and ambiance to the sound."

Here's a quickie translation of the terms used above. Most sound cards use some form of amplitude envelope when producing musical sounds. It allows sounds to be manipulated four ways: attack, decay, sustain, and release. During attack, the amplitude of the sound rises to its highest point, then it dies down a little (decay), holds for a while (sustain), then fades out to nil (release). How these states are handled can change how an instrument sounds. For example, if you eliminate the attack of a piano, it begins to sound like a string instrument being bowed. Creative Lab's auxiliary envelope uses the same techniques to hone pitch and timbre independently.

Pitch-shifting changes the frequency of a sound. For example, a recorded F note can be made higher ($F^{\#}$, G) or lower (E, E^{b}, or D). By storing one note and turning it into five, the amount of ROM you need for your wave table is drastically cut.

Two low-frequency oscillators per voice allow for independent control of vibrato and tremolo. Vibrato and tremolo add life to the sound and you can only do one at a time if there is only one LFO per voice channel.

And that brings us to the programmable digital signal processor (DSP). Whether supplied by or based on designs by Motorola, Texas Instruments, Analog Devices, or AT&T, these little marvels are to sound cards what video accelerator chips are to video cards. They're special processors tuned to handle the mathematics of digital audio, and their purpose is to cut down on the amount of time your computer's CPU has to spend feeding your sound card. Creative Labs sometimes calls its DSP an ASP (audio signal processor), but it does the same thing.

The current generation of DSPs, running in mostly the 10 to 20 million instruction per second (MIPS) range can emulate Sound Blaster compatibility, provide "3-D sound" (QSound), and handle wave table synthesis. When designed into a sound card, these devices can be upgraded by software instead of by replacement. Does a DSP make a sound card more efficient? Yes. Does it cost more money? You betcha.

What you'll need if you want your sound card for high-end DOS games is one that uses both FM and wave table synthesis, because many of them use both techniques for voice and music. You might also note that even though a sound card may use wave table synthesis to play back previously stored MIDI recordings, that doesn't mean it also has a MIDI connector to allow you to plug a keyboard into it.

Gamers should also take note that there are several standards for game sound including AdLib, Sound Blaster, Windows 3.1, MPC, DOS, and VAPI. Read the boxes or you could end up wondering what the game really sounds like. Also keep in mind that while the Windows Sound System 2.0 claims DOS-Sound Blaster/AdLib compatibility, you won't like how it – or other cards that work the same way – do the deed.

The Windows Sound System 2.0 gets it Sound Blaster compatibility by running a small terminate-and-stay-ready (TSR) program in DOS. For reasons known only to Microsoft, they set it up so that the TSR won't work unless you are also running a version of EMM386.EXE (a memory manager) that comes with the card. In order to run EMM386, you must also run Microsoft's HIMEM.SYS. This means you cannot use other memory management software such as QEMM, 386Max, or Netroom. The only upper memory management you're left with is Microsoft's MemMaker, and according to tests I've run on several systems, it's the least efficient of the four schemes. The result, once you've loaded various other software drivers, such as those needed by a mouse, a CD-ROM drive, some (but not all) sound cards, a SCSI adapter, and various other bits of flooby dust, is that you may not have enough DOS memory left over to play the game you wanted to hear (sometimes, companies do stuff that makes you want to weep).

The Windows Sound System 2.0 card works well in Windows, and if that's the only place you're planning to use it for business applications, it's a good buy. For DOS games and MIDI music, look elsewhere. Any sound card manufacturer offering FM synthesis as their MIDI synthesizer is hoping you're tone deaf.

Making connections

If you're ignoring the advice to buy your sound card as part of a multimedia kit, where presumably the sound card and CD-ROM drive are designed to work together, you're going to have to figure out how to make them do that on your own. You will have to look at both devices when you purchase either one.

If you purchase a sound card and CD-ROM drive that have to be mated in order for both to function properly, then your ability to upgrade either one independently may be restricted, and if it's the sound card you're keeping and it has a proprietary connector, you may not have a lot of choice of which CD-ROM drive to buy.

Purchasing a separate SCSI (small computer systems interface) adapter to run the CD-ROM drive is a more expensive alternative and it will occupy an extra expansion slot in your system, but the ability to upgrade both components independently, the ability to add six other SCSI devices later, and the fact you will encounter relatively few compatibility problems with this combination make it an attractive choice.

Some sound cards offer a SCSI interface, but do not allow other devices to be added. Others provide a full interface with the ability to expand (although only with internal devices). This also sounds attractive, but presents the same difficulties as a proprietary interface. How eager will you be to upgrade the sound card if something better comes along in the future if you know it will cost you extra for a SCSI adapter as well?

Beware of the bite

Don't take anyone's word for how good the sound card is. By all means read the ads, the reviews, and the marketing bumpf, but then go to the store and listen to the card. Take some headphones with you to cut out the distractions. If it sounds good, has drivers for your operating environment, supports the software you plan to use with it, and you can afford it, buy it.

If the salestype or the manufacturer's ad material says the card does CD-quality recording, ask to hear a sample. Does it sound like a CD or an AM radio? Check your headphones. Are you hearing stereo or mono?

Beware of tricks. Some folks may try to scam you by playing selections directly from a CD-ROM drive and suggest to you that the sound you hear is being produced by the sound card. That's a no-no. You don't need a sound card to play a CD-ROM (you can pipe it directly to an amplifier). If during the demonstration, you see the CD-ROM drive light come on, thank the salesperson for the demo of the CD-ROM and then ask to hear the card playing a file from the hard drive.

Make sure you can return the card within a reasonable period if you're not satisfied with its performance – particularly if the store didn't allow you to listen to it first to compare it with other alternatives, or if the actual performance of the card doesn't match its hype.

For example, one brand of sound card sold a few years ago advertised full stereo, 16-bit, 44.1 KHz sampling, but when you opened the box, the manual suggested it might not perform that way in Windows full 386 enhanced mode. If the vendor allows returns, get it written on the receipt. Did you tell the seller you planned to run the card under any flavour of OS/2, and did the product blurb say it was OS/2 compatible and had OS/2 drivers on the box?

Keep in mind that in order to get twenty-four sound cards that worked properly for one of their reviews, *PC Magazine* had to order thirty-nine units. Some of the manufacturers are less attentive to quality control than others.

Speakers

What are you going to do for speakers?

A few sound cards pre-amplify their output, and tiny little speakers to go with them come as part of the package. Most don't pre-amp or supply speakers. Check what your choice does and shop accordingly.

Price doesn't always determine quality, but it doesn't make a whole lot of sense to hook up a sound card and CD-ROM drive combination, which may have cost between $600 and $1,000, to a pair of $20 speakers with a one-inch-diameter diaphragm. You may want to splurge a little here.

Speakers usually contain magnets. Unless they've been specially shielded, having them right next to your monitor may produce unpleasant results and you may have to learn what degaussing means. Placing them too close to floppy or hard drives and using them as a place to pile up diskettes can produce interesting effects, too.

CD-ROM Drives

Before we get started, a couple of notes: First, spelling – Webster's *Dictionary of Computer Terms* is quite specific when it comes to the words disc and disk. When referring to optical media (CD-ROM, Magneto Optical, and others), it's a disc. When the storage media is for a mechanical/magnetic device such as a floppy drive or hard drive, it's a disk (short for diskette). Don't ask me why. I didn't make the rule.

Secondly, lest it get lost in the technical discussions that follow, let's talk about why you might want a CD-ROM in the first place. I bless every company that ships software on CD instead of forcing me to install umpteen disks – and find it comforting to work from time to time with everything from Iron Maiden and Gregorian chants to Mozart and my kid's latest hiphop in the background. The presentations I do at various computer shows are more fun to do with music included from CD as well.

If this is too limiting, consider the following: there were 3,000 new CD titles released in 1993, 8,000 in 1994, and there will be well over 12,000 in 1995. Although, according to *PC Magazine*, 68 per cent of the CD titles are developed on the Mac, over 90 per cent are released exclusively to run on a PC in Windows. Like all else in life, a lot of them are shlocky dross, but some of them are highly entertaining and useful as well.

Try some; you're bound to find one or several that you like.

Now the tech stuff

CD-ROM is an abbreviation of Compact Disc-Read Only Memory. All by itself, the name is slightly misleading. A CD doesn't contain memory; it is a storage medium for holding information. The "read only" part of the name is significant, because it indicates that your computer can read the information, but you can't write new information back to the compact disc (unless you pay a whopping amount of cash for a writable CD-R drive – more on this later).

The discs themselves are identical to the CDs used to hold music and were developed using the same technology. Standard CDs are 5.25 inches in diameter, and are made out of plastic substrate with a thin mirrored coating.

Virtually all CD-ROM drives will allow you to play audio CDs as well as those containing computer programs and data. However, you can't use an audio CD player with your computer. CD-ROM drives use a different set of custom-designed integrated circuits to handle a requirement for greater accuracy. Data errors in music CDs can be hidden when they are brief, but similar errors in computer data would give you fits. The circuits in a CD audio player provide only four layers of data correction, compared to five layers of error-correction encoding on CD-ROM drives. Ironically, new developments in CD-ROM technology will soon change this rule slightly (see the discussion of CD-Plus, below). You still won't be able to use your audio player to load the data on CD-ROM discs into your computer, but you will be able to use CD-ROM discs in your audio player to hear music.

New technology

For several years, CD-ROM was dismissed by the PC industry as being too slow and cranky to be worth the effort. Introduction of the first set of Multimedia PC standards (MPC I) in 1992 began a change in attitude, and as we approach the second half of 1995, the changes in technology and the standards being developed to handle them just keep on coming.

Multimedia for the PC started to come into its own in late 1993 when the MPC II standards were introduced with something a little more reasonable – calling for a 386 processor with a minimum of 4 MB of system RAM, a 160 MB hard drive, a 16-bit sound card, and a CD-ROM drive with a minimum data transfer rate of 300 KB/sec and access times of 400 milliseconds (ms) or better with 60 per cent CPU usage.

The result, according to the market research firm Info-Tech, was that the number of installed CD-ROM drives worldwide grew 137 per cent to over 25 million. CD-ROM drives are also becoming standard equipment for new computers. *PC Magazine*, in its June 27, 1995, edition, estimated that more multimedia-equipped PCs were sold in 1994 than upgrade kits.

The second half of 1995 will see five major trendsetting developments that may affect your CD-ROM drive purchasing decisions: (1) Windows 95 will provide three new enhancements that will affect how CD-ROM drives are installed, how they load software, and what they can play; (2) the American National Standards Institute (ANSI) will finally complete the ATA-3 standard, including sections dealing with ATAPI (AT Attachment Packet Interface) and ATASPI (AT Attachment

CD-ROM

Terminology	Meaning
CD-ROM	Compact Disk-Read Only Memory (you can't save data on a CD-ROM disk; you can only read it).
CD-R	CD-Recordable. Look for a slew of products this year, but don't expect speed (they're mostly double-speed units). Expect to spend big.
CD-E	Two consortia are fighting to see who will set this double-sided, erasable, high-density standard. Don't expect the war to be over until sometime in 1996 or later. If and when the dust clears, you can expect to see CD-ROM and CD-R disappear, eventually.
Transfer rate	The speed at which data, once found on the CD surface, is passed to the computer. Single-speed units achieve 150 KB/sec, not fast enough for video. Double-, triple-, quad-, and six-speed units can exceed 300 KB/sec, and the higher the number, the more suited it is for video playback. Single-, double-, and triple-speed units are toast. The best bang for the buck is a quad, but check magazine reviews to see how fast the unit really is, and how many frames of video it drops when playing them back.
Access time	CD-ROM tracks are laid in a spiral with data starting at the centre. Information is read sequentially, not at random like a hard drive. That's why they're so slow. The lower the number for access time, the better the performance and the faster you'll get your data.
Multi-session Photo-CD	When you have pictures transferred to Photo-CD, an index or "session" is created. When you go back and add more pictures, another index or session is created. Multi-session CD-ROMs can read the multiple indexes, while those that are not multi-session stop at the first and can't see anything else.
CD-ROM - XA compatible	So what? There is virtually no XA-compatible software available. It was another "standard" that failed to catch on. You don't care.
Multi-spin	The drive changes speeds as it works. So what? All CD-ROMs change speed as they work. See "access time" above. As the read head moves to the outer tracks on the disk, it has to slow down to keep data coming at the same speed as when the head was on the inner tracks. A hype statement.

Software Programming Interface) that will determine how "enhanced" IDE CD-ROM drives function; (3) speed is going up – both Plextor and NEC have already introduced six-speed CD-ROM drives and the horde can be expected to follow; (4) CD-R (CD-recordable) drives will enjoy a short-lived reign as prices fall below $2,000 Cdn.; and, (5) a war is developing among CD disc manufacturers for a new high-density, double-sided format that will, when the dust clears, blow everything else we use now out of the water.

CD 95

Windows 95 promises to fundamentally change the way we install and use CD-ROM. If *plug and play* (PnP) lives up to its advanced billing, you'll be able to pop sound cards and CD-ROM drives into systems equipped with a PnP BIOS (basic in/out system) and PnP controller (either IDE or SCSI) with the same ease you make toast. According to Microsoft and other PnP proponents, a properly equipped system will automatically detect what you've done and will sort out things like IRQs (interrupt request channels) and both base and upper memory conflicts without you or me ever having to worry about them again. If you've ever had to install these hardware components your-self in the past – and particularly if you've heard the industry's long-time promises of performance – you will understand why my tone is a tad sceptical here, but we can always hope they've done it properly this time.

AutoPlay is another function waiting in Windows 95. The idea is that when you put a new CD in the drive, it will start loading imme-diately. I can see both advantages and disadvantages to this particular trick, but developers of CD products will have to add support for this feature to their CDs before it will work.

Finally, Windows 95 introduces a new CD-audio format, called *CD-Plus* (CD+), a new standard developed jointly by Philips and Sony that will make it possible to play the audio portion of mixed data/audio/video CDs on a standard CD-audio player as well as taking advantage of some of the 32-bit multimedia subsystems in Windows 95 (and AutoPlay). It still won't allow you to use your standard audio CD player to load data into your computer because the technical differences outlined above will continue to prevent it. However, all CD-ROMs contain data on their first track that can, with the static it produces, potentially blow your audio CD player's speakers. The new discs apparently will be smart enough to prompt the audio player to skip the first track.

Enhance me, please

"Enhanced" IDE (integrated drive electronics) CD-ROM drives began creeping into the PC market in late 1994 as early adopters of the format attempted to carve out market share. However, as of June 1995, the ANSI X3T10 committee in charge of providing the ATA-3 standard covering these devices still hadn't finished its work, and various members of the committee were still arguing over some of the standard's fine details. What we do know about enhanced IDE to date is that utilizing all of its features without compatibility problems still requires some consumer research before you buy. You'll want a computer with a BIOS that is both compliant with ATA-3 and PnP (see above) and, particularly if the two IDE connectors are directly attached to the motherboard, allows them to use the (preferably) PCI local bus. If you're using a separate IDE controller slotted into the motherboard, you'll want to make sure it has two connectors, that it can independently address devices along the cables (i.e., set access and data transfer speeds for both fast and slow devices) and that it is fully compatible with the BIOS. You'll want to check with the vendor to make certain that both the enhanced (i.e., over 528 MB capacity) IDE hard drive(s) in the system, *and* the CD-ROM drive have been certified to work correctly with the BIOS as well. It wouldn't hurt you at all and shouldn't task the vendor much also to have a written assurance that the whole system will be compatible with whatever operating system you plan to use (i.e., Windows 95 or OS/2).

What's Latin for six, daddy?

Six-speed drives are the new leading edge. Selling on the street for around $880 Cdn for an external model (slightly less if internal), both Plextor and NEC were first out of the gate with the new units. Plextor's

6Plex claims 900 KB/sec throughput, a random access speed of 145 ms, and a random seek time of 115 ms. It utilizes a 256 KB cache buffer (not large), uses SCSI-2, and supports CD-XA, CD-I, "VideoCD," and Photo CD multisession compatibility.

NEC's MultiSpin 6X is also a SCSI device and boasts nearly the same characteristics, except for a random seek time of 130 ms. The unit is PnP compatible and will also support CD-I, VideoCD, multisession Photo CD, QuickTime, and the new CD-Plus audio format. If you happen to own a Future Domain TMC-1610 SCSI controller, however, don't try to connect this unit unless you've upgraded the controller's own internal BIOS to version 3.6 or greater (call FD at 800-879-7599 and ask for item #867. NEC says you'll get a new BIOS at no charge). NEC reports the "estimated Canadian selling price" at $871 for the external model (6Xe) and $725 for the internal version (6Xi).

Gimme that old-time recorder

While Sony and a few others have announced CD-R drives for the future, the biggest splash in mid-1995 was made by Pinnacle Micro. Its RCD-1000 was being advertised in a number of U.S. publications for $1,895 U.S. (and sold in Canada for about $2,995). It's a SCSI-based double-speed drive with 1 MB data buffer, and its specification sheet claims 307 KB/sec throughput with 300 ms access time. Sony's addition to the party has an "approximate retail price" of $2,499 (Cdn) for the internal CSP-920S (including Corel's new CD-Creator software) and $2,799 for the external CSP-921S. Like the Pinnacle offering, Sony's CD-recordable drive is also a double-speed unit with 300 KB/sec data transfer rate. Both drives double as recorders and readers.

Just hovering on the horizon as this book went to print is a development that may make all of these drives things of the past. The development, loosely called CD-E, was represented by two competing technologies under development by consortiums comprised of Sony and Philips on one hand and Time Warner, Toshiba, and some other folk on the other. Both were striving to develop a recordable, high-density (we've heard capacity figures exceeding 5 gigabytes), double-sided format designed to hold and play back full-length movies with MPEG (Motion Picture Experts Group) 1 and 2 compatibility.

Several things are clear: the future will offer high storage capacity, faster access and data transfer, and full-length movies in your PC. What is not so clear is how long this will take or which competing scheme will emerge as the winner (although both Sony and Philips have reputations for making their standards stick – Beta format videotapes notwithstanding).

If you can't wait for recordable CD-ROM to become affordable or for rumoured new technologies to emerge from the technobattlefield (and I wouldn't), here are some time-honoured, tried and tested guidelines for buying a new CD-ROM drive or to apply to the one being offered with your new computer.

Transfer rate versus access

As a class, CD-ROM drives are far slower at retrieving information than hard drives or floppy drives. It takes them longer to find the data and longer to lift it from the CD and get it into your computer. That's because of the way information is placed on the CD.

The CD is laid out in one continuous track, starting at the centre and spiralling out to the edge. To find anything and read it, the laser head in the drive must start at the beginning and read along the track sequentially until it arrives at the requested data. A standard floppy or hard drive, on the other hand, can locate data placed on disk randomly. Each time a new request for information is received, the CD-ROM drive head has to follow the track (backwards or forwards). How long this takes can be affected by how fast the disc spins (e.g., single speed, double speed, triple speed, quad speed, six speed – it's enough to make your head spin – and we'll talk more about it, below).

A CD-ROM drive's transfer rate (also called throughput) – the speed at which it moves data from the surface of the disc to your computer – is more important than how fast it finds the data on the disc surface. The higher the transfer rate (as far above 300 KB/sec as you can afford), the more smoothly video images will play back on your system. This is important if you plan to run a lot of games and/or multimedia encyclopedias with video images or animations in them.

However, single-, double-, triple-, quad-, and six-speed ratings do not necessarily indicate commensurate throughput. For instance, if we know that single-speed drives deliver roughly 150 KB/sec, and that double-speed drives should deliver 300 KB/sec, it should follow that the transfer rate for triple-, quad-, and six-speed drives should be 450, 600, and 900 KB/sec respectively. 'Tain't necessarily so. It is not uncommon for triple-speed drives to deliver rates in the 360 to 370 KB/sec range. Only extraordinary quad-speed drives deliver more than 450 KB/sec (although I've seen one in a Compaq system that pumped out a whopping 582 KB/sec).

A slight advantage in access is not a substitute for faster throughput. When it's a toss-up between two models of CD-ROM drives, always pick the one with faster throughput over the one with the faster access time. Both single- and dual-speed drives may appear for sale with the data transfer rate missing, and just the access time quoted. This won't give you any idea of how quickly the drive will appear to operate and you get the data on screen.

This doesn't mean that you should ignore the access speed figure entirely; this number will go down (under 240 ms is good) depending on whether the drive is spinning at double, triple, quadruple, or six times the speed of the original "single-speed" drives, and it may be important if you are doing repeated searches of items such as a legal database or national telephone directory. However, if the drive's specifications don't list both figures, transfer rate, and access time, you need to find out why.

You might also have a close look at how the company came up with its access time figure. At one time, the CD-ROM drive industry used a standard "$1/3$ stroke" convention when testing access speed. In this test, the drive's laser pickup head was programmed to move repeatedly (up to 100 times) $1/3$ the length of a disc's radius from random starting points across its surface. The specification number was derived from an average of the scores reporting the combination of the time it took to get the head in place, plus the time to have the drive slow down to the proper spin rate to read data from the disc. When everyone used this testing method, you could at least compare apples to apples.

Today, there is some funny stuff afoot. CD drive manufacturers kept wincing when their performance was measured against hard drives (typically, these days, in the 12 to 9 ms range), which don't store their data in a continuous track the way CDs do and don't have to slow down for the magnetic read head to operate. So, in late 1993, several companies abandoned the $^1/_3$ stroke method in favour of a more random access test. Unfortunately for consumers, however, they haven't settled on a standard way of measuring. Some companies use figures based on $^1/_{10}$, $^1/_{25}$, or even $^1/_{50}$ the length of the radius of the disc. The results look good, but only on paper.

It gets even stranger. Some companies have begun quoting only the seek time in their advertising, ignoring the inconvenient fact that the drive has to alter its speed to read the data. While the old access-time figure calculated both factors (seek and read), these clever folks don't. To quote material supplied by Plextor, "to leave [the time taken for the disc to reach the correct rotational speed] out of the calculations is unconscionable." Ironically, this doesn't stop the company from using the seek figure in its own advertising, although they do include both access time and data transfer rate as well.

One last point. All CD-ROM drives speed up and slow down when in operation. There is nothing special about NEC's MultiSpin drives. That's because CD-ROM drives use something called constant linear velocity. If the drive didn't slow down as the head approached the CD's outer edge, the data would flow by too quickly to be used. A CD-ROM typically spins about 2.65 times faster when data is read from the inner part of the disc as it does when the head approaches the outer edge.

1, 2, 3, 4, or 6?

The most commonly asked question by prospective purchasers of new CD-ROM drives is: "Do I need a quad- (or a six-) speed drive or can I get away with a single or a double or a triple?"

Computer CD-ROMs don't just hold video. They can hold audio, text, and still graphics. When playing CD-audio, the drive has to slow down to the 150 KB/sec rate, otherwise the music would be gibberish. Higher spin rates are useful only for limited applications and video playback.

The advice given by a former sales manager of Hitachi Canada puts the case quite simply. "If the majority of the data you'll be getting from CD is video, then high spin rate and high throughput is desirable. If, however, you're operating in a mixed data environment with a combination of data types – for instance a multimedia encyclopedia with data searching, text, still graphics, and audio – then a single-speed drive will be more efficient because it doesn't spend as much time speeding up and slowing down for the various data types and operations it performs."

You can get away with a single-speed drive if all of the following are true: (a) you can still find one for sale, (b) you're absolutely certain that all you're ever going to use it for is to install new software on your hard drive, (c) you're never, ever going to want to play back video, (d) all you ever want to do with it is to play CD-Audio discs through your computer, and/or (e) you want an attractive high-tech bookend.

I've had quite a few conversations with both manufacturers and vendors of CD-ROM drives that have left all of us scratching our heads, trying to come up with applications, other than video playback, that would benefit from anything higher than a double-speed drive. Aside from running CorelDRAW from CD instead of a hard drive, we're stumped. Despite this, as an "industry standard" the double-speed drive is on its way out.

Not a few of them almost, but not quite, reach the MPC II level of 300 KB/sec throughput when they're tested independently, despite advertising claims to the contrary. Even if the drive does struggle over the 300 KB/sec mark, it is still an anchor holding back the rest of your computer. Despite being double the speed of the original CD-ROM drives, it is still far slower than the CPU, memory, or hard drive of today's typical entry-level PC. At an entry level, they are affordable for newcomers who are still uncertain about the "advantages" of multimedia computing, but you can do better.

What ever happened to the triple-speed CD-ROM drive? NEC still sells 'em, but the price to performance ratio is better with both double- and quad-speed units. Treat triple-speed drives as an orphaned historical accident and you have it about right.

Quad-speed drives are last year's state of the art and, given the rate at which I expect six-speed drives to appear over the next few months, may be the wisest choice of power for the money. What you'll want to watch carefully, however, is the discrepancy between advertised claims of 600 KB/sec performance and actual benchmark figures provided in some of the U.S.-based glossy magazine roundups. Given that the price point for these units hovers around $500, it would be a good idea to head for the library and look up tests reported in past issues of *PC Magazine*, *Windows Magazine*, and others. Have a look at tested throughput, access time, and, for even more fun, the number of video frames dropped by each drive under load.

SCSI versus IDE connections

CD-ROM drives can be connected to a PC using a variety of hardware technologies. When they first appeared on the market, virtually all the drives were connected through a SCSI adapter. Today, they may use a proprietary interface (one invented by the drive manufacturer), be connected through the printer (parallel) port, or be connected to a PC sound card. You'll also see models for the new "enhanced" IDE standard. Each of these schemes has advantages and disadvantages.

I had a lot of trouble from local vendors over the carping I did in the first half of 1995 about enhanced IDE hard drives and other devices and how the industry standard committee overseeing the ATA standard was botching the job it set out to do. However, by the time you read this, the issues should be history, so let's leave the carping aside and simply look at the two standards on their individual merits.

No doubt about it, IDE storage solutions are less expensive than SCSI (small computer systems interface). The vast majority of PCs come with either a separate IDE controller card or chip set built into their motherboards, and with an IDE hard drive. If you're buying a new complete system today, getting a reasonably stable "enhanced" IDE BIOS such as the Phoenix Technologies NuBIOS and a two-connector controller should allow you to take advantage of larger hard drives and up to four internal devices, including a CD-ROM drive now and tape later. Both the hard and CD-ROM drives will be marginally less expensive than a SCSI alternative.

If you're retrofitting an existing system, however, particularly if it was purchased before mid-1995, then the cost of upgrading a BIOS and drive controller to utilize enhanced IDE fully may not make it worth the effort, and SCSI is a serious possibility to consider.

Cost aside, SCSI offers several real advantages over IDE: seven devices per controller instead of four (hard drives, CD-ROM drives, tape drives, Bernoulli and Zip drives, magneto optical and WORM drives, scanners, digital cameras, and printers have so far made the SCSI list compared to hard drives, CD-ROM drives, and, sooner or later, tape for IDE); external as well as internal devices (IDE only allows internal); high-capacity hard drives (up to 18 GB for SCSI, up to 8.4 GB for IDE); faster throughput (up to 20 MB/sec for SCSI compared to an upper limit of 13 MB/sec for IDE); and greater stability. SCSI has been around longer than enhanced IDE, and while no system guarantees perfect compatibility with all products in all circumstances, the SCSI industry's ASPI – advanced SCSI programming interface – has had more time to work out the bugs than the brand-new IDE equivalent, ATASPI. In short, with the new revisions to IDE, SCSI has become the elder technology with a longer successful track record.

Proprietary interface adapters may be less expensive than SCSI adapters and less controversial than enhanced IDE schemes, but they offer none of their advantages. You still end up dedicating an expansion slot to an adapter card which only has one purpose – running the CD-ROM drive. You probably won't be able to run more than one, and if the manufacturer loses interest, you may not be able to get software driver support for your drive when you update your operating system or applications.

Connecting CD-ROM/sound card combos

One of the most popular methods for connecting a CD-ROM drive, particularly in older systems you're retrofitting yourself, is to buy the drive and sound card together. Depending on the models you choose, you may run into a couple of problems that extra time and knowledge can fix. In broad strokes, the sound card manufacturer may offer one of two solutions: a proprietary interface requiring one of a few brands of CD-ROM drive and specific cabling or a built-in SCSI interface.

If the solution is a proprietary connector, and you buy one of the limited number of CD-ROM drives the card supports directly, you may have further limitations placed on how fast the drive can be and whether you have a choice of internal or external model. You may also have a dilemma should you ever decide to upgrade either the sound card or drive in the future, as you may have to jettison both in order to replace one. If you decide to take your chances and get a brand of CD-ROM drive the card doesn't support directly, both may work right up until you try to get the two hooked together. There is no standard determining how many pins the internal audio connectors on the devices use. Either the sound board or the CD-ROM drive may use three-, four-, or five-pin audio connectors, and trying to find a dinky little audio cable that hooks up company X's sound board to company Y's CD-ROM drive can be a daunting task. Do your homework first.

A sound card with a SCSI connector is a good middle-ground solution. It occupies only one expansion slot and is considerably less expensive than purchasing a separate SCSI controller. Creative Labs, Media Vision, Orchid, Diamond, Cardinal, and Sigma all offer sound cards with SCSI controllers, but unless the others have released new models since June 1995, only Creative Labs offers both a 16-bit audio board *and* 16-bit SCSI adapter together (Sound Blaster 16 SCSI II with ASP and the Wave Blaster). Most others offered only 8-bit SCSI adapters, which are adequate for single- or double-speed CD-ROM drives, but don't provide sufficient performance for a quad- or higher speed CD-ROM drive.

In case I'm wrong about the other manufacturers use of 16-bit SCSI (goodness knows, things sometimes get on the market when I'm looking the other way), go one step further and find out if it's possible to hook up more than simply the CD-ROM drive to it. One of the advantages of SCSI is seven devices per controller and if you don't get that, maybe it's not such a good deal after all.

Another last note: haunting the Internet newsgroups devoted to helping people with installation and compatibility problems reveals that there are fewer complaints about SCSI/CD-ROM drive combinations than with any other method. The methods garnering the highest number of problems with compatibility and plaintive cries for help are proprietary sound card/CD combos and CD/parallel port combos.

Parallel port connections

Aside from proprietary circuit boards (semi-IDE and quasi-SCSI variations), the other way of connecting a CD-ROM drive is through the PC's parallel port – the same place you would normally connect a printer. It's an attractive alternative because you don't have to hassle with an internal circuit board and the drives are invariably external, so you don't even have to lift the computer's cover.

The disadvantages include being unable to connect more than one CD-ROM unit, occasional communications problems with a printer using the same port, and a nagging suspicion that, sooner or later, you'll invest in a new operating system or application that can't find the drive until updated drivers are found. External units, because they need a case and a separate power supply, also tend to be more expensive – all other things being equal – than internal units.

What also tends to be glossed over in the ads is that to make these models deliver their specified throughput, you have to have a high-speed, bi-directional "enhanced parallel port" or EPP in your system. If your computer is more than a year old (as of mid-1995), the chances of your having one are slim. Without an EPP, a quad-speed CD-ROM drive hooked into a parallel port may deliver as little as 100 KB/sec throughput, which is less than even the MPC I standard called for.

Even if you do have an EPP, however, your problems may not be over. The parallel port may be connected to your drive controller, to a separate I/O (input/output) board, or wired directly to the motherboard. Depending on how the manufacturer of whatever it is connected to implemented the design, there may not be enough power flowing to the port to run both the CD-ROM drive and the printer you'll also want to attach to it.

Don't even ask about software driver compatibility. It will just give you and me hives.

Other "standards"

It is highly possible to find CD-ROM drives that are not CD-XA ready, but nobody cares anymore because this standard flopped. If you could find an XA (eXtended Architecture) disc, you'd still need some expensive additional hardware to play it properly. PC-based CD-ROM drives use what is called the ISO 9660/High Sierra format, while Mac systems use a format called HFS, which allows interleaving of data and audio tracks (and that's why you can use the same drive mechanisms on both platforms, but not the same CD-ROM discs).

XA was developed several years ago as a way to extend the ISO 9660/High Sierra format to provide better video playback performance, but it simply hasn't caught on; it's generally been superseded by MPEG (the Motion Picture Experts Group) standard.

Because there is little hardware support for XA, there's virtually no XA software available. If your choice is determined by price and one drive is XA ready while the other is not, let price be the guide unless you want to hedge against the slim possibility that XA may, someday, possibly, get popular all of a sudden. The Kodak Photo CD standard is a subset of XA, but if a drive is Photo CD capable, the feature will usually be mentioned separately.

It is possible, if you search hard enough, to buy a CD-ROM drive that is not Kodak Photo CD multisession compatible. Don't. When photographs are transferred to CD-ROM by the Kodak process, an index (or session) is created on the disc. If the same disc has more photographs added to it later, another index (or session) is added. Multisession drives can read multiple indexes on the same Photo CD. Those that are not multisession stop at the first index and can't see anything else.

CD-I by Philips and CDTV by Commodore are intended as game machines to be connected to your television set. They are not compatible with PCs or Macs and can't use computer software, nor can computer CD-ROM drives use discs made for these systems. They belong with a discussion of Nintendo and Sega and you can safely forget them. The only portion of the CD-I standard to make it into the

PC environment was MPEG, and like PhotoCD from CD-XA, it's been elevated from among the collection to a status of its own. It, too, will be mentioned separately in the literature.

Now we come to a series of standards that might make you think of rainbows instead of computers. Developed by the CD industry, these standards are an attempt to maintain compatibility across a wide range of products. Red Book, Yellow Book, Green Book, and now Orange Book standards determine specifications for storage and delivery of information.

CD-DA (compact disk-digital audio) started it, and all the other standards are based on the Red Book standard for audio CDs. They are recorded by converting analog signals into digital samples at the rate of 44.1 KHz (44,100 samples per second). Each sample is assigned a value in a range of 65,536 possible values (16 bits) and the samples are converted to binary code. If your CD-ROM drive adheres to Red Book standards, it will play audio back in a smooth, continuous stream, and you'll get all of the sound originally recorded.

The only thing you really need to know about the Yellow Book recording standard for CD-ROM discs is that if it hasn't been followed, you won't be able to play the disc at all. The Yellow Book sets the various recording specifications for the Apple HFS format, the ISO 9660 format used by PCs, and the DEC VMS format (which you can ignore). Essentially the Yellow Book defines the physical properties of the discs, the arrangement on the spiral, the speed at which they are read, error correction, and sector size. It also sets two data modes to determine how text and computer data is handled (mode 1 – stringent error correction) and how audio and video data are dealt with (mode 2 – less stringent error correction).

The Green Book standard defines specifications for CD-I and some CD-XA specifications. Forget it. Photo CD also borrows from the Green Book standard, but is recorded under the Orange Book specifications – which determine how digitized 35-mm photographs are recorded to CD-ROM.

If a product says it is Photo CD compatible, what it really is saying is that it can recognize and play discs recorded under the Orange Book standard.

If you can find a drive with MPEG compression/decompression

hardware built in, jump on it. Likewise, grab CD-Plus audio support, PnP, CD-I, and QuickTime.

I don't know of any PC-based CD-ROM drive that won't play audio CDs.

Other "funny" stuff

Regard all MTBF (mean time between failure, or might they be fibbing) figures with prejudice. The numbers are one part voodoo, a sprinkling of actual science, two parts witchcraft, plus a whole whack of marketing mumbo jumbo and public relations fact-bending mixed in. If the company actually ran a drive for three years and five months (that's about the time represented by an MTBF of 30,000 hours) to see if it would break before they sold it, its competitors would have the market sewn up before they got it out the door (a six-month turn-around on models is considered pushing the edge).

MTBF for the drive, therefore, is calculated based on the MTBF of the drive's components – which in turn is calculated on the components' components – and the presumption is that somewhere at the end of the chain is a stopwatch held by a little guy or gal wearing a lab coat, thick glasses, and a very bored expression, waiting for something to go *pfzzt*! I'd be much more interested in the length of the warranty and whether the company has an 800 number for both the United States and Canada for technical support.

There are various claims made about the alleged capacity of CD-ROM drives. I've seen ads proclaiming 540 MB, 682 MB, 580 MB, 703 MB, and 650 MB. Which number is accurate? The correct answer is, none of the above.

Once again, we're caught in old hard drive habits. Hard drives are sold in capacities – 350 MB, 528 MB, 1 GB, and so on. A bigger hard drive can hold more data. In the case of CD-ROM drives, however, there can't be a correct answer because the premise of the question is incorrect. A CD-ROM drive has no "capacity." Only the CD-ROM disc, not the drive itself, holds data and suffers from capacity restraints.

The range of numbers is a function of how data is laid on the disc and where it is placed. The disc maker can elect to use – or not to use –

EDC/ECC (error detection code/error correction code). Without EDC/EEC, more data can be placed on the disc (with a greater danger of inaccuracy). CD-ROM discs can also follow the music industry standard of putting the rough equivalent of 74 minutes of material on the disc instead of 60 minutes worth (which is considered more reliable). Different combinations of these factors account for the varied numbers.

Some over-enthusiastic suppliers of shareware discs, trying to cram as much as possible on one CD-ROM, may try to write information right out to the edge of the disc. That's not a good idea because slight warping at the disc edge can affect the quality of the data – and some drives are better than others at reading material there. You shouldn't run into this problem with commercial software because most of the companies providing it know better.

Bottom line: when you see advertisements for drives with a "capacity" of 682 MB or 553 MB, one isn't better than the other; they're both wrong. The ad writer has simply slipped some bogus specifications into the copy hoping you have the capacity to be fooled.

Odds and ends, buttons and doodads

The biggest enemy of your CD-ROM discs and drives is dust, grit, and grime. It is virtually impossible to break a CD by dropping it, but you can give it severe problems if you twist or bend it (it cracks), or if you scratch the surface. If dust accumulates on the lens of the laser or the read head, the quality of the data will suffer.

You'll want to look for a drive that has an automatic lens-cleaning feature that clears the lens each time you insert a new disk. A door on the front of the drive that closes after you insert the disk also helps to keep dust out.

Some models of CD-ROM drives will come with built-in caddies to hold the discs while playing; others use external caddies that you remove from the drive in order to change discs. Both methods have advantages and disadvantages. The internal models offer less protection against dirt and dust, while the external models sometimes feel as though you need three hands to handle them.

I prefer the external caddies for a simple reason. I can buy extra ones and leave my CDs in the caddies when not in use. This limits their exposure to the outside world and prevents my fingers from smudging the surface. There is also something to be said for reducing the number of moving parts in the drive that might break later.

Your decision about whether to get an internal CD-ROM drive or an external model may depend on how you plan to use it, the size of your computer's case, and the number of drive bays you have available. Internal models are generally less expensive (no need for a separate case and power supply), but if you plan to share your CD-ROM drive across a small network, having it internal to one system may make that awkward. So far as I've been able to determine, there isn't any particular quality issue here, and your choice will be entirely subjective unless you are on an extremely tight budget.

Other features it is a good idea to seek include both a power-on and a power-off eject button (in case of software ejection difficulties or when a disk becomes jammed in the drive), external line connectors to carry the audio signal directly to a sound card or external amplifier, a headphone jack, and separate volume control.

Does the manufacturer provide easily accessible technical support or do you have to rely on the retailer you bought the drive from? This may not be a large concern today, but a year or two from now, when your retailer has closed up shop, it might.

Shopping tips

There are a large number of CD-ROM alternatives from which to choose and an equally wide range of prices and features.

If I were shopping for a new drive today, given that I use my current model for a wide mixture of data types, I'd look for a double- or triple-speed model with a standard SCSI interface. Six months after Windows 95 ships, assuming that an internal drive is what I want, I'd take a hard look at the enhanced IDE models – but not before.

If I were going to be using the drive primarily for video playback, then a quad- or six-speed model would be better (with at least 350 KB/sec transfer rate or higher), but I'd check the benchmarks carefully to see which models are worse than others when it comes to dropping video frames (even at quad speeds).

The drive would be multisession Photo CD compatible and capable of using external caddies. I wouldn't care if it were CD-XA ready, but it would not be CD-I or CDTV compatible.

For further information, I'd also get a brochure published by Plextor titled *15 Questions to Ask Before you Buy a CD-ROM*. It is the most objective and even-handed document I've ever seen from a manufacturer (and you may recognize some of it if you've read all of the material above). You can order it by calling Plextor at (800) 886-3935. Hurry before somebody in the company finds out how good it really is.

8

Things That Click When They Move, Bop When They Stop, and Whir When They Stand Still: Pointing Devices and Keyboards, Modems and Scanners

In this chapter, we're going to look at some of the additional items that you will get with your computer, as well as some you may want to think about very seriously. It's time to look at pointing devices such as a mouse, and at keyboards, modems, and scanners.

Mice

A mouse is an electronic pointing device attached either to a serial port (serial mouse), to a circuit board inside the computer (bus mouse), to a small, round PS/2 port (PS/2 mouse), or occasionally through a keyboard (some proprietary mouse designs and most Macs).

A pointing device allows the user to manipulate the on-screen pointer, select objects, and perform many other tasks. It's optional in DOS and virtually impossible to live without in Windows, OS/2, or Mac environments.

The mouse was originally designed by Xerox at its Palo Alto Research Centre (PARC) for the first graphical user interface —which the company's researchers also designed, and its marketing geniuses then nixed, believing it wouldn't go anywhere. It was later adopted by Apple for use in their original Macintosh systems, and is now an almost indispensable component in the PC world.

Computer mice don't eat crumbs; they hate them. Dirt and grime kill mice – dead. The mechanics of both mice and their upside-down cousins – trackballs – are the same. A rolling ball moves against pressure-sensitive rollers (usually three, but sometimes four). From the movement of each roller, the mouse generates binary codes representing two-dimensional movement coordinates. Other mechanics in the device also generate signals to indicate when one of its buttons has been clicked and released.

When these signals reach your PC, it hasn't the foggiest idea what to do with them. The computer's CPU knows what a keyboard is and has hardwired instructions in system ROM that tell it what keystrokes represent and how it's supposed to respond – but the signals coming from the mouse or any other pointing device need a software driver to interpret their signals for the CPU.

As important as having a driver is the ability to get an updated version when other software (such as the operating system) changes. Nationally advertised name brands, with telephone numbers you can call easily, have a better record of providing this needed service. They also cost slightly more, but that doesn't make them last longer.

Over the years that I've used various pointing devices, I've never found a successful method of keeping anything with a ball alive for any appreciable length of time. It may be the acid in my perspiration, the fact that I smoke (leave me alone), the number of children who have visited my systems, or the amount of time they're used. All of these factors may have had a small part in their early demise. One thing I do know is that neither the amount of money they cost nor the recognizability of their brand name has anything to do with longevity. Mice and trackballs alike all die, sometimes within a weekend, soon after they reach me (and I have a box of dead ones in my office as a constant reminder).

A couple of alternate technologies for moving the pointer around in Windows deserve some mention. For example, there is the whole class of pointing devices known as graphics tablets. For a number of years now, I've been using one by Wacom, together with both pressure-sensitive and non-pressure styluses or its four-button cursor "puck." Tablets are very popular among the CAD (computer aided design) crowd, and I find them valuable given the amount of artwork I do for various publications (anything I can sketch with a pencil, I can duplicate with a stylus because it handles the same way). It took me over three years to kill a stylus (a record) and the tablet itself shows no signs of wear aside from a slight abrasion of its surface. Tablets are available in a variety of sizes from a variety of manufacturers, but none of them are as inexpensive as a generic mouse and some cost several times more.

One innovative approach to arrive in the past several years has been the "eraser head" pointer found embedded in the keyboard of various models of notebook computers. While they take some retraining time to learn to use smoothly and can be awkward when attempting to do any kind of drawing, they have the advantage of also being hardier than any trackball I've ever tried.

Last but not least is the most innovative approach of all – and one I recommend trying if all else fails – the GlidePoint "mouse" by Cirque Corporation in Salt Lake City. The GlidePoint is a small platform, about three inches wide by a little longer, with two buttons on the bottom edge. It looks like a miniature graphics tablet, but you don't use a stylus; you use your finger instead. As you move your finger over the surface, the cursor moves. Tap the surface and it's the same as clicking the primary mouse button; double-tap and it's the same as a double-click – or you can use the buttons on the edge. The small size of the GlidePoint makes it ideal for use with a notebook and, unlike both a mouse and graphics tablet, it doesn't require a lot of desk space (and there are few moving parts to gum up and expire). A special button-tap sequence allows you to make it behave as though you were holding the left button down continuously, so it is also suitable for drawing (although not if very fine resolution is needed). Neat product.

For special needs, such as presentations, there are a variety of mouse-like devices using both extremely long cables and infrared beams to allow you to control a notebook from a distance. I've tried several but haven't been overly impressed by any particular brand or model.

The Key's the Thing

Short of the Microsoft "natural" keyboard, there been few major innovations in keyboard technology since someone finally figured out that having cursor controls integrated into numeric keypads or function keys available only on the left side was a bad idea.

Some PC manufacturers (notably Compaq) have tinkered with attaching a mouse directly to the keyboard or building speakers into it, but the layouts have remained roughly the same for several years.

Virtually all PC keyboards now have roughly the same layout: Twelve function keys across the top, separate alphanumeric, cursor, and numeric keypads, and dual CTRL, SHIFT, and ALT keys on either side of the spacebar. To get this on an Apple system, you still have to pay extra, but it's fairly standard for a PC, even though you'll still see this style referred to in ads as "enhanced."

Early IBM keyboards had a spring in each key that clicked when the key was pressed far enough to send a signal to the computer. I've spoken to some touch typists who prefer clicking boards because they know the keys are working without having to look at the screen. At a very early point in my use of computers, however, I transcribed audio tapes – and the clicking of the keyboard interfered with hearing faint or distorted voices.

Whether you want the keys to click or merely thud softly is largely a subjective choice. Most people tend to favour the style they used when they first started computing. The important thing is to try out the keyboard, if how it works is important to you, before you leave the store.

Other points to ponder include feet and the board's orientation. For example, most standard keyboards have feet at the far edge and tilt up from the back towards the user. Whether these feet are rubber-capped (good because it prevents slipping) or whether they have a range of positions (best if you have a choice of not tilted, tilted a little, or tilted a lot) will affect the price and how pleasant they are to use.

The Microsoft keyboard doesn't tilt towards the user; it is raised on the edge closest to the user and tilts down and away to the back and sides. The alphanumeric keys are arranged in a hump or mound that fits into the cup of your hands. This was hard to get used to at first until I realized that both the tilt and the wrist-rest on the front put far less strain on my wrists. I'm told by some people (including Microsoft folk) that the physical layout of the keyboard is difficult for self-taught, hunt-and-peck typists to master. However, a full-hand typist should become accustomed to it in no time flat, and even prefer it. Now all we have to do is encourage someone else to license the look, then produce the thing for a reasonable price.

Modems

Internet, Internet, where have I been?
I used Telnet to London to talk to the Queen.
We were routed through Saturn
(Or somewhere between),
Now I'm typing to something
That's eating my screen.

A modem – MOdulate DEModulate – is an electronic communications device that can be either internal or external to the computer. It is designed to convert the digital signals produced by the computer into analog signals the telephone system can understand (modulate), then to reverse the process so it works the other way around (demodulate).

Despite the growing popularity of on-line services, the Internet, and computer-based faxing (with a resulting steady increase in demand for modems), both the hardware and the software developed for modems remain the least user-friendly (and sometimes downright unfriendly) component most of us ever encounter.

The only explanation I can offer for this is that computer-based telecommunication has largely remained in the hands of a dedicated segment of the computer-user community. It started out being more complicated than most computer tasks and, because the segment of the market that used and understood it was relatively small, remained that way long after most day-to-day tasks such as using a word processor (or blowing up a space nasty) got simpler.

All this is due for a change, probably faster than most of us realize, now that hardware manufacturers and software developers are becoming aware of the new market for telecommunications products spawned by interest in the Internet (and faxing and on-line services and so on).

In this section we'll try to cover the basics: shopping for a modem, connecting one to your system, useful hardware for your system to contain, and sorting out hardware interrupt conflicts (or how come my modem and mouse won't work together under Windows?).

Shopping tips

There are three basic flavours of modem to consider, two for desktop systems and one for notebook and portable systems.

If you have (or are buying) a desktop system, your choices are external (a modem that sits separately next to the computer, connected to it via a cable) and internal (the modem is on a circuit board that fits into one of the computer's internal expansion slots). It is possible that in the near future you may also see a trend towards directly wiring them to a computer's motherboard, but this is not a method I'd recommend (and I'll explain why below). Notebook systems can also be connected to an external modem, but the more practical solution is a PCMCIA (Personal Computer Memory Card International Association) card, a credit-card sized unit that slips into a slot in the side of the notebook.

Modems today also come with three different functions, depending on the features added to them by the manufacturers. Modems may transmit and receive text or binary data (datacom), facsimiles (faxcom), and voice (voicecom). Each of the three functions requires the modem to handle different sets of command signals, and one that will send and receive data may not send or receive faxes. A modem capable of data and fax may not also handle voice mail. Some modems, such as those most commonly shipped with the multifunction offices in a box (see Chapter 6, on printers), may fax only without doing anything else. The more things it will do (and the faster it will do them), the more it will cost.

The rate at which new standards and speed ratings for modems appear is the primary reason I don't recommend having them as an integral component of the motherboard. As you become more familiar with what your modem can do and begin to feel constrained by the speed at which it can do it, you are more likely to want to upgrade this component to a faster model than any other component in or attached to your computer.

So, we run into standards again. If any piece of hardware has suffered by an overabundance of "standards," the lowly modem has to top the list. To make it worse, the jargon associated with the standards is so impenetrable it makes you wonder whether there was a plot to keep most folks from joining the circle. Standard names such as V.32, V.32bis, V.42, and V.42bis simply aren't tossed around in most people's casual conversation.

Part of the problem has been the industry's attempt, mostly successful, to keep modems "backward compatible" to earlier developments in the device's history. While today we can have a modem capable of sending and receiving data at a rate of 28,800 bits per second (also written as 28,800 bps or 28.8 kilobits or 28.8 kbps), we still expect to be able to communicate with folks who haven't kept up to the fastest rates and have modems with top speeds of 2,400, 1,200, or even 300 bps.

The other part of the problem is that most modem communication uses standard telephone lines, which have a top speed of 2,400 bps and only token noise suppression. To move data faster requires techno-magic such as compression – and to keep the speed of transmission up and the rate of errors down, error correction strategies as well.

All of these factors would be bad enough, but the real killer for the user community has been a lack of development of a common method of telling modems how to do what they do. You can instruct modems (and this by no means is a complete list) to use tone or pulse dialling, to send and receive at specific speeds, to answer or not answer the phone (on the first or a specified ring), to use a specific speaker volume (or not use it at all), to respond back to the user in codes or text strings, to store telephone numbers, and to perform a variety of other tasks. At last count there were fifteen standards, plus several proprietary ones.

The telecommunications section of the market is nowhere near a solution to this problem. To date, there is no common pool of modem drivers available through Windows (or OS/2 or System 7). Major software developers such as Delrina, DCA, Datastorm, and deltaComm (WinFax, Crosstalk, ProComm Plus, and Telix) have tried the printer industry's approach of supporting as many modem brands as possible. Some products even try to interrogate the modem to see what it is. Unfortunately, that still leaves many people with odd-brand modems scratching their heads while they try to figure out how to enter the correct initialization commands so that the durn thingmy will work.

If there is any "standard" way to talk to modems at all, it's the basic command set originally developed by Hayes Microcomputer Systems (recently purchased by Boca Systems). It's been around since modems for microcomputers first started appearing on the market, and the instruction set for its brands has been dubbed the "Hayes AT Command Set" because all commands start with the letters AT (meaning, "Hello, modem? Wake up!"). Because of Hayes' past dominance of the market, manufacturers would claim that their products were "Hayes compatible" and, because most telecommunications software had a driver for one or more Hayes models, they could be used with the same commands.

It doesn't quite work that way. While most modems can be jogged into life by being given the command, ATDT (Wake up, dial using tone), followed by a telephone number, and this can technically be called compatibility with the Hayes AT command set, specific commands to carry out various functions after that point can be anything at all.

When all modems operated at 300 bps, none of them had fax or voice capabilities, and all the end user had to figure out was how to tell it to stop answering the phone (or start), minor differences in the command sets could be overcome without too much skull-sweat. That was then and this is now.

Until there is either development of a large pool of Windows modem drivers or the combined players in the telecom hardware/ software industry can forget enough of their rivalry to develop a common driver, modem buyers need to do their homework, starting with what software they plan to use, before acquiring the hardware.

28,800 bps modems

Modems started out slow and got faster and faster. We've seen speeds jump from 300 bps to 2,400, to 9,600 to 14,000, and a few speeds in between. Most recent models communicate at 28,000 bps, and it's this speed you'll most likely be eyeing in the stores. However, there were some false starts by the industry as it sought ways to implement the higher speed, which left many consumers wondering whether it was safe to buy the new 28,800 bps modems The answer is yes – with three conditions.

Attempts by some manufacturers to jump the market using a method of achieving 28,000 bps called V.FAST or V.FC (V.Fast Class) were premature. Models using V.terbo and proprietary high-speed standards such as the USRobotics "HST" models are also out in left field; they can only communicate at high speeds with each other. Avoid 'em.

The commonly accepted standard today for 28,800 bps data communications centres around a standard called V.34 and a corresponding chipset developed by Rockwell International. V.FAST or V.FC modems (also developed by Rockwell) are not compatible with V.34, and unless the modem you purchased using this scheme was specifically designed to be upgraded to the V.34 standard later, you're out of luck.

When V.34 was first introduced, it had some minor glitches, and there were actually two versions of it – one with glitches and one glitch-free – which could lead to connection problems such as modems backing down to a slower transmission speed (thereby losing the advantage you've paid extra to get), or a complete failure to connect. By the time you read this, the earlier, buggy version should have passed through the market. But regardless of which version of the chipset the modem has, a model with a flash ROM (read-only memory that can be changed) will be upgradeable (and may also be upgradeable for other features as well). These modems cost more.

As of mid-1995, V.34 covered only data communications – sending and receiving text or binary data between two modems, calling out to an on-line service or BBS, or using the Internet. It didn't cover fax or voice. V.34 fax (i.e., fax transmission at 28,800 bps) was just around the corner and was expected to start arriving in new models by the fall 1995 or spring of 1996. Even then, I'd be cautious about buying one until the standard matures.

There is no "standard" for voice communication (voice mail) using a modem. This is a relatively new development in the telecom industry, and the various schemes developed to meet it are all over the map. I can't recommend one over the other because of the lack of standards (and I hate voice mail, so I'm not the best person to consult, anyway).

Internal versus external

Whether to get an internal modem (one that fits into an expansion slot) or an external model (connected to a serial port by a cable) is largely a subjective choice. Assuming the modem comes from a reputable manufacturer, there should be little difference, if any, in how external and internal models operate. While its location may have something to do with hardware or software compatibility, it has nothing to do with speed of operation, and very little to do with day-to-day use.

I've used both, and each method has advantages and disadvantages. Unless you're in an environment with a client-server network (such as Novell NetWare or Banyan VINES), you won't be doing much networked telecommunications today. Next year may be different, because getting telecom software to work properly on peer-to-peer networks such as Windows for Workgroups and Windows 95 is the next hurdle we expect the software developers to jump in the near future.

Nevertheless, if you're buying the modem for a multicomputer office, an external modem will be easier to use. I used to use a fairly simple switching box with lines running to it from three computers. It sensed an attempt to contact the modem and activated the line coming to it from whichever computer was trying to call out. Sadly, it wouldn't automatically detect which of the three computers had telecom software running in automatic receive mode, so we were constantly tinkering with it to force it to send to one system or another. Getting two more modems solved that problem, but it's not an ideal solution.

External modems cost more than internal models (you are paying extra for the case, the lights to indicate usage, the power supply transformer and electrical cord), but if you're reluctant to open your computer to install an internal model, or all your expansion slots are already occupied, or you shudder at the thought of sorting out IRQ conflicts (see below), and if you have a reason to move the modem around often, these benefits may outweigh the additional expense. Because they rely on the computer's serial port to get data from it and send data to it, you may have to know more about what's driving your serial port than you wanted to know (see the discussion of UARTs below).

An internal modem costs less, but it occupies an expansion slot, requires opening the computer to install it, may be more difficult to hear through the computer case, and has no external lights to indicate operation. Because it is designed to work in addition to your existing serial ports, an internal model will often have its own UARTs. But it may also fight with your existing serial devices, so you will almost certainly have to consult the manual that comes with it and the manual that came with your drive controller or separate I/O board (whichever is the source of your serial ports) to sort out inevitable IRQ conflicts.

When (and if) "plug and play" modems actually work, when both operating systems and devices use the same standard to make them work, these considerations may become historical footnotes. Today they're anything but.

UARTs

Universal asynchronous receiver/transmitters (UARTs) are required for serial communications. An external modem may have two; one for internal operations (error control, compression, flow control, and protocol processing), and another to control signals between the modem and the computer. These are not the UARTs we care about. For the purposes of this discussion, you can ignore them and relax.

The UARTs we do care about are connected to each of your computer's serial ports (and/or internal modem card). UARTs are buffers (temporary holding areas) that operate on the first in, first out (FIFO) principle. They are necessary to the operation of a serial port because your computer can generate information faster than your modem (or mouse or serial printer or anything else) can handle it. (The fastest modem you can buy is still slower than the slowest old XT computer to which you may want to attach it.)

For the UART to function properly, the PC's operating system has to be able to read and flush each character quickly (something MS-DOS does well enough, but Windows doesn't). When you get FIFO overruns (the next incoming character overwrites the buffer and the previous character is lost), data transmission speed and accuracy suffer.

At slow telecommunications speeds of 9,600 bps or lower, older 8250 and 16450 UARTs can keep up, but at speeds over 9,600 bps, they can't. These UARTs, still found in older systems or low-end internal modems, use single-byte FIFO buffers. If the communications application you're using is running under Windows and you want to communicate at 14,400 bps or higher, you won't like the results.

The problem will become apparent as soon as you acquire a modem that operates faster than 9,600 bps and you try to download a file or accept an incoming fax sent at the higher rate. FIFO overruns and CRC (cyclical redundancy check) retry errors abound. If the data transfer succeeds at all, it may take even longer than with an old 2,400 bps modem.

As telecommunication speeds have increased, UARTs have had to change to allow you to take full advantage of the increased speed – and that brings us to the 16550. It was originally developed by National Semiconductor and its real name is the Ns16550A.

The 16550 UART has separate, 16-byte transmit-and-receive FIFO buffers and shorter access cycle times than the 16450 or 8250. It can run reliably at transmission rates up to 460,800 bps. Given that today's consumer-level, high-speed modems run at 28,800 bps to the outside world, and that PC modem-to-computer rates (the speed at which the modem and computer communicate) generally top out at 115,200 bps (although many modems have a maximum modem-computer rate of 57,600), that leaves a lot of room to manoeuvre.

On a PC you can find out what the UART of your serial port is if you have DOS 6 or higher by running the MSD (Microsoft Diagnostics) program, which, if you followed the default installation, should be in the DOS subdirectory on your hard drive. If you have an earlier version of DOS, ask yourself why. MSD is one of the few tools that will interrogate and return UART values. Other system information programs, such as both DOS and Windows versions of Norton Utilities and PC Tools, current in mid-1995 couldn't and neither could the more exhaustive CorelBOOK utility shipping with the CorelSCSI 2.0 application suite (nor could various benchmark test suites such as *PC Magazine*'s Winbench or *Windows Magazine*'s WinTune).

If you have an internal modem, it may not have a UART *per se*, but may be emulating UART functions another way. MSD should still report the emulation, but its success rate is spotty, depending on how well the modem emulation performs. MSD may also produce incorrect results if you run it as a DOS task from Windows. Start it from the DOS prompt *before* you start Windows for more accurate results.

How (or whether) you can change an UART depends on what you have now and where it is located. If your serial ports are connected to your hard drive controller (not uncommon) or to a separate I/O card, the UART may be a separate chip socketed into the card. If so, it will be clearly labelled with the model number. Because the 16550 is pin-compatible with both the 8250 and 16450, removing the old chip and replacing it presents little difficulty unless for some unfathomable reason it's soldered in place. If the idea of fiddling with your computer's innards scares you, or if the serial port isn't working anymore, take either the circuit board or your whole computer to your dealer.

If the UART is soldered on to the board, integrated into a surface-mounted chip along with other circuits, or is an integral part of the computer's motherboard, you've got a problem. Desoldering chips from anything is risky and best not undertaken by inexperienced folks.

UARTs integrated into other circuits can't be replaced. The best you can hope for is that the device containing it allows you to turn the associated serial port off and that you've kept the manual that tells you how to do it. Then you can either purchase a new serial port card with 16550s on it, or an internal modem with a 16550 built into it.

If you go to your dealer and the salesperson's eyes glaze over when you mention UARTs of any type, don't be surprised. A lot of them still don't understand what they are, where they're located, or why the heck people would want any. You may have to shop for a dealer with more experience.

Ports

It's possible to be confused by the references to COM ports, serial ports, and RS232C ports used in various product manuals. An RS232C serial port is the connector on the back of your PC to which you might attach an external modem or a mouse. RS232C is an engineering standard that defines how information is sent and received through serial connectors and the cables between them. It defines the nature of the information and specifies which signal uses which wire.

COM port, on the other hand, is a more general term. Short for communications port, it refers to the computer's internal way of keeping track of the number of serial devices the central processor needs to watch. There are four of them available in today's PCs (COM1, COM2, COM3, and COM4). They may be routed to an external RS232C serial port connector, to an internal modem, or they may be idle.

IRQ conflicts (or why won't my modem and mouse work anymore?)

You've read the articles, plumbed your wallet, purchased an internal modem, and plugged it in expecting to find the world on the other end of your phone line. You fire up Windows and it either fails to run, your mouse goes dead, or no matter what you try the modem won't respond.

You saw some vague reference to IRQ and port conflicts in the modem manual, but it's written in offshore pseudo-English or in engineering technobabble. In desperation, you finally break the plastic wrap off the Windows manual hoping that reading it will help – all to no avail. What do you do?

Welcome to the unfriendly side of the world of telecommunications and one of the best reasons in the world for the computer industry to get busy developing operating systems and hardware that can recognize each other without user intervention. Unfortunately, that day is still in the misty future, and you're going to have to solve this problem yourself.

The CPU has a number of specific access points through which the activities of your computer's other components and peripheral devices can get its attention and through which it can send them instructions. These interrupt request channels (IRQs) are limited in number and aren't terribly flexible. They can usually handle only one thing at a time.

Don't ask me why it was designed this way; I couldn't tell you. Ask Intel and IBM. But back at the dawn of computer history, some group of otherwise intelligent people thought that four COM ports could share two interrupts. COM1 and COM3 share IRQ4, while COM2 and COM4 share IRQ3. For the insatiably curious (such as this book's editor) a list of common PC IRQ assignments follows:

IRQ0 – system timer; IRQ1 – keyboard; IRQ2 – cascade to IRQs 9-15; IRQ3 – COM2, COM4; IRQ4 – COM1, COM3; IRQ5 – second parallel port (LPT2), may be available for other uses; IRQ6 – floppy disk(s); IRQ7 – first parallel port (LPT1) – printer; IRQ8 – real-time clock; IRQ9-12 – may be available; IRQ13 – redirect to nonmaskable interrupt (NMI) used to check memory parity errors; IRQ14 – fixed (i.e., hard) disk; IRQ15 – may be available.

Since most computers come with two external serial ports, set to COM1 and COM2, you usually don't have a problem connecting a mouse to one of them and an external modem to another. The mouse on COM1 uses IRQ4, while the modem on COM2 uses IRQ3. No conflict, no hassle. Windows recognizes both and you can move on to fighting with your software over the type of modem you have and with

Windows if you want to communicate at high speeds (see UARTs above).

When you connect an internal modem, however, everything goes to pieces. Even though the modem should – and probably does – allow you to configure it for COM3 or COM4, you still have a problem. Assuming you keep your mouse on COM1, that means IRQ4 is in use (and COM3 will collide with it when you try to use it). So you try to use COM4 instead.

Oops! Even though you weren't using COM2 before and didn't have it connected to anything, it hasn't gone away. The CPU still knows it's there and keeps IRQ3 occupied checking to see if it wants to do something. Along you come with a modem (which also uses IRQ3) and it's collision time again.

You only have a limited number of options. You could stop using the mouse (bad idea) or give up on using a modem (equally bad). You could find the manual that came with whatever your existing two serial ports are attached to (it could be your drive controller, separate I/O board, or the motherboard itself), then figure out how to disable one of them. Open the computer case and follow the diagrams to change whatever dip (dual inline pull) switch or jumper is on the device, then keep the manual handy while you turn the computer back on.

You could try the Windows Control Panel and change the IRQ used by either your existing serial port or the one on the modem. If you aren't using a sound card, a second parallel port, a SCSI adapter, scanner, or other device that wants it, you might be able to use IRQs 5, 7, or 9 through 12 and 15, instead of IRQ 3 or 4, but only if the device driving the serial port supports this.

An external modem is simpler.

Shopping tips

By now you should be prepared to do the following: Before you buy your computer, pester the salesperson to make sure you have a 16550 UART attached to the serial ports, regardless of where they're connected. This is a good idea whether you plan to jump into telecommunications immediately or later.

If you're going to jump in immediately, and you want an internal modem, it makes sense to have the vendor install it and test it under Windows, before you take it home, to make sure all conflicts are resolved.

You're going to do whatever it takes to get some sense of what brand and model of modem is supported by as wide a range of telecommunications software as possible (keep in mind that manufacturers often produce more than one model, and that the one the software supported last month may not be the one you'll be offered next week). At the very least, look for a modem that supports 14,400 bps for both data and fax communications.

If you want the fastest modem you can find, decide that 28,800 bps sounds fast enough, but can't wait for the standard to settle down, search for models using the V.34 standard. If the vendor can't tell you which flavour of V.34 the modem has, at least get one with a flash ROM so you can upgrade it later (although by fall 1995, most of the flaky ones should have exited the market).

If you're shopping for V.34 data, 14.400 bps fax and voice, you'll want about $600 in your jeans to cover the hardware and taxes. Prices go down from there depending on speed, internal versus external, how much and what kind of software is bundled with the unit, and recognizability of brand name. By the time you're under $100, you're probably buying something without a lot of support that's about to fall off the market because it's too slow.

Scanners

Ever since computers first appeared and went into general business use, people have been consumed with two tasks: getting material out of the system and getting new material into it. Getting stuff out has its own set of tasks (get it on the screen, get it to the printer) and headaches. ("But it didn't look like *that* when it was on the screen. Honest!") What we're concerned with in this section is getting material *in*.

Whether your task involves word processing, spreadsheets, or graphics (forget databases for a while), the standard limit of how quickly you can get data into a program is how quickly you can type (or draw or trace). The technology of computer voice recognition is simply not advanced enough yet for us to speak into our computers and have them take dictation flawlessly without a lot of training time (both for the software and the user), nor have pen-based systems advanced far enough to recognize handwriting (most treat our scrawls as pictures). Voice recognition is nifty for people who can't use their hands fully, but for the time being the rest of us should avoid it.

For both graphics and text, that pretty much leaves the scanner as the only alternative. Scanners come in three sizes and two flavours. The sizes include hand scanners with a typical scanning width of about four inches, and two types of desktop scanners – those with a flat bed and cover (similar to a typical photocopier) and those with a sheet-feeding mechanism (similar to most stand-alone fax machines). To add a wee bit of complication, you can sometimes purchase an optional "automatic document feeder" for flat-bed models as well. All three types come in monochrome and colour versions.

Scanners of all sorts, in the simplest sense, operate the same way. They shine a light on a page, then photosensitive receptors in the scanner differentiate between the amount of light returned from the objects on the page (more comes back from light-tinted objects such as the page itself, less from type and pictures). Electronics in the scanning system and special software translate the electrical pulses produced by the photosensors into digital numbers.

The number of photosensors and how often the scanner "looks" at an image while you scan it will determine the resolution (in dots per inch or dpi). For example, a unit with 600 photosensors, scanning at $1/_{1200}$ of an inch, will deliver a 600 by 1,200 dpi image and one heck of a hit on your hard drive if it's in 24-bit colour.

You can get bogged down by various tech-weenie arguments about the colour of the light (red, green, or yellowish) used by mono-chrome scanners or the number of passes a colour scanner makes (whether it's three or one, when you come right down to it, doesn't make a heck of big difference, because the time required is about the same in most cases).

How you distinguish between models in each class will depend on how you want to use the device. For example, professional scanning of 24-bit colour photographs will require a colour unit capable of very high-resolution scans (1,200 dpi or higher). Most optical character recognition (OCR) software, however, won't thank you for a colour image or for one with a resolution of much more than 200 dpi (since a higher resolution scan is more likely to pick up the kinds of extra data, such as ink bled into the paper or creases, that the OCR software detests).

If you're engaged in high-volume work, a model with an SCSI interface may be more suited to your needs than one with its own proprietary circuit board or one that connects through your system's parallel port. However, particularly if you're settling on an SCSI model, you'll want to see what kind of SCSI drivers it uses, whether it requires a proprietary adapter, and, if not, how it connects to your existing SCSI adapter (there are three different connectors, 50-pin SCSI-2, 25-pin parallel, and a huge Centronics connector – and it would help if the scanner came with a cable compatible with what you already have).

If all your work is in black and white, colour scanners may make you crazier than you need to be – they're often not very happy with monochrome images (not to mention being slower).

Scanners take pictures of pictures and text. Any image you acquire with your scanner/PC/Mac system is going to arrive in the computer as a picture, regardless of what it started out to be. That means when a document is scanned into the system, all you get is a picture of the words, not the words themselves. You can see them, but you can't edit them in your word processor.

OCR

That brings us to optical character recognition (OCR) software (and sometimes hardware). OCR, in essence, translates the digital picture codes that the scanner produces into digital alphanumeric codes. However, OCR is not simply a convenient excuse to avoid typing on a keyboard. For single documents, most accomplished typists and even experienced hunt-and-peck artists can generally type faster than most of today's OCR software can read a picture, decipher it, and make it part of your electronic document store.

Remember the buzzwords "paperless office?" It's the driving force behind OCR – visions of empty in-baskets and empty file cabinets with documents stored electronically and available at the tap of a button started some folks wondering what they could do with the tons of paper already on hand. It would be prohibitively expensive to have someone keyboard them, and the prime candidates for these services (legal firms, governments, insurance companies, publishers) could afford to pay $30,000 to $50,000 for complicated systems that would do the work for them.

It also didn't take long for someone to notice that computer printers had entered the world with the sole task of creating even more paper. The same industries and agencies with a massive pre-computer store of paper were producing and receiving tons more of it.

Early developers of OCR systems faced a world of mainframes and minicomputers or desktop systems with limited 8-bit processors and 64 KB memory capacities. Their approach to page recognition focused on hardware – combining scanners, customized processing systems, terminals, and high-capacity storage systems in stand-alone, dedicated page recognition systems.

While these developers recognized the need to accommodate desktop systems with lower-cost, software-only products, their initial offerings were tied to customized hardware. Creating a software-only product meant they had to transfer their page recognition algorithms from hardware to software – a task that required significant effort. Many of the high-end (very costly) products still use special hardware to aid in the task.

For the more cost-conscious among us, however, the advent of the 386/486 PC processors and faster Macs, both with full 32-bit processing and plenty of memory, meant that lower priced, software-only schemes were a viable alternative.

Before you jump to the conclusion that scanning, plus OCR, will make your life better, it would help to understand how difficult it is to do. *Despite what salesfolk will tell you in the shop, you will seldom be able to scan in a document that doesn't require some sort of correction before it can be used.*

When you or I look at a printed page of material, we focus on the portions that interest us. Our minds can handily dismiss anything on the page that isn't text (such as drawings or pictures), and it doesn't really matter that the type may be in different orientations (sideways, angled, vertical, upside-down), or different weights and heights, or italicized or underlined, or in a fancy font (like Olde English), or in a cursive font (like Zapf Chancery).

OCR software, however, doesn't read the way you and I do – before it can recognize anything, the original document has to find its way to the computer – usually via someone else's hardware, such as a desktop or hand scanner, or fax machine.

Computers are very literal about what you feed them. Use a keyboard to produce the digital code recognized as an alphabetic character, and a character is what you get on screen. Word processing software is written to use the same codes. The end result of a scanned image, however, is a picture of the words (and anything else that happens to be on the same page – including creases and coffee stains).

To make matters even more interesting, it isn't necessarily a good picture, either. To begin with, it's composed of dots, because the scanner (unless it is very, very expensive), only samples the image at about 400 to 1,200 dots per inch. Any higher scanning rate would both take forever and eat disk space at an incredible rate.

If the paper is tinted or contains areas of differing tint, if there is a mixture of font types, if it's a bad photocopy with parts of the letters missing, you get a degraded image to start with. Further problems occur if the text is too tight – letters so close to each other that they touch – or too loose – letters far enough apart so that the OCR package thinks they are different words. As well, various paper types that absorb and spread ink (such as newsprint) can produce blotched characters that are too smudged to read. This all makes the task for the OCR software, which has to translate these pictures into characters, that much more difficult.

Fax input is even worse. At low quality, material is scanned at 100 dpi, then sent over noisy phone lines – and even at high quality produced by a computerized fax system such as WinFax, the output is still only 200 dpi.

Scanner shopping tips

Here are a few rules of thumb to observe if you are seriously considering setting up an OCR system (and even if you're not).

Hand scanners don't make it. Don't even think about using a hand scanner for OCR. They have their place in low-cost scanning of small drawings and pictures for home and occasional small-business use, but their 4-inch scan width is simply inadequate for most serious document scanning.

Coupled with the difficulty imposed by having to scan an 8.5-inch page twice is the difficulty of manually controlling not only the scanning speed (the faster you move the scanner, the worse the image) but the alignment as well (I defy you to scan in a perfectly straight line every time, even with some kind of holder). Finally, if you are going to scan a lot of material, there is no hand scanner on the market with any kind of document feeder to save you time.

Desktop scanners are better for OCR. Look for a desktop scanner with a page size large enough to handle at least standard 8.5 by 11 inch paper. For full flexibility, I'd recommend a flat-bed scanner with detachable document feeder. The combination will allow you to feed a stack of ordinary business documents, but will also allow you to scan larger items and smaller ones, as well as from sources such as those that fold or are bound (unless you really enjoy slicing pages out of whatever you're scanning). Vendors of sheet-fed scanners just scream when I say things like this and you can ignore my advice, but only if you know with absolutely certainty that you'll never want to scan anything other than standard single-page documents no wider than 8.5 inches, that they'll never be large, small, or printed on anything other than bond paper (e.g., card stock, transparency, slide, newsprint, stamps, or a cocktail napkin).

Automatic document feeders save time, but if you are going to scan a mountain of material, look for a scanner with both an automatic document feeder and software that understands that you may wish to scan into one file both one-page and multipage documents. Here's a neat trick to try on the vendor when you ask for a demonstration: Just about any document feeder will handle pristine documents, so take some with you that have been folded over a staple or paperclip. For even more fun, staple some pages together, then rip 'em apart with gusto – make sure they have tattered edges. Want to see the salesperson's eyes glaze over? Try pages that have been three-hole punched.

Colour just gets in the way. You will be able to save some money if you are absolutely certain you won't ever want to scan colour. Grey-scale scanners are less expensive (and their file sizes for finished images are smaller, too).

Have some idea of the nature of the material you wish to scan. Simple documents with straightforward typefaces on white paper are relatively easy. Documents with a mixture of paper shades and fonts, with material that came off a press (nice solid type) or a dot-matrix printer (jagged dots), bad photocopies, smudged originals, or old and faded documents require special handling. You may have to invest in equipment with either Hewlett-Packard's Accu-Page or Caere's Any-Page technology – both of which are designed to overcome just these problems.

Money. Don't go shopping for a scanner unless you have between $1,000 and $2,000 in your pocket for starters. Have a serious look at products by both Microtek and Hewlett-Packard (after reviewing HP's ScanJet 3c, I bought it instead of giving it back).

If all you need is a software solution, you won't be disappointed by Xerox's TextBridge; it's one of the best OCR software applications for Windows that I've reviewed in the past several years and works with both fax and scanned files.

TWAIN

TWAIN answers a major problem faced by people trying to get print-ers, mice and other pointing devices, modems, and other hardware peripherals to work together with the software applications in their computers.

At several points in this book, I've yelped about software drivers to the point where both you and I are probably sick of hearing about them. Nevertheless, hardware and software need a way to talk to each other so that what you get out of your computer is something that at least vaguely resembles what you put into it. The traditional method is for either the hardware manufacturer or the software developer – or both – to include software drivers designed to help the device and the application (the program) communicate. Where this solution falls down is when either the hardware or the software is upgraded to a new version that the driver can't handle – or when you purchase a product for which there is no driver.

TWAIN literally means technology without an independent name (although the committee overseeing it now insists it is not an acronym, but is instead a word designed to illustrate the union of applications and input devices). Regardless, the original committee was worried that if scanning fell into this bind over drivers, consumer frustration would result in low or no sales of their products. Neither side wanted to have to ship multiple drivers for the other. They also felt that users would appreciate being able to scan directly into an application without having to start a second application to handle the scanning – then worry about translating the result into a format they could use.

The result was a common software driver, TWAIN. The best thing about TWAIN is that it generally works and works well.

If a scanner is TWAIN compatible or if an application is TWAIN compatible, the company will usually mention it in advertisements, promotional material, and on the box. *If the product isn't TWAIN compatible, you don't want it.*

The following lists definitely don't cover all TWAIN-compliant products – just those with which I'm personally familiar:

Windows-based word processing software with TWAIN compatibility includes WordPerfect 6.1, Microsoft Word 6.0a, and Lotus Word Pro.

Desktop publishing applications with TWAIN include Adobe PageMaker 5.0 (which used to be called Aldus PageMaker), CorelVENTURA 5.0, and Microsoft Publisher 2.0 (although you won't find this out by reading the box – you have to open the manual to discover it).

Fax programs include Delrina's WinFax Pro 4.0 and Phoenix Technologies' Eclipse Fax SE, as well as BitFax Professional.

Drawing/design programs include CorelDRAW 5.0 and Photo-Paint 5.0; Micrografx Designer 4.0, PhotoMagic 1.0, and Picture Publisher 4.0; Adobe Illustrator, PhotoStyler, and Photoshop. Presentation graphics applications include Microsoft PowerPoint 4.0, Lotus Freelance 2.1, Novell Presentations, and Micrografx Charisma 4.0.

On the hardware side, there are far more scanner models with

TWAIN compliance than exist in my head. Virtually all products from AFGA, Epson, Logitech, Hewlett-Packard, Microtek, UMAX, and a long list of others come with TWAIN compliance. Today, it is rarer to find a scanner without it than with it. In order to impress upon the industry its feelings about TWAIN, *PC Magazine* for one won't review non-TWAIN models (and neither will I).

When choosing a TWAIN scanner, however, you should know that while compatibility between hardware and software likely won't be an issue, the driver's abilities might be – because not all TWAIN drivers have the same features. Basic TWAIN drivers provide elementary pre-scan and scan capabilities, but don't have tools for fine-tuning images. Many image scans can be improved before they arrive in your computer by pre-selecting optimum resolution and colour, so some vendors add value to their drivers by providing tools that help the process at the scanning end.

Additional features may include highlight and shadow controls, colour pre-scanning (which can be switched on and off) and auto-adjustments for colour correction and shadows. Also useful are black-point and white-point setting tools (to set absolute black and white values), pre-scan zoom controls, and cropping tools (which let users type in desired dimensions).

All in all, TWAIN takes a lot of the sting out of finding a scanner-application combination that will work for you.

9

More Things That Click . . . and Some You Can Take on the Plane: Cases, Power Supplies, and Notebooks

Cases, uninterruptable power supplies, and notebooks didn't fit anywhere else in the book, so I've artfully collected them here!

Down to Cases

We take computer cases for granted, but there are a few pointers that will help you enjoy your computer as time goes by.

There is no standard way to determine whether a case is a desktop or a tower other than the way the label is attached and the orientation of the drive bays – but in most instances, it really doesn't matter. Floppy and hard disk drives don't care whether they lie flat or on their sides (but they do care about being upside-down or at an angle). So, even if you have a desktop case, you can turn it on its side anytime. Some people insist that your hard drive should be formatted in the orientation in which it is going to operate, but I haven't had any bad experiences that lead me to worry about this. Most vendors will sell you an inexpensive plastic stand if you're nervous about the system tipping over, but under most circumstances you won't need this either unless you live with a large, boisterous dog or small kids.

About the only component that may not thank you for altering its orientation is a CD-ROM drive. The discs it uses like to lie flat, so that the distance between the laser reader and the underside of the disc surface remains constant. I have seen one drive in a Compaq system mounted on its side, but it had special clips designed to hold the disc in place and, although there may be separate drives sold with this attachment system, I'm unaware of them.

If for aesthetic reasons, or because of space considerations, you want a tower case, there is no scale used to determine whether it's a full, "server-sized" tower, a mid-sized tower, or a mini-tower. All sizes are in the eye of the beholder.

The larger the case you get the more it will cost – simply for the materials – but the more room you'll have to move around inside it when upgrading components later. You'll have less of a chance of crimping a device cable when you put it back together. You'll have room to attach additional cooling fans. Depending on where you put it, you'll also have a greater chance of it taking a chunk out of your shins.

If you know or even suspect that you'll be opening the case frequently to upgrade parts or to clean it out (a good idea), then a case with snap-off sides or easily removable top is something you can get if you hunt for it.

It's what is sold with the case and should accompany it that's of greater concern. Most PC systems will be quite happy with a 200-watt power supply. That's sufficient for a hard drive, floppy drive, CD-ROM drive, and most components that come with the motherboard. If, on the other hand, you even suspect that in the future you'll want to add another hard drive, a tape drive, additional internal SCSI or IDE devices, and so on, then look for 230 to 250 watts or more.

It's also worth noting again that the LED readout numbers on some cases, which appear to be clocking the speed of either the motherboard or CPU, are almost invariably set with jumper blocks or switches on the inside of the case itself. The vendor sets them; you can set them – to any number you fancy.

Of course, in order to do this, you'll need the manual that should come with the case. It's also going to be highly useful to you the day you open the case to add a component or to gently run the brush from a vacuum cleaner around the inside of the computer to clean up the dust that makes it run hotter than it should. When you accidentally knock a wire loose connecting the motherboard to the system speaker, turbo switch, keyboard lockout, power, drive or other lights, the manual for both your motherboard and case will come in very handy.

Notebook PCs

One of the fastest evolving and most expensive ways you can buy a PC is to get it in a small package. Notebook and sub-notebook computers (the term "laptop" is *passé*) exact a price premium for two reasons: You always pay extra for convenience and popularity and, because of their miniaturization, you're paying for a lot of proprietary engineering as well. It's rarer to find locally assembled house brands of notebooks than nationally advertised name brands. Of these, the following manufacturers dominate the notebook market: Toshiba, IBM, AST, Canon, NEC, Hewlett-Packard, and Dell.

Notebooks have a shelf-life of about six months before a wave of new models takes over at the leading edge and pushes everything else down. The price for the leading edge in desktop systems hovers around $5,000, but the price for leading-edge notebooks with the latest toys is $7,500 or more. Again, like their larger siblings, notebooks and sub-notebooks also have a point at which they fall out of the market, except that finding anything worth having for less than $2,000 will be difficult.

Most notebook users report that their priorities when purchasing one are different than for a desktop system. While CPU, memory, and hard disk capacity are important issues, they pale by comparison to concern over battery life and screen type.

Batteries

Batteries play a big part in your use of a notebook system. You'll want to examine how long the battery will keep your system alive, how quickly it recharges, how long it lasts before it dies completely, how much it costs to get a backup or replacement when the original wears out, and whether they're easily available from either the original manufacturer or from other vendors (batteries for some of the lesser known brands can sometimes be difficult to find).

From my tests and long-term use of a variety of notebook and sub-notebook systems, the batteries I prefer are lithium ion (L-ion), nickel metal hydride (NiMH), and nickel cadmium (NiCad), in that order.

NiCad batteries tend to go flat quickly, suffer from memory effect (see below), and die early; NiMH batteries also go flat fairly quickly and suffer from memory effect, although they take a little longer to die than NiCads; L-ion batteries last a long time, don't suffer from memory effect, and love short charges.

As we were going to press, a new battery type, zinc air, was being talked about, but no one had produced a system using it.

Virtually all rechargeable batteries, except L-ion, suffer from memory effect. After repeated partial discharges, the battery "remembers" how flat it got, then won't discharge past that point anymore. Over time the point moves up until the battery will neither discharge nor recharge. When that happens, it's dead. This is useful to know because in order to achieve miniaturization most notebook manufacturers design their own battery shapes and sizes. Before yours dies (and preferably before you ever own it), it's very important to determine how easily you can find a replacement at a reasonable price, assuming you can find a compatible battery at all.

Screens

There are four types of screen, ranging from the hideously expensive to the simply hideous.

Active matrix (also referred to as thin film transistor – TFT) is a horrendously expensive colour screen technology that uses individual transistors (three of them) for each pixel on screen. TFT adds $1,500 to $2,000 to the cost of each notebook that has one, but if you're engaged in colour-sensitive work on the road, such as preparing electronic slide presentations, the colour fidelity may be worth the added cost.

Dual scan is a type of passive-matrix screen technology that divides the screen into horizontal halves and scans both halves simultaneously in order to improve refresh time, so that your mouse cursor doesn't constantly get lost.

Passive matrix screens use LEDs (light emitting diode – a crystal in a semi-liquid medium that glows when power is applied) rather than transistors to supply colour. They're slower to react to changes than active-matrix or dual-scan screens and the result is ghosting of moving images and cursors that disappear when you move them too quickly. Their only advantage, given their washed-out colour, is that they're relatively inexpensive.

LCD (liquid crystal diode) screens use a diode that doesn't light up when power is applied. Instead, it twists and becomes more or less opaque to light passing through it, depending on how much power is applied and when. Screens using LCD technology often have no light source of their own, tend to be monochrome, and don't work terribly well under dim lighting conditions.

PCMCIA cards

Personal Computer Memory Card International Association – or people can't memorize computer industry acronyms – are sometimes called Smart cards (although this term can also apply to things such as credit cards and other identification devices), PC cards, or Pickme cards. These miniaturized hardware devices are still often described as new gimmicks, but have now been around for so long (in computer terms) that they are hardly new.

Today you'll find them used in everything from handheld organizers to notebook computers and full-fledged desktop systems. About the size of a credit card (and in some cases not much thicker), PCMCIA cards can contain all manner of goodies, including (but not limited to) additional memory, modem, sound card, SCSI adapter, network interface adapter, or a hard drive as large as 340 MB. There are also flash memory cards (i.e., no moving parts) holding 10, 20, 40 MB, and higher storage capacities, which could end up making floppy disks obsolete – but this little scenario is unlikely to happen until their cost comes down.

Because of the flexibility of PCMCIA cards and the fact that their 68-pin connectors directly access the system bus, we haven't even scratched the surface of what they may be capable of doing. In 1995, a host of multifunction PCMCIA cards began to appear on the market. You can now acquire units containing both network interface and modem, sound board and SCSI adapter, and so on. Watch for this trend to continue.

On the other hand, since their introduction a few short years ago, they've already gone through versions 1, 2, and 3 (and Toshiba is pushing a version 4), so they just could die under a welter of standards that keeps everyone confused to the point where we all give up and go do something else.

All PCMCIA slots in notebooks are not the same. While the majority of systems will include one Type III slot that's able to accept one Type III card or two Type I or Type II cards, several models of Toshiba notebooks won't allow more than one card of any type.

One factor slowing migration of PCMCIA cards to desktop systems is the software interface required to service them. "Card and Socket Services" device drivers use a huge amount of upper memory and can get quite cranky about other software invading the territory, even though with one or two cards, only a small section of the memory is actually used. This, like the problem of standards, needs fixing.

What else?

Other factors to bear in mind when thinking about buying a notebook are processor speed, keyboard layout, and pointing devices:

The processor speed is always going to be slower than what you can get at the equivalent edge for desktop systems. CPUs use power, and because battery life is so important, notebooks tend to be behind the development of larger systems (it took nearly eighteen months after the Pentium was introduced before manufacturers got around to putting them in notebooks), and then they used slightly slower chips (again, even though 133 MHz Pentium CPUs were available and 90 MHz systems were fairly common in 1995, most notebook manufacturers were confined to the 75 MHz version of the chip until Intel released a special low-power version of the P90 later the same year).

As you add toys to a notebook, you'll find that concerns over battery life once again dominate choices. For example, an active-matrix colour screen eats power like candy compared to the less gorgeous dual-scan alternative. The size of a hard drive isn't relevant to battery life, but adding a floppy drive, CD-ROM drive, sound system, PCMCIA slots, and other gizmos takes a toll.

Some design points to ponder

An "eraser head" mouse embedded in the keyboard, plus a shelf on which to rest your wrists, will provide less grief than a trackball or plugging in a mouse. As noted under the section covering pointing devices, trackballs, and mice die.

Some sub-notebooks save space by leaving out little things, like external ports for a full-sized monitor, keyboard, or mouse. Others often don't include a floppy disk drive, and you'll have to check carefully to see if an external model is (a) available and (b) included in the price.

Virtually all notebook and sub-notebook manufacturers offer some sort of external docking port to allow you to keep connections for various devices back at the office and to hook them up quickly. Some of the ports cost hideous amounts, are almost as big as a full desktop system, and offer only a skimpy list of connectors. Others (notably the Dell Latitude XP) have small port replicators that cost under $300 and include SCSI and Ethernet (network) connectors along with a full compliment of external monitor, serial, parallel, and PS/2 connectors for mouse and keyboard (small, round canon-style connectors first introduced by IBM in its PS/2 line of computers that take up less physical room on a PC than 25- or 9-pin serial port connectors).

How big are your fingertips? When you make something smaller, something usually suffers. Pay attention to the keyboards and your habits. Notebook systems often make compromises about the size of function keys and cursor controls, and the software you normally use might make these awkward.

Cramped keyboards are the bane of notebooks. Hunt-and-peck typists may have no problem with them, but anyone used to typing with all fingers on both hands is going to have some trouble adjusting. IBM has come up with one notebook model – the 701C and CS – that has a split keyboard that nests under the screen when the notebook is shut, but slides out to a full-size keyboard when it's open; handy, but more moving parts that can break.

What happens when your notebook does break? Various manufacturers have different warranty policies dealing with everything from active-matrix screens (how many pixels have to die before it's considered defunct) to catastrophic failure. Fixing one if you're in Winnipeg or San Francisco may not be a problem, but it's something you'll want to consider carefully if you make a habit of going to places like Pago Pago or Rangoon. Samsung, for example, has a support system arrangement with a global courier to supply replacement systems anywhere on the planet within a remarkably short time.

What you get at the leading edge of the notebook genre may depend on future developments, but towards the end of 1995 you could look for an 11.3-inch TFT screen, an "eraser-head" pointing device; either a hardened steel eyebolt or a plug for a Kensington security lock so you can tie your expensive notebook down; a 750 MB to 1.2 GB hard drive; a dual-purpose internal docking socket that allows you to use either a removable floppy drive or CD-ROM drive; 16 MB of RAM; 28.8 kbps internal modem with fax and telephony; infrared port for wireless connection to a network and/or stand-alone desktop system to allow you to transfer files; a PCI-based graphics controller with 2 MB of graphics memory; lithium ion battery; 90 MHz Pentium CPU; 256 KB processor cache; at least one Type III PCMCIA slot capable of handling one Type III card or two Type I or Type II cards; 16-bit wave table synthesis sound controller (with a full panel of line-in, line-out speaker and microphone ports); docking station port; full-sized, enhanced, high-speed, bi-directional parallel port (not a small proprietary port); external VGA monitor port; external 9-pin serial port; external PS/2 port for keyboard and/or mouse; and an internal transformer (so you don't have to lug a brick around). Have around $8,000 or more in your pocket when you leave the house.

What you'll get in a sub-notebook includes all of the above with the following substitutions: a smaller 10.4-inch TFT screen, an external rather than internal floppy/CD-ROM, a 486DX4/100 or 75 MHz Pentium CPU, a removable 540 to 750 MB hard drive, an expanding keyboard, and in order to keep its weight under six pounds, an external power transformer. Forget the sound system ports, PS/2 port(s), and processor cache, and you can leave about $2,000 at home.

Uninterruptible Power Supplies and Power Conditioners

Once upon a time, the uninterruptible power supply (UPS) was regarded as something only corporate systems would ever need. This was in the days when certain widely used database applications would trash their records if not shut down properly and a sudden loss of power could be a company-wide disaster. But it was difficult for home users to justify the $350 (and up) cost. After all, if the computer shuts down while you're playing *Doom*, who cares?

If you plan to use Windows 95, Windows NT, or OS/2, you'll care. All three operating systems will yell at you and perform other kinds of crankiness if not shut down properly.

While protection against blackouts will become more important when using these systems, there are other electrical phenomena your local power company will send you that can be worse.

Dirty power comes in a variety of flavours (all of them bad):

Sags: Also known as brownouts, sags are short-term decreases in voltage levels and the most common type of power problem. A sag can "starve" a computer of the steady power it needs to function, causing frozen keyboards and unexpected system crashes with the end result of lost data.

Sags are typically caused by the start-up power demands of many electrical devices (including motors, compressors – such as in refrigerators – elevators, shop tools, automatic washers and dryers, and so on). They are also the electrical utility's short-term solution for coping with extraordinary power demands (during the supper hour as people turn on electric ranges or on especially hot days when folks run their air conditioners).

Blackouts: This is a total loss of utility power caused by excessive demand on the power grid. Sudden blackouts can cause databases to scramble their files, will result in loss of any work currently in memory, may cause a hard disk crash and loss of the file allocation table (with subsequent scrambling of all data on the hard drive), and will give networks the screaming fits –particularly if it takes place during a system backup.

If you are using OS/2, Windows 95, or Windows NT, a blackout will also prevent the orderly shutdown of your computer(s) that these operating systems require in order to keep their files straight.

Spikes: Also known as an impulse, a spike is a virtually instantaneous, dramatic increase in voltage. Akin to the force of a tidal wave, a spike can enter electronic equipment and damage or completely destroy components. Typically caused by a nearby lightning strike, spikes can also occur if utility power lines are downed.

Surge: A short-term increase in voltage, typically lasting $1/120$ of a second or longer (anything less is a spike) usually caused when electrical appliances switch off and the extra voltage is dissipated through the power lines – and into your system .

Computers and other devices (such as monitors, printers, modems, and so on) are designed to receive power within a certain voltage range. Anything outside of the range will stress the components. They may not fail immediately, but prolonged and multiple stressing can cause premature failure of things like memory chips.

Noise: Although not in the same league as sags, surges, spikes, and blackouts, electromagnetic interference (EMI) and radio frequency interference (RFI) are still power problems. The effects are sometimes difficult to judge, but could result in programs executing improperly, premature discharge of memory contents, weird patterns on your monitor, and print jobs that suddenly produce gibberish.

How to tell if you have a power problem

Power problems may masquerade as other problems – no one knows how often flaky program execution is blamed on other software or hardware when bad power was to blame, nor how often a scrambled hard drive is blamed on viruses when a sag may have been the culprit.

(1) Flickering lights are easy to dismiss because they literally occur in the blink of an eye. They may be symptoms of temporary power sags or even very short power outages. It may take a power loss or sag of hundreds of milliseconds to cause a fluorescent tube to flicker, but in the computer's terms that may as well be forever.

(2) Data transmission errors between network nodes is a common problem for local area networks (LANs) and can have a couple of different causes: EMI/RFI (see above) and ground loops.

Ground loops can occur between any two devices linked by a data cable, especially if the two devices are a considerable distance apart. When a significant voltage difference develops between the two devices, the difference will equalize as an impulse travelling on the cable. The result will be scrambled data in the cable and, if the voltage difference is large enough, could result in fried circuit boards at either end.

EMI/RFI can also be a factor of distance. For instance, it is common practice to connect a printer to a computer by a parallel cable. Unless heavily shielded, parallel cable runs of more than ten feet are chancy because of a tendency for the cables to pick up both EMI and RFI noise. In essence, the cable acts as an antenna and pulls the noise out of the air. The same phenomenon can affect network cables.

(3) Unexplained system lockup and random system crashes may also be signs of flaky power quality. While this can also be caused by software that doesn't work and play well with others, it's possible that a power sag has done funny things to your computer's memory.

By the way, spikes can enter your system through power lines, obviously, but might also come to visit via printer cables, modem cables, or telephone lines (a phone line spike once killed one of my modems dead – how about something coming through the data line connecting your external CD-ROM drive?).

(4) Hard drive crashes and mysterious data loss may be blamed on viruses but may also be caused by sags or short blackouts. Today, most hard drives have floating heads that require power to force them close to the disk surface. This doesn't mean you're safe, however. Just about everyone using a version of DOS later than 5.0 is using SmartDrive or some other disk caching software (or you may have a cache on the hard drive itself).

One of the things disk caches do is to hold the file allocation table (FAT) in memory for faster access. If the power goes out before the cache updates the FAT, pieces of data will still be on the disk, but without an address in the FAT, they may as well be on the far side of the moon, because you won't be able to find them. If the power goes out while the cache is writing to the disk, the whole FAT could go missing.

As well, disk drives like to spin at a constant velocity. Just like having an audio tape running at a funny speed will distort the sound you hear, data written to a disk that is spinning too slowly will be distorted when you try to read them back later at the proper speed.

(5) Loss of data in the CMOS isn't solely caused by your battery dying (see the clock/calendar section in Chapter 2). While the computer is turned on, the CMOS draws its power from the same supply as the rest of the system. Spikes, surges, and static discharges can clean a CMOS out completely (just another reason why you should print the contents of the CMOS out tonight, write information like hard disk type, cylinders, heads, write precompensation, and sectors per track on a disk label and paste it under your keyboard for safekeeping).

By the way, the CMOS isn't the only memory in your system that is subject to this sort of damage. The EPROM (erasable programmable read-only memory) chips that control your keyboard, serial ports, BIOS, and other vital components (they're in printers and modems, too) are equally susceptible to power glitchery.

(6) System devices behaving erratically when too many are turned on is another sign of a power problem. Harmonics aren't just what you get in a choir. They'll also show up on an oscilloscope as current or voltage disturbances when too many connected devices are drawing fluctuating amounts of power.

LANs are prime victims of this sort of thing, particularly when too many workstations are powered from the same circuit, because computer power supplies don't draw power smoothly; they suck it up in big gulps, then use capacitors to feed it to the system until they need another gulp (once about every $^1/_{120}$ of a second or so).

(7) Frequently aborted modem transfers are also a sign of power trouble. Nothing twists my crank faster than losing a modem transmission in the middle (or just before the end). Spikes and surges and EMI/RFI are particular problems in telephone lines. They scramble data and cause excessive bad block errors that may end up terminating the transmission.

A less catastrophic result is that the two modems may step down their transmission rates in order to compensate for the line noise (annoying enough with a local call, but expensive if you're on long distance or logged into a system that charges for time on-line).

(8) If the display on your monitor wavers, flickers, dances, or sparkles, it could be a sign that there is low voltage (the size of the image shrinks), or that there are strong EMI fields nearby (move that telephone and those speakers – not to mention the power supply in your computer! – away a few feet).

You may be able to put up with this, but keep in mind that the same disturbance showing up on your monitor may be slowly turning your expensive RAM chips into nothing more than curious jewellery.

Power conditioners

You may not, despite the warnings above, decide on an uninterruptible power supply, but I've always believed that everyone who owns a computer should have some type of power-line conditioner.

Power line conditioners come in a range of prices and with a range of features. Some may offer limited protection from the worst spikes and surges, while others may also offer EMI and RFI protection. Power line conditioners do not protect against sags or blackouts.

One of the first things to understand is that the multiple-plug extensions sold at many stores for $19.95 or less and *called* power conditioners may only be expensive extension cords. They may carry certification by either or both the Canadian Standards Association (CSA) or U.S. Underwriter's Laboratory (UL), but that certification may come only under the extension cord section of both agencies. In order to qualify for surge and spike protection, conditioners must be able to withstand repeated 6,000-volt hits without passing them through. At least one consultant I spoke to says he advises his clients that if the power conditioner costs next to nothing, that's about what it will protect.

These are some of the gizmos you'll want to find inside the conditioner to protect your system: *metal oxide varistors* (or MOVs) act as shock absorbers, clipping the tops off spikes and surges (one is not much good; you want the model to have several.); *capacitors* act to back up the MOVs in toning down surges and are also used to filter out EMI/RFI line noise; and *rod core inductors* are additional EMI/RFI filters (think of a metal core with wire wrapped around it acting like a sponge).

The more of these items the power conditioner has, the more expensive it will be. The cost will also go up if it has additional connectors to ground a telephone line, but you can purchase relatively inexpensive phone-line grounders that plug into one of the extension sockets.

Uninterruptible power supplies

Good uninterruptible power supplies will protect against spikes, surges, and EMI/RFI, as well as dealing with sags and blackouts.

Aside from considerations of capacity (we'll get to it in a moment), you're going to be faced with two basic flavours of UPS. Even though everything that supplies power when the main current goes away is *called* a UPS, some of them don't supply the power instantaneously. The industry calls these standby power supplies (SPS).

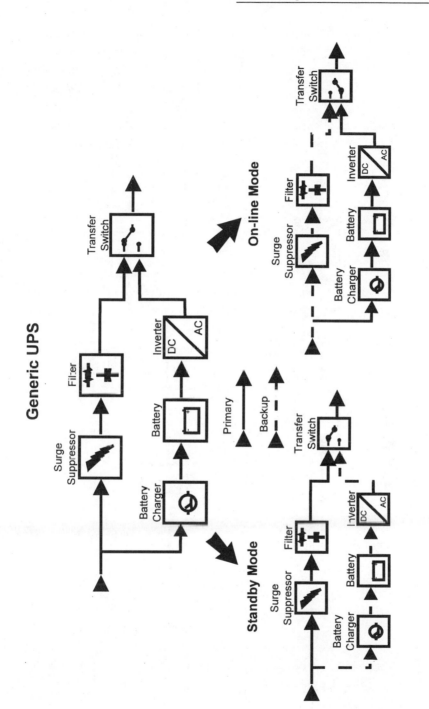

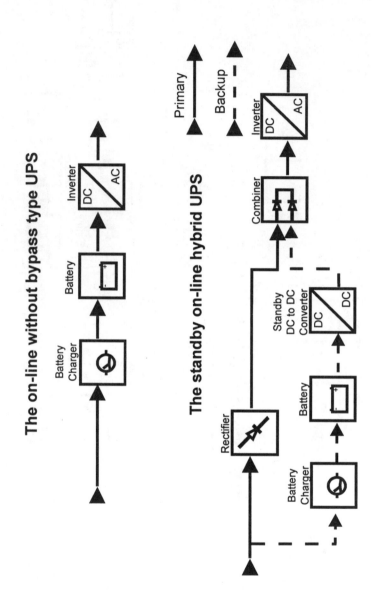

The on-line without bypass type UPS

The standby on-line hybrid UPS

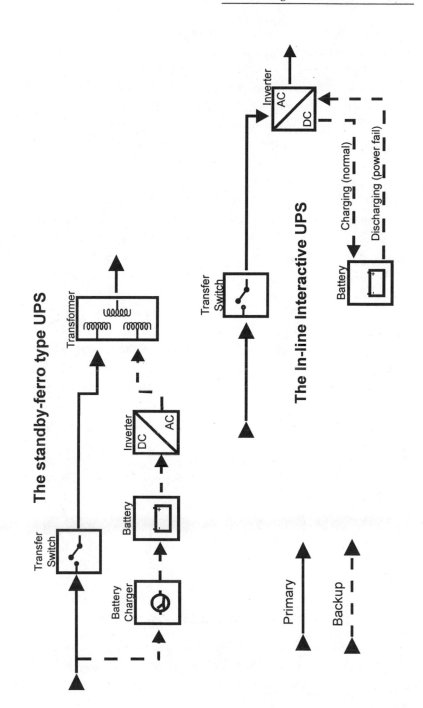

The standby-ferro type UPS

The In-line Interactive UPS

The UPS has a sensitive static transfer switch used to detect the loss of power during a deep sag or blackout. When the AC power from the wall goes away, it switches to the AC power available from the unit's battery/inverter, generally so quickly that your PC never knows the difference. Typically, a UPS will provide enough battery power to allow for five to fifteen minutes of operation – just enough for you to shut the system down in an orderly fashion. The longer the battery lasts, the more you'll pay for the system.

In an on-line UPS, the primary power source is the battery/inverter and you only get AC power directly if the battery gives out. This type of system generally provides cleaner power more consistently. Because of the way it is configured, a loss of AC power doesn't affect output. Classic on-line UPS systems include some models from APC, Sola, and Toshiba. On-line systems tend to cost more than standby (SPS) systems.

The transfer switch in an SPS unit doesn't instantly sense the loss of AC power from the wall. The pause may be measured only in milliseconds, but there still needs to be time for the transfer switch to operate and for the battery to come on line. SPS units tend to have smaller battery chargers than on-line UPS systems, as well as producing less heat. As a class, they are less expensive than the other systems. SPS units include the APC Back-UPS, Emerson Accupower, and Sola Sidekick.

There are four additional methods of managing power supplies: "on-line without bypass" and "line interactive," which are both variations of an on-line UPS system, and "standby on-line hybrid" and "standby ferro," which are, as the name implies, standby types (although with the hybrid, the line gets fuzzy). Some of these – the line-interactive models in particular – can get very expensive. But check 'em out.

How large a UPS/SPS will you need?

If everyone measured everything in the same way, this would be a simple matter, but they don't. Electrical equipment power usage is measured by the voltage it requires and by the amperes (amps) it uses. Watts are what you get when you multiply volts by amps. If you look on the back (or bottom) of all of your pieces of equipment, you may see the number of watts they use, or it may be expressed in volts and amps. For example, my CD-ROM drive uses 115 volts and 0.2 amps (for a total of 23 watts).

If I go to every piece of equipment I plan to plug into a UPS and perform the same calculation, I'll eventually find out how much power I need to provide. I'll want to include the power supply in the computer itself, any external peripheral devices (such as CD-ROM drive, modem, and so on). I'll definitely want to add my desk lamp, but I'll have to think about whether or not to add my laser printer (it can use over 600 watts if it happens to be heating up its fuser when the lights go out). I'll probably want to add about 25 per cent to my calculations to allow for some future expansion. Then I'll know how large a UPS to get, right?

Not necessarily. There's a trap. Quite a few UPS manufacturers have adopted a scheme of measurement called volt/amps. They say it is a more accurate measurement of the amount of current required. You may see volt/amps expressed as V/A, V-A, or simply VA (and of volt/amps in the thousands expressed as KVA).

During my research I've found several confusing ways of explaining the difference between VA and watts. Several manufacturers suggest simply multiplying watts by 1.4, while others went on for pages carefully explaining that there was no precise way to measure the difference except that the wattage for PC equipment was generally between 60 and 70 per cent of the VA rating. Sheesh!

Keep in mind that as you're recording the volts and amps or watts used by your equipment, that it too may report its power consumption in volt/amps (so if you see VA after a number where you might have simply expected to see V, it's not necessarily a spelling mistake).

To keep it as simple as possible, a 300 VA power supply is really only putting out somewhere around 180 to 200 watts.

For more – and sometimes conflicting – information: American Power Conversion Corp., (800) 800-4APC (4272) or (401) 789-5735; fax (401) 789-3710. Best Power Technology, Inc., (800) 356-5794 or (608) 565-7200; fax (608) 565-2221.

10

Upgrade or Replace?

When I conduct seminars, I get a lot of questions from folks looking for their first computer – but everyone else is there to find out how to upgrade an existing system.

Today, there are somewhere between 135 and 139 million PCs on the planet, but in late 1994 only about 35 million of them had 80486 or higher processors. Whichever way you slice it, this leaves one heck of a lot of XTs, 286s, and 386s lying about, struggling to run Windows effectively.

People who have older, slower computers often have emotional attachments not only to the box they've been using for lo these many years, but also to the cash they're afraid they'll have to spend to replace the old beast. Nevertheless they often start dreaming of newer, wilder, and more powerful toys each fall when the new lines start to ship.

If you are dreaming of a faster system, the obvious first question to ask is whether to upgrade or replace the old one. While your choice will largely be financial (upgrading can be less expensive), it will be also be conditional on the age and type of your present system.

XT and AT-286 systems

I don't recommend that you try to upgrade an old XT or AT 286. It would be like spending good money on a few new parts for your rusty, old car. It may run better for a little while longer, but it is still an old car.

Your XT or 286 may not be unsafe to drive, but I'm willing to bet that you're not too comfortable with it anymore. Even if you don't want to join the people running Windows or OS/2, your internal sense of how fast your computer should be working must be driving you nuts.

There are several things you can do with the old system (and I'll share those with you in a moment), but let's first look at all of the things you'll want to replace if you actually do try to upgrade instead.

If you have an old XT, practically none of it can be moved to a newer environment. Your drive controller and hard drive are both 8-bit systems. Neither will make the leap to a 16- or 32- or 64-bit computing environment – assuming that they would work in the new system at all.

If your computer is between five and ten years old, the chances are that you have either a monochrome, CGA (shudder), EGA, or very early VGA graphics card in it. It won't keep up in the new environment, so sooner of later – and quite probably sooner – it will have to go. And if you're upgrading the graphics card, you probably won't be able to use your old monitor, either.

The whole motherboard and all of the system memory will have to go, too; you can't simply add a processor or more memory chips to speed things up. The chances are also better than average that you'll have to abandon your old case because it's unlikely that the new motherboard's holes will match the location of the attachment points in the old case – and besides, that 120-watt power supply in the old unit is unlikely to be up to the demands of your new components.

Still, not everything is lost. You'll probably be able to keep your keyboard (unless of course it will only produce XT, and not AT, scan codes). To read all those 5.25-inch disks you still have, you'll want to take your 5.25-inch floppy drive – and if you have them, you might possibly want to take your mouse and modem as well – but that's about it.

Things are not quite as cut-and-dried with an AT-286. Depending on when you bought it (i.e., if it was at the end of the 286 production cycle when some more modern techniques were being applied), you might, just might, be able to take your system memory if it is comprised of at least 80 nanoseconds or faster single in-line memory modules (SIMMs); otherwise, forget it. If you're upgrading to virtually any motherboard sold in 1995 or later, it will have 72-pin memory slots and your SIMMs will be the older 30-pin units, so you may as well forget it anyway.

If you're really lucky, a new motherboard might fit your existing case, but have a close look at the power supply; a 150- or 175-watt supply may not be adequate if you're also planning to add extra devices such as an additional hard drive and/or a CD-ROM drive and/or a tape backup system.

If your existing hard drive and controller are relatively new IDE-type units, and the drive has an average access speed of 19 milliseconds or less (i.e., faster) and a capacity of 120 MB or more, they may be worth keeping. Of course the controller won't be a local bus model (there were no local bus 286 or 386 systems), so it will work more slowly than newer units. It also won't be enhanced IDE or Plug 'n' Play (PnP) compatible. Sounds like it's toast to me!

Got a fast video graphics card in that 286? It also won't be a local bus card, and even the slowest PCI-based video controller on the market will make your current graphics adapter appear dead slow.

And so on and so on and so on. The bottom line here is that old XTs and AT-286 systems aren't worth upgrading. By the time you've replaced enough parts to bring them up to today's standards, you'll have practically built a new system from the ground up (and have enough parts left over to re-build your old one).

Granted, building a system piecemeal may solve your cash-flow problems, but if your whole point was to save money, you won't have saved any. Building a computer yourself – although it's a good way to get a powerful system with nothing but the best of all possible components – costs about 15 to 20 per cent more than buying a complete system because retailers charge a slightly higher margin for component parts. When you consider the cost of new systems (see the price ranges below), it hardly seems worth the effort – particularly when you think about what you can do with the old computer instead of gutting it.

Reuse, recycle

Older systems that are still working have a lot of life left in them. The software designed when these computers were new still runs well on them. In fact, if your only reason to upgrade is because there is newer hardware and software on the market, you might want to rethink a bit. A simple rule of thumb in the computer business is *you only upgrade to a new hardware or software product when you have a problem with the old stuff that you can't solve any other way.*

On the other hand, perhaps you've had enough and crave more speed and fancier functions because, well, dammit, you've earned them. However, there might be a member of your family – perhaps older or younger than you – who would love what you consider to be a system that's too old and slow. Your kids may not thank you for a system that can't run today's high-end games or Windows, but you may be surprised by the reaction of your mother, your uncle, or your granny (show her how to get in touch with the Grey Panthers on the Internet, then stand back!).

Have you thought about networking that older system and using it as a print server? How about using it as a dedicated fax or telecommunications server? Even an XT works faster than the fastest modem you can connect to it, and using it to receive faxes won't tie up your other system.

Most North American charities aren't interested in older computer technology for their own use for the same reason that you're thinking about upgrading – they don't have the time to waste with old, slow systems. However, there are all kinds of agencies, some supplying domestic non-profit organizations, some engaged in Third World development, who can recycle older technology and put it to use. If you're serious about making a donation, start by calling any local volunteer agency. Sooner or later, someone will put you in touch with the right party.

386 systems

If you have an older 386 system, you have some intriguing options.

Again, depending on its age, you may be able to keep memory, hard drive, drive controller, floppy drives, and so on. In fact if all you're replacing is the motherboard with new memory and processor, you have a better than average chance of being able to keep – and to keep using – everything else, including the case and power supply. You're looking at well under $1,500 for a leading-edge motherboard, including the processor (but maybe not memory). Everything else costs less.

One other alternative is to turn a 386 into a quasi-486 system by replacing the 386 CPU on your existing motherboard with one of Cyrix Corp.'s DRX2 processors. I have no direct experience with this particular method of upgrading, but *PC Magazine* once reported that they were happy with the approach when tried on systems in their offices. So long as it's a less expensive alternative to replacing the entire motherboard and your expectations don't exceed the chip's abilities (remember, it still won't have a math coprocessor), it might be worth a serious look – but my own feeling about this is that you're simply spending money to turn one obsolete system into a slightly less obsolete system.

486 systems and above

If you have an existing 486 or Pentium 60 (or just about anything else, for that matter), there are a number of things you can do to improve its real and apparent performance.

Keep in mind, however, that older 486 system designs may make it impossible for you to take 30-pin SIMMs or VESA local bus devices with you into your next computer, and you may want to give some thought about whether upgrading is simply pouring money into a hole from which it will never return.

Nevertheless, for well under $1,000 you have several alternatives.

If you can still find 30-pin SIMMs, you might add more memory. If you double whatever you have, up to 16 MB, it will make running either Windows or OS/2 more efficient – and so will increasing the amount of external cache memory in the system, particularly if you have less than 512 KB now. Check your motherboard – if some of the cache memory slots are empty, or if some of them are longer than the chips currently installed, you may be able to add more or replace your low-density chips with higher density models.

If the CPU is an Intel 486, but less than a DX2/66 (i.e., a DX or SX of either 25 or 33 MHz), think about a CPU upgrade using the Intel DX4 OverDrive. Despite its need for 3.3 volts, it is pin-compatible with all Intel 486 sockets and includes a voltage regulator to allow it to run on your 5-volt motherboard. Some 486 motherboards will run at either 25 or 33 MHz. I can't tell you if yours will, but check your manual to make sure. The DX4 OverDrive comes in two flavours – a 75 MHz model for 25 MHz motherboards and a 100 MHz model for those running at 33 MHz.

As time passes and prices drop, upgrading a 486 CPU to a Pentium OverDrive might make sense if (a) your system has a 35-, 37-, or 38-pin "P24T" socket designed for it, (b) the system was certified as "Pentium Upgradeable" by Intel, and (c) the price of the part is less than the cost of a new motherboard designed for the Pentium architecture. As with the Cyrix upgrade noted above, don't expect the result to act like a full-fledged Pentium – the rest of the architecture for this chip (i.e., the supporting chipset on the motherboard) still won't be there – but you will get, according to Intel, about 50 per cent better performance than a 486DX2/66 in the same system.

If you have a 60 MHz Pentium now, don't despair. Intel promises to produce an OverDrive chip for you, too (sometime in 1996), based on the 120 MHz Pentium processor released in 1995. It was designed to run on a 60 MHz bus and will also come with a voltage regulator to handle the difference between your 5-volt socket and its 3.3-volt requirements. If the pricing is reasonable, this could be a way to double your system's performance for under $1,000.

Also for under $1,000, assuming you have either a VESA or PCI-based local bus scheme, you'll be able to find a very fast, accelerated local bus video adapter (they topped out at around $800 at the leading edge in 1995 and may be cheaper by the time you read this). Fast local bus hard drive controllers, even with lots of onboard cache memory, also cost well under $1,000 and will leave you with enough left over for a 528 MB standard IDE hard drive (and the same is true of enhanced IDE/PnP components). One note to folks with VESA local bus slots, however. When you finally upgrade to a Pentium or higher system, the chance that you will be able to – or would want to – take VESA components with you into what will inevitably be a PCI environment is slim.

Thinking about adding a SCSI adapter to your system? This also would cost you well under $1,000 (even for a local bus model with cache) and you'll have enough left over for a good, quad-speed CD-ROM drive, or a nice gigabyte-plus hard drive (or, the way prices have been falling for each product, maybe both).

How about a tape backup system, so you can protect your data against hard drive malfunction, theft, fire, or other disasters such as errant software, a visitor's fat fingers, or your cat? High capacity tape subsystems in the 1 to 3 gigabyte range are all under $1,000.

So are uninterruptible power supplies (UPS), which will keep your computer running long enough for you to shut it down properly in the event of a blackout (something Windows 95, Windows NT, and OS/2 all want you to do). For far less than $1,000 you can find models that will also bring voltage up to the proper level in the event of a brownout – and they'll all protect your system against radio frequency interference and electrical surges and spikes that can ruin your system.

You Work Hard for the Money

An old business adage says you can do anything you want so long as you have enough time and enough money. The only problem is that you never have enough time or money. Technology is expensive and, in the economic climate of the 1990s, neither large corporations, institutions, governments, nor individuals have bottomless bank accounts. So what can you expect to get for your hard-earned coin?

First, you'll want to take note of the points raised in the section on reading computer ads under the subheading "prices always go down."

No matter whether you're considering a complete system or an individual device or component, there is always an upper price point at which new products are introduced.

As each new product arrives, the price of existing products gets pushed down and, unless it is vital for some reason to buy at the leading edge, you'll always get the biggest bang for your buck by shopping for products one or two steps back from it. Keep in mind, however, that buying a product when it's at its lowest price, just before it disappears from the market, simply means it will be out of date faster and the time to replace it will arrive sooner, instead of later.

So, if you have $1,000, $2,000, $3,000, $4,000, $5,000, or more to spend, what can you expect? Note: you can play games with these numbers. By upgrading or downgrading the quality of any component, by increasing or decreasing the capacity of hard drives, by adding or subtracting the amount of both external cache and system memory, and particularly by quoting prices from a nationally advertised manufacturer versus a local system assembler, you can push the prices in both directions. So, if you can find a better deal than I've listed here, good. If a vendor wants to charge you more than I've suggested for fewer goodies, don't yell at me – prices on components (especially memory) can change up or down weekly. Simply chalk it up to market varities and let it go or continue to shop around. Also, note that the price ranges and estimates for systems below do not include taxes.

$1,000

If you want a brand-new computer capable of running today's and tomorrow's software and you have only $1,000 or less to spend, keep saving.

Unless you find a store specializing in remaindering old stock, or take the risk of buying a used system (shudder), you won't find an up-to-date PC or Mac for that little. The bottom price point for a complete PC system, before current technology falls off the market, is around $1,200 to $1,800 (with minimal performance components). If you do go the route of purchasing an old system, all you'll buy for yourself will be frustration when it proves to be slow and incapable of running software you hadn't planned to need before you got it, but discovered later you just had to have.

Used computers aren't like used cars. There are no government guidelines for minimum standards of safety. Even assuming every component in it is still in good working condition, my guess is that if it was too slow for someone else, it will soon be too slow for you as well.

If I had an existing PC that was already a 486 or better and $1,000 to spend, I would put the money into upgrading some of its components, extending its useful life, and deriving real benefit from it (see above).

$2,000

Do you have a PC and up to $2,000 in your jeans? With less than a 486, keep your present system and plan to network it to a new one. If your existing system has PCI local bus peripherals (i.e., video and drive controller), 72-pin SIMMs, and an up-to-date hard drive, you have another alternative.

In this case, replacing the motherboard makes sense. Two thousand dollars will be more than enough to buy you a new motherboard with whatever the leading edge CPU is at the time, with enough left over to add memory or replace the graphics card (but probably not both). Unless you're technically gifted or have a friend with the skills, get a shop to do the work for you.

No PC? Keep saving. Two thousand dollars will get you into something about to fall off the market within a few months (or weeks) with a few extras added to it. It might even be enough to get into the low end of the third step back from the leading edge, but you'll have precious little left over for any sort of decent quality graphics card or monitor, extra memory, a large hard drive, or multimedia components – not to mention a printer and some software to run on the system.

$3,000

Three thousand dollars? Now we're talking, and you get to start making decisions. At $3,000 and up, you start balancing processor power against memory, graphics subsystem quality, hard drive size (and type), multimedia components, and so on.

For this kind of money, it should be possible to put together a third-tier system with lots of nice toys or a second-tier system with fewer toys. If you have an industry-specific need (i.e., music or commercial graphics), $3,000 will also get you into a low-end Mac LCS or Quadra.

$4,000

Between $4,000 and $5,000, you're definitely into sailing into leading-edge territory, and if you're buying a locally assembled system instead of a nationally advertised name brand, you'll have enough to add a few nice toys to it as well. A second-tier system costing this much money will have fast graphics, large storage capacity, plenty of multimedia goodies, tape backup, and a good monitor. You won't be able to get quite as much extra if you're looking for the leading edge Pentium or leading edge P6. You're also within sailing distance of a PowerMac (unless you also want it to run PC software).

$5,000 and up

If you have over $5,000 to spend on a computer, you can have the locally assembled system of your choice. For between $6,000 and $7,000, you can have a nationally advertised name brand on it, too. Printers are extra. So is software. We aren't at the leading edge for PowerMacs, yet, but we're getting there.

You have $8,000 to $10,000? Now we can talk about whatever the leading edge is for PowerMac technology. Or, instead, how about a dual P6 processor-based PC with the top quality component of every one we can find, plus a printer, plus software?

Recap

The following is a recap of various pieces of advice found in elsewhere in this book, but assembled here as a reward for those who made it all the way through:

The only wise time to upgrade hardware is to solve a problem you can't fix any other way (if it ain't broke, don't fix it). However, the time to buy a computer is when you need one (yes, the price of what you want today will always be lower in six months, but your friends or business competitors will be six months ahead of you if you wait that long).

Let what you're going to do and what software you need to do it determine your hardware, not the other way around. Then, get what your friends have (or better and make them really envious).

Some processors are too expensive for you right now, but there is no such thing as one that is too powerful for you. However, you can't get the fastest processor there is; it isn't in the store yet; it's on a truck somewhere between the lab and the factory (but every time you want to have your cake and eat it, too, someone will allow you the opportunity to pay for the privilege).

To optimize performance in your new system, while maximizing the effectiveness of your budget, the money gets spent in the following priority order (each section in brackets is also ranked by importance):

- CPU (type and speed); motherboard architecture (speed, amount of external cache memory, type of local bus, and more speed);
- RAM (random access memory – amount, type and speed);
- video (acceleration, range of resolutions, and number of colours);
- storage (hard drive and drive controller type, hard drive capacity, drive/controller speed and amount of onboard cache);
- monitor (size, dot pitch, refresh rate, number and location of controls, features);
- input devices (keyboard, mouse),
- printer (type, speed, resolution, monochrome versus colour);
- multimedia components including CD-ROM (throughput, spin rate, and internal versus external) and sound card (bit-depth, sampling rate, MIDI scheme);
- fax/modem (speed, internal versus external);
- other (tape backup, power conditioner/supply, other toys).

Remember, you don't have to have all the latest gizmos and gadgets to enjoy your computer, just one that's fast enough to run the programs you'll be using and with the peripheral devices you need. As I said way back at the beginning of this book, the point of using a computer is to make your work so efficient, you'll have time to do other things. So, buy or upgrade – and enjoy!

INDEX

Company:		Address	
Salesperson:		Telephone:	Fax:
Component	Brand Name or Style	Features or Amount	Price
Motherboard			
CPU			
BIOS			
Cache memory			
DRAM SIMMs			
Case			
Power supply			
Hard Drive			
Disk Controller			
Floppy Drive(s)			
Graphics Card			
Memory			
Resolutions			
Colours			
Monitor			
Mouse			
Keyboard			
Ports			
Printer			
CD ROM			
Sound Board			
Tape Backup			
Operating system			
Word Processor			
Spreadsheet			
Database			
Utilities			
Other			
"Free" software			
Warranty			

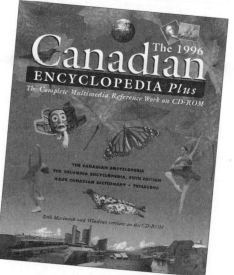

SPECIAL REBATE ON YOUR PURCHASE OF

The 1996 Canadian

ENCYCLOPEDIA *Plus*

The Complete Multimedia Reference Work on CD-ROM

When you buy *The 1996 Canadian Encyclopedia Plus* (available at your local bookstore or computer software retailer), just send in this coupon along with a proof of purchase and get a rebate of $19.99 – the cost of this book.

Send your coupon along with a proof of purchase for *The 1996 Canadian Encyclopedia Plus* to:

CD-ROM Sales Department
McClelland & Stewart Inc.
481 University Avenue, Ste. 900
Toronto, Ontario
M5G 2E9

Please send me my rebate of $19.99.
You will find enclosed my proof of purchase and receipt for
The 1996 Canadian Encyclopedia Plus.

Name: _____

Address: _____

City: _____ Prov.: _____

Postal Code: _____ Phone: _____

Offer not valid in conjunction with any other promotional offer.